# JavaScript

## Introductory Concepts and Techniques

**Gary B. Shelly**
**Thomas J. Cashman**
**William J. Dorin**

**COURSE TECHNOLOGY**
**ONE MAIN STREET**
**CAMBRIDGE MA 02142**

*an International Thomson Publishing company*  **I(T)P**

SHELLY
CASHMAN
SERIES®

CAMBRIDGE · ALBANY · BONN · CINCINNATI · LONDON · MADRID · MELBOURNE

MEXICO CITY · NEW YORK · PARIS · SAN FRANCISCO · TOKYO · TORONTO · WASHINGTON

COURSE
TECHNOLOGY

Course Technology
One Main Street
Cambridge, Massachusetts 02142, USA

ITP Europe
Berkshire House
168-173 High Holborn
London, WC1V 7AA, United Kingdom

ITP Australia
102 Dodds Street
South Melbourne
Victoria 3205 Australia

ITP Nelson Canada
1120 Birchmount Road
Scarborough, Ontario
Canada M1K 5G4

International Thomson Editores
Saneca, 53
Colonia Polanco
11560 Mexico D.F. Mexico

ITP GmbH
Konigswinterer Strasse 418
53227 Bonn, Germany

ITP Asia
60 Albert Street, #15-01
Albert Complex
Singapore 189969

ITP Japan
Hirakawa-cho Kyowa Building, 3F
2-2-1 Hirakawa-cho, Chiyoda-ku
Tokyo 102, Japan

ISBN 0-7895-4693-0

**PHOTO CREDITS:** *Project 1, pages J 1.2-3* Mountain lake, twisting road, Courtesy of PhotoDisc, Inc.; boulders, dirt road, Courtesy of Digital Stock; road sign, Courtesy of KPT Metatools; BMW, web site, ©1999 BMW of North America, Inc. used with permission. The BMW name and logo are registered trademarks; *Project 2, pages J 2.2-3* Piggy bank, checkbook, calculator, money, man working at computer, Courtesy of PhotoDisc, Inc.; computer monitor, Courtesy of KPT Metatools; *Project 3, pages J 3.2-3* Barbie® doll, Barbie Web site, Ruth Handler, Courtesy of Mattel, Inc.; Barbie and associated trademarks are owned by and used with permission from Mattel, Inc. ©1998 Mattel, Inc. All Rights Reserved. All screens shown © Mattel. Fashion Avenue is a trademark of Newport News, Inc. a member of the Spiegel Group.

1 2 3 4 5 6 7 8 9 10    BC    03 02 01 00 99

# JavaScript
## Introductory Concepts and Techniques

# C O N T E N T S

## ● PROJECT THREE

## ENHANCING THE USE OF IMAGE AND FORM OBJECTS

# Preface

The Shelly Cashman Series® Internet books reinforce the fact that you made the right choice when you use a Shelly Cashman Series book. Earlier Shelly Cashman Series Internet books were used by more schools and more students than any other series in textbook publishing. Yet, the Shelly Cashman Series team wanted to produce an even better book for JavaScript, so the step-by-step pedagogy was refined to include larger screens (800 x 600) to present material in an even easier-to-understand format. Features such as Other Ways and More Abouts, with links to JavaScript and Web design sites, enhance the book to give students an in-depth knowledge of JavaScript. Each project opens with a fascinating perspective of the subject covered in the project. Completely redesigned student assignments include the unique Cases and Places.

## The World Wide Web

In the several years since its birth, the World Wide Web, or Web for short, has grown beyond all expectations. During this short period of time, the Web has increased from a limited number of networked computers to more than twenty million computers offering millions of Web pages on any topic you can imagine. Schools, businesses, and the computing industry all are taking advantage of this new way of delivering information and they are using JavaScript to bring their Web pages to life by adding dynamic content and interactive elements. This book shows you how to use JavaScript to add functionality to your Web pages by inserting code within an HTML document.

## Objectives of This Textbook

*JavaScript: Introductory Concepts and Techniques* is intended for use in combination with other books in an introductory course on creating and enhancing Web pages. This book also is suitable for use in a one-credit hour course or a continuing education course. Specific objectives of this book are as follows:

- To expose students to adding functionality to Web pages
- To teach students how to use JavaScript
- To illustrate common Web page interactivity
- To encourage students to use their creativity in developing Web pages
- To develop an exercise-oriented approach that allows students to learn by example
- To encourage independent study and help those who are learning how to enhance Web pages in a distance education environment

## Organization of This Textbook

*JavaScript: Introductory Concepts and Techniques* is comprised of an introduction to JavaScript section and three projects that step students through enhancing Web pages. This book assumes students have a working knowledge of HTML. Each project begins with a statement of Objectives. The topics in the project are presented in a step-by-step, screen-by-screen manner. Each project ends with a Project Summary

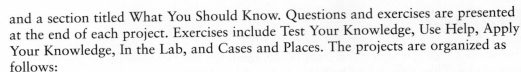

## Other Ways

1. Press ALT+F, S

### More About

### Scripting Languages

Netscape's JavaScript and Microsoft's VBScript are the two main client side script languages used today. To read more about scripting languages and why many organizations want one common language platform, visit www.scsite.com/js/p1.htm and then click scripting languages.

and a section titled What You Should Know. Questions and exercises are presented at the end of each project. Exercises include Test Your Knowledge, Use Help, Apply Your Knowledge, In the Lab, and Cases and Places. The projects are organized as follows:

**Introduction to JavaScript Programming** The Introduction provides an overview of JavaScript. The differences between Java and JavaScript and between JavaScript and VB Script are discussed. This section presents the basic concepts of JavaScript variables, conditionals, functions, objects, properties, methods, event handlers, forms, frames, and arrays.

**Project 1 - Integrating JavaScript and HTML** In Project 1, students are introduced to integrating JavaScript into an HTML file. Topics include placing JavaScript tags and comments within HTML; placing HTML tags within JavaScript statements; using the document object; setting the background colors property; extracting the system date; setting the substring property; defining variables; writing user-defined functions; and using the setTimeout() and Alert() functions.

**Project 2 - Creating Pop-up Windows, Adding Scrolling Messages, and Validating Forms** In Project 2, three common uses of JavaScript are presented: creating pop-up windows, adding scrolling messages, and validating forms. Topics include using JavaScript to conduct data entry validation on the client computer; working with the document object, forms, string length, and focus properties; the If-Then-Else control structure; user-defined functions; event handlers; and the parseInt(), isNaN(), and pow() functions.

**Project 3 - Enhancing the Use of Image and Form Objects** In Project3, students learn more about functions and the common objects used in JavaScript. Topics include writing a function that calculates the number of days to a future date; changing graphic images; using the index from a select list in an If-Then-Else control structure; passing a value to a function that sets a value in a text box; and calculating an estimated cost for services.

# End-of-Project Student Activities

A notable strength of the Shelly Cashman Series Internet books is the extensive student activities at the end of each project. Well-structured student activities can make the difference between students merely participating in a class and students retaining the information they learn. These activities include all of the following sections.

- **What You Should Know** A listing of the tasks completed within a project together with the pages where the step-by-step, screen-by-screen explanations appear. This section provides a perfect study review for students.

- **Test Your Knowledge** Four or five pencil-and-paper activities designed to determine students' understanding of the material in the project. Included are true/false questions, multiple-choice questions, and two short-answer exercises.

- **Use Help** Any user of JavaScript must recognize the importance of the JavaScript Web sites that discuss JavaScript and illustrate algorithms. Therefore, this book contains two Help exercises per project that have the student visit JavaScript Web sites. These exercises alone distinguish the Shelly Cashman Series from any other set of instructional materials.

- **Apply Your Knowledge** A substantive exercise intended to be completed in a few minutes that provides practice with project skills.
- **In the Lab** Several assignments per project that require students to apply the knowledge gained in the project to solve problems.
- **Cases and Places** A set of unique case studies allow students to apply their knowledge to real-world situations.

# Shelly Cashman Series Teaching Tools

A comprehensive set of Teaching Tools accompanies this textbook in the form of a CD-ROM. The CD-ROM includes an electronic Instructor's Manual and teaching and testing aids. The CD-ROM (ISBN 0-7895-4695-7) is available through your Course Technology representative or by calling one of the following telephone numbers: Colleges and Universities, 1-800-648-7450; High Schools, 1-800-824-5179; and Career Colleges, 1-800-477-3692. The contents of the CD-ROM are listed below.

- **Instructor's Manual** The Instructor's Manual is made up of Microsoft Word files that include lecture notes, solutions to laboratory assignments, and a large test bank. The files allow you to modify the lecture notes or generate quizzes and exams from the test bank using you own word processor. The Instructor's Manual includes the following for each project: project objectives; project overview; detailed lesson plans with page number references; teacher notes and activities; answers to the end-of-project exercises; test bank of 110 questions (50 true/false, 25 multiple-choice, and 35 fill-in-the-blank); transparency references; and selected transparencies. The transparencies are available on the Figures in the Book described below. The test bank questions are numbered the same as in Course Test Manager. Thus, you can print a copy of the project and use the printed test bank to select your questions in Course Test Manager.

- **Figures in the Book** Illustrations for every figure in the textbook are available. Use this ancillary to create a slide show from the illustrations for lecture or print transparencies for use in lecture with an overhead projector.

- **Course Test Manager** Course Test Manager is a powerful testing and assessment package that enables instructors to create and print tests from the large test bank. Instructors with access to a networked computer lab (LAN) can administer, grade, and track tests online. Students also can take online practice tests, which generate customized study guides that indicate where in the textbook students can find more information for each question.

- **Lecture Success System** The Lecture Success System is a set of files that allows you to explain and illustrate the step-by-step, screen-by-screen development of a project in the textbook. The Lecture Success System requires that you have a copy of Notepad, a browser, a personal computer, and a projection device.

- **Instructor's Lab Solutions** Solutions and required files are available for all the Apply Your Knowledge and In the Lab assignments at the end of each project and the projects themselves.

- **Student Data Files** All the files that are required by students to complete the projects and the Apply Your Knowledge exercises are included. See the section titled JavaScript Data Disk on the next page.

- **Interactive Labs** Eighteen hands-on interactive labs that take students from ten to fifteen minutes to step through help solidify and reinforce computer concepts. Student assessment requires students to answer questions about the contents of the interactive labs.

# JavaScript Data Disk

The JavaScript Data Disk is required for some of the projects and exercises. Students can obtain a copy of the JavaScript Data Disk by following the instructions on the inside back cover of this book. The Shelly Cashman Series Teaching Tools CD-ROM contains a copy of the files that comprise the JavaScript Data Disk.

# Shelly Cashman Online

Shelly Cashman Online is a World Wide Web service available to instructors and students of computer education. Visit Shelly Cashman Online at www.scseries.com. Shelly Cashman Online is divided into four areas:

- **Series Information** Information on the Shelly Cashman Series products.
- **Teaching Resources** Designed for instructors teaching from and using Shelly Cashman Series textbooks and software. This area includes password-protected instructor materials that can be downloaded, course outlines, teaching tips, and much more.
- **Student Center** Dedicated to students learning about computers with Shelly Cashman Series textbooks and software. This area includes cool links, data that can be downloaded, and much more.
- **Community** Opportunities to discuss your course and your ideas with instructors in your field and with the Shelly Cashman Series team.

# Acknowledgments

The Shelly Cashman Series would not be the leading computer education series without the contributions of outstanding publishing professionals. First, and foremost, among them is Becky Herrington, director of production and designer. She is the heart and soul of the Shelly Cashman Series, and it is only through her leadership, dedication, and tireless efforts that superior products are made possible.

Under Becky's direction, the following individuals made significant contributions to these books: Doug Cowley, production manager; Ginny Harvey, series specialist and developmental editor; Ken Russo, graphic designer and Web developer; Mike Bodnar, Stephanie Nance, Mark Norton, and Ellana Russo, graphic artists; Jeanne Black, Quark expert; Nancy Lamm, copyeditor/proofreader; Marlo Mitchem, production/administrative assistant; Cristina Haley, indexer; Sarah Evertson of Image Quest, photo researcher; and Susan Sebok contributing writer.

Special thanks go to Jim Quasney, our dedicated series editor; Lisa Strite, senior editor; Lora Wade, associate product manager; Tonia Grafakos, associate Web product manager; Meagan Walsh, editorial assistant; and Kathryn Cronin, product marketing manager. Special mention must go to Becky Herrington for the outstanding book design; Mike Bodnar for the logo designs, and Mark Norton for the cover design and illustrations.

Finally, a special thanks to our reviewers Larry Manning, Abul Sheikh, and Dwight Watt, and to Judy Knapp, Elyn Rykken, Andrea Dorin, and Caroline Ruhs for reading the manuscript and providing valuable comments.

Gary B. Shelly
Thomas J. Cashman
William J. Dorin

JavaScript

# Introduction to JavaScript Programming

You will have mastered the material in this project when you can:

- Describe JavaScript
- Define HTML and explain the use of HTML tags
- Define attribute
- Differentiate between JavaScript and VBScript
- Define JavaScript cookies and variables
- Describe string, numeric, and Boolean JavaScript variable types
- Discuss the rules for naming variables
- Differentiate between variables and literals
- Discuss special codes and how they are used in a literal
- Discuss the advantages and disadvantages of using JavaScript
- Define expression and describe the arithmetic operators
- Discuss the order of precedence in an expression
- Define concatenation
- Define conditionals and the use of If and While statements
- Discuss the use of JavaScript functions
- Discuss If, If . . . Else, and While statements and loops
- Define objects, properties, methods, and events
- Describe how event handlers and forms are used
- Define frames and arrays

**OBJECTIVES**

# JavaScript

# Introduction to JavaScript Programming

## Introduction

**JavaScript** is a programming language that allows you to add functionality to your Web pages by inserting code within an HTML document. Whereas **HTML (hypertext markup language)** tells your browser how to display text and images, set up lists and option buttons, and establish hyperlinks, JavaScript brings your Web page to life by adding dynamic content and interactive elements. Using JavaScript, you can enhance a Web page by adding items such as:

▶ scrolling messages
▶ animations and dynamic images
▶ data input forms
▶ pop-up windows
▶ interactive quizzes

JavaScript is a product of a joint venture between Sun Microsystems and Netscape Communications Corporation. Netscape originally began development of a script language called *LiveScript*, while Sun was trying to simplify its *Java* programming language. Today, JavaScript is endorsed by a number of software companies. It is an open language that anyone can use without purchasing a license. JavaScript thus allows you to improve the appearance of your Web pages without spending a large amount of money or learning a high-level programming language.

Several other programming languages allow you to add functionality to Web pages. One such language is Sun Microsystems's **Java**, which is a full-fledged, object-oriented programming language. Java is similar to more traditional compiler programming languages such as C or COBOL, in that you can use it to create stand-alone applications. Java also is used to create a special type of mini application, called an applet. An **applet** is a small program designed to execute within another application. Unlike a JavaScript statement, which is embedded in the HTML document, an applet is sent to the browser as a separate file alongside an HTML document. The applet adds functionality, such as an interactive animation or game, to a Web page. To write a Java program or applet, you must use the Java Developer's Kit (JDK) from Sun Microsystems or Microsoft's Visual J++.

Although it shares many of the features of the full Java language, JavaScript is a simpler language that supports less functionality. You cannot use JavaScript, for example, to create applets or stand-alone applications. In its most common form today, JavaScript resides inside HTML documents and can provide interactivity to otherwise static HTML documents.

Unlike Java, JavaScript is an interpreted language, meaning it does not end up as an executable file (like a typical program). Instead, the code runs only on a JavaScript interpreter built into your browser. The **interpreter** translates each line of a language and converts it into machine code line by line as it is executed. When you request a Web page, your browser retrieves and reads the page from top to bottom, displaying the results of the HTML code and executing JavaScript statements as it goes.

Because the interpreter is a built-in feature of the browser, the version of JavaScript you use depends on the version of your browser. JavaScript is supported by recent browsers from Netscape and Microsoft. Because Internet Explorer supports additional features, Microsoft calls its version *Jscript*. Many older browsers are unable to handle newer JavaScript codes.

# JavaScript and HTML Tags

This book assumes you have a basic knowledge of HTML (hypertext markup language). You can build very sophisticated Web pages with the WYSIWYG (what you see is what you get) editors such as Netscape Composer, Microsoft FrontPage, Corel Web Designer, and others without knowing any HTML. A basic understanding of HTML is important because it allows you to correct errors and bugs that may occur in the coding of the page.

The script code is embedded within the HTML tags. A **tag** is an instruction that is surrounded by less than (<) and greater than (>) symbols. As the browser reads the HTML file and encounters these tags, it formats the page according to the instructions given by the tags. These instructions are called attributes. **Attributes** are characteristics of a tag that have values assigned to them. Figure I-1 shows a typical BODY tag with two attributes: text (for text color) and background (to name the image used for a background). In general, these attributes instruct in formatting text, placing headings, paragraphs, images, links, and creating and establishing tables and frames to format the page layout. In this book, attributes and tags are shown as all uppercase. The example figures show mixed case to demonstrate that tags and attributes are not case sensitive.

More *About*

## Tags and Attributes

HTML tags and attributes are not case sensitive. Some browsers do not recognize lowercase or mixed-case tags and attributes. If an error occurs and the syntax is correct, try changing the tag and attributes to all uppercase characters.

```
<BODY Text = "00008B" Background = "image.gif">
```

**FIGURE I-1**

In HTML, you use tags in pairs. You must have a beginning tag and an ending tag or formatting will be incorrect. For example, to make text display bold on a Web page, start with a <B> tag, enter the text, and then end with a </B> tag. The bold tags are simple and do not use any attributes. Others, such as the INPUT tag, have attributes associated with the tag.

Figure I-2 shows the INPUT tag for a text box found on the typical form for data entry. Type, name, and size are all attributes of the INPUT tag. In this example, the TYPE attribute indicates whether a text box, option button, check box, image, SUBMIT button, or RESET button is created. The NAME attribute assigns a name or variable (PhoneNumber) to the text box. This variable stores the data entered until it is needed. In addition, you will use the variable name later in the JavaScript code to validate the data entered into that text box. You may assign an initial or default value to the VALUE attribute on the form. For example, in Figure I-2, a blank value is being assigned to the text object of the form. The SIZE attribute indicates the size of the text box, which is based on the number of characters to be placed in a text box.

```
<INPUT Type = "text" Name = "PhoneNumber" Value = " " Size = 17>
```

**FIGURE I-2**

### SCRIPT Tags

To use JavaScript, or any scripting language, in the HTML code, the browser needs to be told that a script language is being used. Most Web page designers place an initial SCRIPT tag in the heading of the HTML document. This initial script includes the various JavaScript functions that will be defined. In addition, a SCRIPT tag must be used again in order to place JavaScript code in other areas on the Web page. Every time you use the SCRIPT tag, it is recommended an HTML comment is used to hide the code from the user's browser in case it does not support JavaScript. Figure I-3 shows the code for the SCRIPT tag to identify JavaScript.

```
<SCRIPT LANGUAGE = "JavaScript">
<!-- Hide from old browsers
place your JavaScript code here
//-->
</SCRIPT>
```

**FIGURE I-3**

One of the attributes for the SCRIPT tag is LANGUAGE. In the **LANGUAGE** attribute, the word, JavaScript, with no version number indicates version 1.0. To indicate a different version, you must add the version number to the JavaScript value. For example, JavaScript1.1, indicates version 1.1 and, JavaScript1.2, indicates version 1.2. The version of JavaScript to use depends on which browser the users are expected to have.

# JavaScript Versus VBScript

Because of the popularity of its Visual Basic programming language, Microsoft has developed a script language called **VBScript** (VB stands for Visual Basic). JavaScript follows syntax similar to the programming language C, while VBScript uses syntax similar to Visual Basic. For example, you write functions with JavaScript (as in C), and you write subroutines with VBScript (as in Visual Basic). In JavaScript, functions begin and end with braces ({}), while in VBScript, a subroutine begins with the word, SUB, followed by the words, END SUB. As of this writing, version 4 or higher of Microsoft Internet Explorer executes JavaScript, but Netscape Navigator does not execute VBScript.

# Why Use JavaScript?

Using JavaScript enhances a Web page by adding interactivity to HTML. Users can be provided instant feedback without complicated CGI (Common Gateway Interface) scripts and languages. A **CGI** script is any program that runs on a Web server for the purpose of processing data. The Web page sends the data to the server that processes the data and may return a result to the Web page. CGI scripts are powerful tools useful in searching databases or processing purchase orders for companies doing mainstream business on the Internet.

CGI scripts are a waste of resources, however, when the needed task can be processed on the user's computer. For example, with JavaScript, you can validate a data entry form, such as a purchase request, immediately on the user's computer. The need to send the data back to the server for validation is eliminated. The user receives feedback instantaneously and is not waiting for a response during heavy Internet traffic times.

## JavaScript Cookies

Forms are not the only types of data a Web browser handles. Some generated data is not part of an HTML defined object, such as a data file. One type of data is the cookie file. **Cookies** are pieces of data sent and stored in files on the user's computer. Web developers use these pieces of data to track a user's preferences while visiting a Web site. Navigator stores cookies in the cookies.txt file. Internet Explorer stores cookies as separate files in the Cookies folder.

Internet Explorer and Netscape Navigator use cookies to help users build personal start pages. Companies use cookies to remember what a person wants to buy. If you have shopped for items on the Internet, then you have used a cyber-shopping cart, which is a cookie. You collect things in the cart and then pay for them when you check out. Cookies also help Web developers identify dead-end paths. **Dead-ends** are sections on the Web site a user visits, which apparently cause them to leave the Web site for lack of interest. Advertisers like to use cookies to profile your interests. Certain advertisements record cookies. Clicking certain advertisements eventually will determine what type of advertisement you will see in the future.

JavaScript cookies cannot get data from the user's hard drive, read e-mail, or steal other sensitive information. The JavaScript code limits access to the user's hard disk for security reasons. JavaScript only has one way to write cookies, which the browser controls through a predetermined cookie location. Because the cookie information is embedded in the data sent to the browser, the browser can block cookies. Some sites give limited access if the cookie information is blocked, however.

# JavaScript Basics — Variables, Literals, and Expressions

Much of the processing with forms or functions you will perform requires the use of variables. A **variable** represents a value stored in memory for use by the script. The more common types of values stored in the variable are numbers, words, or a combination of both. Values that hold numbers are called **numeric** and values that hold words or combinations of letters and numbers are called **strings**. JavaScript also uses **Boolean** type variables that represent a state or condition as being True or False (Yes or No).

**More About**

**CGI Scripts**

The CGI script specifies the communication between the server and Web browser. Many functions of CGI scripts can be accomplished through ActiveX controls and Java applets.

**More About**

**Cookies**

For more information on cookies, visit www.scsite.com/js/int.htm and then click cookies.

Unlike many other programming languages, when you define a variable in JavaScript you do not have to indicate its type. The variable assumes its type depending on the type of data it stores. This flexibility means you can use a variable for one type of value in one instance, and then use the variable again for another type of value in a different instance. This practice is unwise, however, because it can lead to confusion. As in other programming languages, it is best to use unique variable names in developing JavaScript pages.

### Rules for Naming Variables

Various names may be used for a variable, but adhere to the following simple rules:

▶ The name must begin with a letter or an underscore.
▶ The rest of the name is made up of letters, numbers, or underscores.
▶ Avoid naming variables with reserved words. **Reserved words** are predefined words that have special meaning to JavaScript.
▶ Do not place any spaces or punctuation in the name.

The reason that a period cannot be used in a variable name is that periods separate objects, properties, and methods. Table I-1 shows examples of valid and invalid variable names. In addition, remember that in JavaScript, variable names are case sensitive. **Case sensitive** means that if you create a form and use mixed-case spelling, such as State, as a variable name, and later use the uppercase spelling, STATE, as a variable name, JavaScript will determine these spellings as two different variable names.

Variables are declared the first time they are used by inserting the word, var, before the variable name, followed by an equal sign (=), and then the value. For example, if you type, var gpa, this name will declare a variable named, gpa, with no value assigned. Current versions of Netscape Navigator and Internet Explorer display the word, undefined, on the screen for the variable value if it is used without a value having been assigned to it.

**More About**

**Reserved Words**

Reserved words are the names of built-in objects, functions, and methods used by JavaScript. Using these words as variable names would create confusion for the interpreter. For more information on reserved words, visit www.scsite.com/js/int.htm and then click reserved words.

**Table I-1**

| VALID | INVALID |
|-------|---------|
| idnumber | id number (space) |
| Cust_ID | Cust.ID (period) |
| Major | *Major (does not start with a letter) |
| Year2000 | 2000 (does not start with a letter) |
| Passwd | Password (reserved word) |
| _Continue | Continue (reserved word) |

### Literals

While a variable is used to store data or values, a literal is a constant value that does not change. A **literal** is an actual number or character text, rather than a calculated result or value input from a keyboard. If the literal is a number, it is called a numeric literal. Character or text values are called string literals. Figure I-4 shows how to define a variable with a numeric literal value.

```
var width = 3
```

**FIGURE I-4**

The numeral three (3) cannot be changed and always will remain the same. The value of width can be changed from three (3) to some other number either through a calculation or through reassigning it another value.

A **string literal** is text enclosed in pairs of quotation marks. Figure I-5 shows how to assign a string literal to a variable. With string literals the text must be placed inside a pair of quotation marks. Numeric digits may be placed inside quotation marks, but they will be treated as a string, not as a number. Think of the characters between quotation marks as a sequential group of characters, one after the other, forming a continuous string.

```
var browserType = "Netscape"
```

**FIGURE I-5**

If the characters are not enclosed inside quotation marks, JavaScript will try to interpret the characters as having some other meaning. JavaScript might show an error message that says it cannot find the undefined variable, or it might interpret the characters as an object or function.

In addition, JavaScript string literals can use certain special characters or codes. This feature is borrowed from the C programming language, and is convenient if you need to insert quotation marks in the middle of a string. For example, to place quotation marks within a string, use a slash and a quotation mark (\"), placed at the location you want the quotation marks to display. In Figure I-6, a quotation from Shakespeare is placed in a variable called Shakespeare. The \" keeps the quotation marks around the string so they will display if the value of Shakespeare is ever displayed.

```
var Shakespeare = "\"To be or not to be, that is the question!\" Hamlet."
```

**FIGURE I-6**

A number of these special codes exist and are explained in Table I-2. The user, however, must be warned that some symbols act differently depending on the operating system in use. For example, a script needs the \r\n for a carriage return, line feed in the Microsoft Windows environment, but only the \n in the UNIX environment. You may find it easier to use the HTML tags of <P> or <BR> in the write() method for a new line. The **write()** method is associated with the Document object and is used to write text to the Web page. These tags work the same in the JavaScript write() method, as they do in any HTML document, but these tags cannot be used in the alert() method. The **alert()** method is used to display messages in a dialog box. Both of these statements will be discussed in more detail in Project 1. Remember the maximum number of characters in a string is 255. This limit is based on the older browsers, so the developer always must account for them.

| Table I-2 | |
|---|---|
| CODE | SYMBOLS |
| Backslash | \\ |
| Single quotation | \' |
| Double quotation | \" |
| Tab | \t |
| Carriage return | \r |
| Backspace | \b |
| Form feed | \f |
| New line | \n |

## Expressions and Operators

An **expression** is a formula or a way to assign values to variables. The JavaScript expression uses a combination of variables and literals to derive other values. Figure I-7a shows an expression that might be used in a simple math problem. This example assumes that the sum has been defined previously in the JavaScript code. Figure I-7b demonstrates how to initialize a variable to zero (0). This practice is used widely in programming to insure that no unusual values are in the Count variable, which might cause an error in the result.

```
average = totalValue/Count
```

**FIGURE I-7a**

```
var Count = 0
```

**FIGURE I-7b**

An expression operates by taking the values to the right-hand side of the equal sign, performing the arithmetic operation, and then storing the result in the variable on the left-hand side of the equal sign. The action in Figure I-7b on the previous page still is an expression because the value on the right-hand side of the equal sign is assigned to the variable on the left-hand side. In most uses of expressions, you probably will use variables instead of literals.

For example, imagine you have a Web page where you sell used musical compact disks (CDs). Your Web page displays pictures and titles of the CDs with a price. A person browsing your Web site may pick a certain CD with a price of $7.99. This value is stored in a variable called Cost. You ask the user to enter the number of CDs they want to purchase, which will be stored in a variable called Quantity. To calculate the sale price and store it in a variable called SalePrice, you multiply the Quantity by the Cost (SalePrice = Quantity * Cost).

JavaScript uses the same basic arithmetic operators as other programming languages or application software packages. The **arithmetic operator** is the symbol that instructs the expression what to do. Table I-3 describes the arithmetic operators with an example.

## More About

### Modulus

Modulus operations return the remainder of a division. For example, 7 % 2 equals 1 because 7 divided by 2 equals 3 with a remainder of 1.

**Table I-3**

| SYMBOL | DESCRIPTION | EXAMPLE |
|--------|-------------|---------|
| = | Assign values | counter = counter + 1 |
| + | Addition | sum = 4 + 5 |
| - | Subtraction | difference = most - least |
| * | Multiplication | pay = hours * rate |
| / | Division | percent = totalAmt / portion |
| % | Modulus - returns the remainder only in division | remainder = 27 % 12 |
| ++ | Increments the variable by one | j++, ++j |
| -- | Decrements the variable by one | j--, --j |

JavaScript uses the increment (++) and decrement (--) operators borrowed from the C programming language. The use of these operators needs some explanation because j++ is not the same as ++j. The difference can be seen in how the operator is used in an expression. Avoid using this operator until you fully understand how it works. Table I-4 shows how the different expressions are evaluated. The initial values of m and x are equal to seven.

**Table I-4**

| m | x | EXPRESSION | RESULT | EXPLANATION |
|---|---|------------|--------|-------------|
| 7 | 7 | m = x++ | m = 7, x = 8 | m is assigned first, then x is incremented |
| 7 | 8 | m = ++x | m = 9, x = 9 | x is incremented, then m is assigned |
| 9 | 9 | m = x-- | m = 9, x = 8 | m is assigned first, then x is decremented |
| 9 | 8 | m = --x | m = 7, x = 7 | x is decremented, then m is assigned |

Like the programming language C, JavaScript allows expressions like x + = y. This expression is the same as writing x = x + y. Table I-5 shows how this style of expression is written with other arithmetic operators. Writing expressions in this format can be confusing. Using expressions you understand is recommended. By writing expressions in an easily understood format, the JavaScript code will be easier to debug in the event of problems.

In addition, the mathematical order of precedence is used in evaluating an expression in JavaScript. Table I-6 shows the order of precedence for the operators discussed thus far.

Proceeding in a left to right order, the first thing evaluated is anything inside the parentheses. If more than one set of parentheses exists, the innermost set is evaluated first. Any increment and decrement symbols are evaluated, followed by multiplication, division, or modulus operators and finally, the addition or subtraction operators are evaluated. The other symbols and levels to the order of precedence are not discussed in this book.

The plus sign (+) is used in another operation called concatenation. **Concatenation** is used to join string literals or variables together as one variable. Figure I-8 is an example of combining two string variables to create a message. The end result is that completeMsg now contains the contents of Message1 and Message2.

| Table I-5 | |
|---|---|
| *EXPRESSION* | *SAME AS* |
| a + = b | a = a + b |
| a - = 1 | a = a - 1 |
| x * = x | x = x * x |
| n / = m | n = n / m |
| remainder % = d | remainder = remainder % d |

| Table I-6 | |
|---|---|
| *SYMBOLS* | *OPERATORS* |
| ( ) | Parentheses, with innermost parentheses first |
| ++ and -- | Increment and decrement |
| *, /, and % | Multiplication, division, and modulus |
| + and - | Addition and subtraction |

```
var Message1 = "You only can put so many letters in a string "
var Message2 = "before you run out of space."
var completeMsg = Message1+" "+Message2
```

**FIGURE I-8**

This technique is useful because older browsers have a limitation on how many characters you can place in a string. You will learn the use of concatenation in Project 1.

**More About**

**Concatenation**

Concatenation sequentially joins string data. The result of the JavaScript statement, *var answer = "3" + "2",* is not 5, but "32".

# Conditionals

One of the advantages to using JavaScript is the capability to validate data entered into a form. To validate data, you compare or test the data entered to a desired value. This test is called a **conditional,** and the result of the test is either True or False. Based on the result of the test, you execute different JavaScript code.

Remember, the test only has two possible outcomes: True or False. JavaScript uses conditionals with If and While statements, to compare or test the values stored in variables (Table I-7 on the next page). The function of the **If** statement is to select and execute alternative sections of code. The function of the **While** statement is to initiate a loop. Notice in the table that the conditions are enclosed in a pair of parentheses, as they would appear in JavaScript code.

**Table I-7**

| OPERAND | EXAMPLE | RESULTS |
| --- | --- | --- |
| = = | (a = = b) | True if a equals b |
| != | (a != b) | True if a does not equal b |
| > | (a > b) | True if a is greater than b |
| < | (a < b) | True if a is less than b |
| >= | (a >= b) | True if a is greater than or equal to b |
| <= | (a <= b) | True if a is less than or equal to b |
| && | (a = = b) && (x < y) | True if both a equals b and x is less than y |
| \|\| | (a != b) \|\| (x >= a) | True if either a does not equal b or x is greater than or equal to a |

## If and If...Else Statements

The first part of the If statement is written as *If (conditional)*. Place the JavaScript code to be executed if the result of the conditional test is True, inside a set of braces ({ }) as illustrated in Figure I-9.

```
var todaysDate = new Date()
var numHours = todaysDate.getHours()
If(numHours>=12) {
   document.write("Good Afternoon")
   }
Else   {
   document.write("Good Morning")
   }
the rest of your code .
```

**FIGURE I-9**

The use of the **Else** clause indicates which code should be executed when the result of the test is False. Though you will not understand some of the statements, Figure I-9 illustrates a way to test the time of day and display a message whether it is morning or afternoon. Not every condition test needs an Else clause. Do not make the mistake of placing code after the Else clause brace that you need to execute, regardless of the results of the conditional.

## While Loop

A **loop** is a set of JavaScript codes that are to be executed repeatedly. The **While loop** tests a condition at the beginning of the loop. If the condition is True, the loop is executed. If the condition is False, the code after the closing brace (}) is executed. The basic form of the While statement is shown in Figure I-10. You will learn more about While loops in Project 2.

```
While (condition) {
     the JavaScript code to be executed while the condition is True
     }
the JavaScript code to be executed when the loop is finished
```

**FIGURE I-10**

# Functions

A **function** is a way to write several lines of script and use them repeatedly as needed. Functions are defined by starting with the keyword function followed by a set of parentheses. Figure I-11 shows a sample function, which displays a message using the alert() method.

The instructions or code for the function are written inside a set of braces ({ }). The left-hand brace indicates the beginning of the function and the right-hand brace indicates the ending of the function. Notice the placement and direction of the braces in Figure I-11.

```
function Greetings() {
        alert("Hello, this is a friendly message.")
        }
```

**FIGURE I-11**

The function name is, Greetings, and it will display a dialog box with the words, "Hello, this is a friendly message." The alert() method displays a dialog box with an OK button. The browser waits for the user to click the OK button and then closes the box. The browser then will continue executing the next set of script codes. You can use the function Greetings() instead of typing the code *alert("Hello, this is a friendly message.")* every time you need to display this message.

By slightly changing the Greetings() function, you can make it an all-purpose message display function. Figure I-12 shows how to pass a value using a variable to a function. By passing a value to the function, the message changes as needed, using the same Greetings() function.

```
messageStr = "This is a customized message."
function Greetings(messageStr) {
        alert(messageStr)
        }
```

**FIGURE I-12**

# Objects, Properties, and Methods

An **object** is a real-world entity. Your book, car, pets, and friends are all objects. JavaScript makes use of objects in its association with Web browsers. This technique is called **object oriented** (**OO**). When it refers to programming it is called **Object-Oriented Programming** (**OOP**). The development of OOP provides a way to represent the world in conceptual terms that is understood easily. People understand their everyday objects and can understand easily that objects have properties and behaviors.

An object is described by its properties. **Properties** are attributes that help differentiate one object from another. For example, a car has a color, a certain body style, and a certain type of interior. These are all properties of the car that can be used to describe it. You separate an object and its property with a period. For example, you would write, car.color = "red", to indicate the car is the object and color is the property. Red is the value of the property.

**More** *About*

**Object-Oriented Programming**

For more information on object-oriented programming, visit www.scsite.com/js/int.htm and then click object-oriented.

A behavior is called a method. A **method** is a function or action you want the object to perform. You either can write your own functions, or use the built-in methods supplied with JavaScript. Methods associated with car, pet, and friend objects might be drive, feed, and talk, respectively. Thus, for a drive() method, it is written, car.drive().

Some methods require what is called an argument. An **argument** is a value given to the method. The argument is the message used in a method that is passed to the object. For example, you might have the cat object and the feed() method, written, cat.feed("Tuna"). The argument, "Tuna", is a message describing what to feed the cat. Just as in the statement document.write("this is an example"), the document is the object, write() is the method, and "this is an example" is what is to be written to the document.

Arguments can be variables or literals. The argument must match the method. This means, the method must be able to use the argument. For example, in the write() method you can add regular HTML tags for special formatting. You must include the tags in quotation marks as shown in Figure I-13.

```
document.write("<CENTER><B>PLEASE READ THE FOLLOWING</B></CENTER>")
```

**FIGURE I-13**

Although JavaScript uses objects, it is not to be considered a complete OOP language. JavaScript provides many built-in objects, even though you can define and create your own. The objects that you define and create are object instances. An **object instance** is the actual object used. For example, instructions for building a backyard shed are an object, but the actual shed is an instance.

The built-in objects include the Date, Arrays, windows, and forms, along with the items on a form such as a text box, a check box, or an option button. One rule about defining objects is to assign unique and meaningful names. For example, it is acceptable to name a form, form1, but not very meaningful.

It makes more sense to name the form based on its activity. A registration form, might be called, regForm, while an order form might be called, ordForm. This naming style easily differentiates the order form from the registration form, especially if several months pass and you need to make a change to the Web page. The form1 name may not have meaning by then.

The confusion about the entire set of objects in JavaScript is that some objects can be properties of another object. For example, a **document** is an object on it own, but it also can be a property of the Window object. The **Window** object is the top-level object in the hierarchy. By using the various properties and methods associated with the Window object, you can manipulate your document. In Figure I-13, the Document object was used with the write() method. The statement could have been written as window.document.write("<CENTER><B>Good Morning</CENTER ></B>"). Because of the hierarchy of the JavaScript object, the Window object is assumed. Figure I-14 shows a small portion of the object hierarchy in JavaScript.

**FIGURE I-14**

# Events

Many applications today require that you do something before an action takes place. These actions are called **events**. In a word processor, you click a toolbar or property button to save the document, print the document, or run the spell check. These buttons actually represent events. The document will not print until you click the Print button, or a new document cannot be opened until you click the Open button.

Table I-8 lists the basic event handlers and their descriptions. Netscape recommends that all event handlers be written in lowercase.

As users read the Web page, they may click a button or move the mouse pointer over an image or a link. By using one of the event handlers, the JavaScript code associated with the event is executed. When you execute the code associated with an event handler shown in Table I-8, you are **triggering** the event.

**Table I-8**

| EVENT HANDLER | DESCRIPTION |
| --- | --- |
| onfocus | Used to draw attention to an object when the insertion point moves to it. |
| onblur | Removes attention when the insertion point moves off the object. |
| onselect | Used when the user highlights text. |
| onchange | Does something when the user changes the value of the object, and moves off. |
| onsubmit | Action performed when the user clicks the SUBMIT button. |
| onclick | Action performed when the user clicks any button. |
| onmouseover | Action performed when the user moves the mouse over something. |
| onmouseout | Action performed when the mouse moves off of something. |
| onload | Action performed when a document is loaded. |
| onunload | Action performed when the user leaves a page. |
| onabort | Action performed when the user clicks Stop to interrupt loading a page. |
| onerror | Action performed when an error occurs in the script. |
| onreset | Used to clear values when the user clicks the RESET button. |
| ondragdrop | Action performed when the user drags and drops an object in a window. |
| onkeydown | Action performed when the user presses a designated key. |
| onkeypress | Action performed when the user holds a key (preceded by onkeydown). |
| onkeyup | Action performed when the user releases a designated key. |
| onmousedown | Action performed when the user presses a mouse button. |
| onmousemove | Action performed when the user moves the mouse. |
| onmouseup | Action performed when the user releases the mouse button. |
| onmove | Action performed when the user moves a window or frame. |
| onresize | Action performed when the user resizes a window or frame. |

## Forms

Because many of the event handlers work with forms, you need to know how the HTML tags work for forms. If you have ever filled out a request for information on a Web site, you have worked with a **form**. The form may have text boxes, option buttons, check boxes, and other buttons. Many Web sites use forms to collect data and transmit it back to the main Web server. These sites might use CGI to submit the data on the form to the server. Then the server runs a program that may validate the values in the text boxes. If a problem is found, an error message is sent back to the user.

To use CGI in this fashion requires fairly extensive programming capability. One of the more popular CGI languages is **Perl**, which is primarily a UNIX-based language. Users of Microsoft Windows NT servers can use C or Visual Basic as their language of choice. With JavaScript, however, the Web page user's browser window can validate the form before the data is sent to the server. The JavaScript code can keep the user on the form until the data is entered correctly to the satisfaction of the Web page author.

Using event handlers in forms is quite simple. For example, suppose you have a form with a dark background color such as dark gray. Knowing that users might have video display units that make it difficult to read the text on this kind of background, you can create a button to change the background color to white or another lighter color. Figure I-15 illustrates the code to change the background color to white.

**More** *About*

**Perl**

For more information on Perl, visit www.scsite.com/js/int.htm and then click Perl.

```
<INPUT TYPE = "Button" Value = "White" onclick = "document.bgColor = 'White'">
```

**FIGURE I-15**

Onclick is the event handler. When the user clicks the button that displays, the background color will turn white. To execute a function with an event handler, simply place the function name between the quotation marks after the equal sign associated with the event handler. For example, in Figure I-16, suppose you wanted to display an image of the sun for someone viewing the Web page in daytime, and an image of the moon if the page is viewed at night. You create a function called timeLine(), which would test the clock and determine whether to display the sun or moon image in a certain location when the Web page is loaded.

```
<BODY bgColor = "White" onload = "timeLine()">
```

**FIGURE I-16**

Many of the event handlers (such as onfocus, onblur, onchange, onsubmit, and onreset) described in Table I-8 on the previous page, usually are used with the INPUT tag. Clicking a form's text box, check box, or option button gives that object the focus. **Focus** means that a text box, check box, or option button has attention drawn to it. For example, a text box that has the focus contains the insertion point. Thus, you would use the onfocus event handler to trigger the script associated with this object.

An object no longer has the focus when you click another part of the form or another object. In JavaScript, when an object loses focus, it is said to blur. **Blur** means that the attention has moved from the object; for example, the user clicks a text box to move the insertion point to the new text box. Thus, you can use the onblur event handler to execute a function to perform a task. JavaScript is capable of knowing when the value of the text box, option button, or check box has changed. You can use the onchange event handler to trigger a function.

Finally, many forms have Submit and Reset buttons. The onsubmit event is the event handler triggered when you point to and click the Submit button. Usually, you will have an action that will transmit the form either to a CGI program or e-mail it to an intended receiver. The Reset button allows you to trigger an event handler that clears the form and allows the user to start over and reenter the data. Figure I-17 shows how the HTML tag creates a Submit button with a JavaScript function set to an onclick event handler. This INPUT tag has several attributes, with an onclick event handler. The function associated with the onclick event handler will be triggered when the user clicks the Submit button.

```
<INPUT TYPE = "Button" Name = "SubmitText" Value = "Submit" onclick = "Transmit()">
```

**FIGURE I-17**

# Frames and Arrays

A **frame** is a feature that allows a browser window to be split into smaller units. These units are not windows. You need to think of the frame as similar to the windows in a house. Some windows are all one large sheet of glass, similarly to picture windows. Others are broken down into smaller pieces called panes. In a browser you might see one large window, or it might be broken into smaller frames.

Frames actually are created with the HTML tags <FRAMESET> and </FRAMESET>. The FRAMESET tag actually takes the place of the <BODY> tag. The FRAMESET tag has one set of attributes, which is used to create columns or rows depending on the attributes used. Each frame created with a FRAMESET tag has its own HTML source page, which is identified by the SRC attribute. The **SRC attribute** identifies the HTML document you want to load. A sample FRAMESET tag is shown in Figure I-18. The figure shows a 25/75 split in the window, with the left-hand side being narrower than the right-hand side. The left-hand side will display a table of contents, while the right-hand side will display the first page.

A concern with frames in JavaScript is that each frame is an object. As such, JavaScript applies properties and methods to the frame object to provide dynamic controlling of the browser window.

**More About**

**Frames**

Netscape Navigator 2.0 introduced frames. Each frame represents a separate document. A common practice uses a frame on the left to serve as a table of contents for multiple Web pages or sites.

```
<FRAMESET COLS = "25%,75%">
  <FRAME SRC = "TOC.HTML">
  <FRAME SRC = "MAINPAGE.HTML">
</FRAMESET>
```

**FIGURE I-18**

## Arrays

To understand and use some aspects of frames, you must understand how an array works. An **array** is a collection of data items that is identified by a singular name. This singular name is used in place of the many different variables that would have to be used if JavaScript did not have the capability of using arrays. JavaScript arrays were introduced with Netscape Navigator 3.0, although an array can be simulated in earlier versions. Creating arrays will be discussed in Project 3.

In the latest versions of JavaScript, arrays are true objects. To define an array, you use the built-in Array object (Figure I-19). Notice in the figure that an argument is used in the object array's parentheses. This value is called the length. The **length** actually represents the number of items stored, not how many characters are being stored. The individual items or elements in the array are indicated by a subscript in square brackets.

```
var currMonth = new Array(13)
currMonth[1] = "January"
currMonth[2] = "February"
.

.
currMonth[12] = "December"
```

**FIGURE I-19**

Notice that the number of elements is 13 and not 12, to match the number of months in a year. As with most other programming languages, JavaScript's first array element is [0]. As mentioned earlier, however, you can simulate an array in JavaScript version 1.0. The problem is that in the older browsers and JavaScript versions, the [0] element contains the size of the array. In the newer versions, which use the built-in Array object, the first element can be used for storing any data. It is recommended always to leave element [0] empty and start with element [1].

Unique to JavaScript arrays is that you can add more items to the array than originally defined. By assigning any value to the intended item, JavaScript extends the size of the array. Netscape Navigator and Internet Explorer display the word, undefined, if you attempt to display an array element outside the original size that does not have data stored in it. Be aware that with this feature, JavaScript does not provide error messages. If you use an undefined array element in a mathematical expression, you can have serious errors that are difficult to find. Therefore, it is imperative you keep data defined to the initial size of the array and do not arbitrarily add elements.

# Summary

This introduction provided an overview of JavaScript and its components: attributes, tags, variables, expressions, operators, codes, functions, objects (Window, Document), properties, methods, events, event handlers, frames, and arrays. This overview provides the basic concepts on how HTML tags are used and how to incorporate JavaScript into HTML code. As you work through the projects that follow you will learn the power of JavaScript. You will learn how to begin developing more interesting, dynamic, and interactive Web pages.

# Test Your Knowledge

## 1 True/False

**Instructions:** Circle T if the statement is true or F is the statement is false.

T   F   1. JavaScript is a product of a joint venture between Microsoft and Sun Microsystems.

T   F   2. Microsoft Internet Explorer can execute JavaScript but Netscape Navigator will not execute VBScript.

T   F   3. A variable is a name given to a value that is stored for use by the script.

T   F   4. You can change the value of a literal with the <var> tag.

T   F   5. In the order of precedence, addition is evaluated before multiplication.

T   F   6. A property is something that describes an object.

T   F   7. In object-oriented languages, methods are used to associate built-in functions with objects.

T   F   8. In JavaScript, an event is a function.

T   F   9. Including the latest version of JavaScript, you can choose from 22 total event handlers.

T   F   10. You cannot mix JavaScript event handlers with HTML tag properties.

## 2 Multiple Choice

**Instructions:** Circle the correct response.

1. _____ is a programming language developed by Sun Microsystems to be the standard for the Internet.
   a. VBScript          b. J++               c. Java                  d. C++

2. Netscape originally started developing a script called _____.
   a. LiveWire          b. HotWire           c. LiveScript            d. VBScript

3. An HTML _____ is an instruction surrounded by less than and greater than sign symbols (< >).
   a. tag               b. instruction       c. file                  d. object

4. A _____ is a name given to a value that is stored in memory for use by the script.
   a. function          b. tag               c. variable              d. frame

5. Values or variables that hold numbers are called _____ variables.
   a. numeric           b. string            c. Boolean               d. array

6. A variable name must begin with a(n) _____ or a(n) _____.
   a. letter, number
   b. letter, underscore
   c. number, pound sign (#)
   d. uppercase letter, number

7. The reason that a(n) _____ cannot be used in a variable name, is that they are used to separate objects, properties, and methods.
   a. underscore
   b. comma
   c. period
   d. slash

*(continued)*

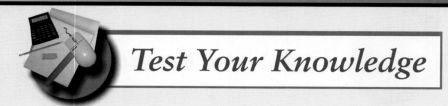

# Test Your Knowledge

**Multiple Choice** *(continued)*

8. One limitation of string variables is they can hold a maximum of _____ characters.
   - a. 40
   - b. 90
   - c. 128
   - d. 255

9. Which conditional operand requires that the results of two conditions both be True in order for the whole conditional test to be True?
   - a. **
   - b. //
   - c. &&
   - d. ||

10. A(n) _____ requires that the user do something before an action takes place.
   - a. event
   - b. method
   - c. property
   - d. subroutine

# 3 Understanding Variables Names and Types

**Instructions:** In the examples below, the first column contains a series of var statements or arithmetic expressions used to define variable names. In the spaces provided in the second column, indicate whether the bold variable name in the first column is valid or invalid. In the spaces provided in the third column, indicate the variable type as string, numeric, or Boolean.

| VARIABLE OR EXPRESSION | VALID | TYPE |
|---|---|---|
| 1. var **userName** = "Fred" | | |
| 2. var **status** = True | | |
| 3. var **Count** = Count + 1 | | |
| 4. **_address** = "10 Downing St" | | |
| 5. **end of file** = "False" | | |
| 6. **cap_size** = 7.5 | | |
| 7. var **1k** + = 1 | | |

# Test Your Knowledge

## 4 Understanding Arithmetic Expressions

**Instructions:** In the examples below, the first column contains one or more variables and their current values. In the second column, the variables are used in an expression. In the spaces provided, determine the value of the expression shown in the second column and enter the result in the third column.

| VARIABLE | EXPRESSION | RESULT |
|---|---|---|
| 1. m = 3 | m = m + 1 | _____ |
| 2. Cost = 0, Price = 3.00, Units = 5 | Cost = Price * Units | _____ |
| 3. Total_Cost = 33.00, Cost = 15.00 | Total_Cost = Total_Cost + Cost | _____ |
| 4. j = 5 | j++ | _____ |
| 5. Sum = 9 | --Sum | _____ |
| 6. counter | counter = counter + 1 | _____ |
| 7. t = 5 | t * = t | _____ |
| 8. a = 15, b = 4, c = 0 | c = a % b | _____ |
| 9. n = 5, x = 2, t = 2 | t = (n + 1) * x | _____ |
| 10. dist = 0, speed = 55, time = 3 | dist = speed * time | _____ |

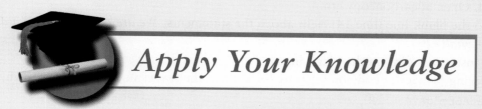

# Apply Your Knowledge

## 1 Add a Greeting to a Web Page Based on the Time of Day

**Instructions:** Start your browser and Notepad. Open the Web page carboncopy.htm on the JavaScript Data Disk. If you did not download the Data Disk, see the inside back cover for instructions for downloading the JavaScript Data Disk or see your instructor. The Web page has a generic greeting. Modify the Web page by adding the JavaScript code that reads the system time. If the hour is between 4:00 A.M. and noon, add the lines, Good Morning. Have a rush job for the afternoon? We can handle it! (see Figure I-20 on the next page). If the hours are between noon and 6:00 P.M., then add the lines, Good Afternoon. We can get that print job ready by tomorrow morning. If the hours are between 6:00 P.M. and 11:00 P.M., then add the lines, Good Evening. We will be here all night if you need us! Finally, if the hours are between midnight and 4:00 A.M., then add the line, Yes, we are working at this hour! (*Hint:* the system type is in European time, so you must compare the hour appropriately. For example, 4:00 P.M. is 16 hours.) Perform the tasks on the next page.

*(continued)*

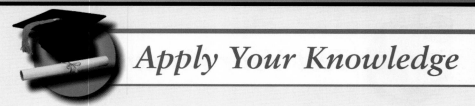

## *Apply Your Knowledge*

**Add a Greeting to a Web Page Based on the Time of Day** *(continued)*

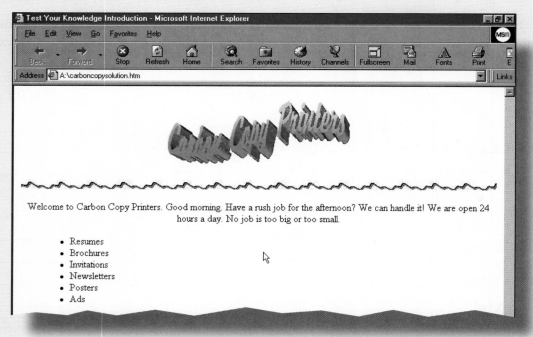

**FIGURE I-20**

1. Start Notepad. Open a:\carboncopy.htm.
2. Scroll down to the blank line (line 14) right above the statements, *We are open 24 hours a day. No job is too big or too small.</p>*
3. Position your insertion point on the blank line.
4. Type the following JavaScript code on separate lines. Press the SPACEBAR to indent as shown.

```
<SCRIPT LANGUAGE="JAVASCRIPT">
<!-- Hide the script from old browsers --
    today = new Date()
    If ((today.getHours() >=4) && (today.getHours() <=12)){
      document.write("Good Morning. Have a rush job for the afternoon? We can handle it!")
    }
    If ((today.getHours() >12) && (today.getHours() <=18)){
       document.write("Good Afternoon. We can get that print job ready by tomorrow
morning.")
    }
    If ((today.getHours() >18) && (today.getHours() <=23)){
       document.write("Good Evening. We will be here all night if you need us!")
    }
    If ((today.getHours() >=0) && (today.getHours() <4)){
       document.write("Yes, we are working at this hour!")
    }
// -- End hiding here -->
</SCRIPT>
```

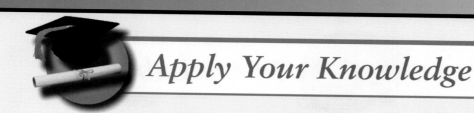

## Apply Your Knowledge

5. Save the revised Web page using the file name, carboncopysolution.htm, on the floppy disk in drive A.
6. To test your Web page, start your browser, and then open the a:\carboncopysolution.htm file.
7. If an error occurs, go back to Step 4 and double-check your spelling, quotation marks, parentheses, and relational operators. Make corrections in the Notepad text file. You must click the Refresh button on your toolbar to reload the Web page and view your corrections.
8. If correct, use your browser to print the carboncopysolution.htm Web page and then print the HTML file using Notepad. Hand in the printouts to your instructor.

## In the Lab

## 1 Using Mouse Event Handlers to Show Images

**Problem:** One of the advantages of using JavaScript is the ability to change an image in a given placeholder. You can use the mouse event handlers to accomplish tasks by calling a function that assigns a new graphic file to the image location in the HTML code. The Pine Wood Country Club and Golf Course would like to add an image on their Web page that displays when the user points to a link and then another image that displays when the mouse pointer is moved from the link (Figure I-21).

**FIGURE I-21**

*(continued)*

# In the Lab

**Using Mouse Event Handlers to Show Images** *(continued)*

**Instructions:** Start Notepad. Open the pinewood.htm Web page on the JavaScript Data Disk. If you did not download the Data Disk, see the inside back cover for instructions for downloading the JavaScript Data Disk or see your instructor. Add a function similar to the LeftSide() function called by the onmouseover event handler. Perform the following tasks.

1. Locate the function RightImage() in the first SCRIPT tag.
2. Position the insertion point under the t in the word function (line 10).
3. Type `document.RightSide.src="golfer1.jpg"` and then press the ENTER key.
4. Find the HREF for the Membership link.
5. Position the insertion point after the onmouseover="LeftImage()" statement.
6. Type `onmouseout="RightImage()"` as the statement.
7. Do not press the ENTER key.
8. Save the Web page using the file name, pinewoodsolution.htm, on the floppy disk in drive A.
9. Start your browser and then open the pinewoodsolution.htm file.
10. Test the Web page by placing the mouse pointer over the Membership link. An image of two golfers should display on the left. Move the mouse pointer off the Membership link and an image of a golfer should display to the right.
11. Print the Web page. Click the Notepad button on the taskbar and then print the pinewoodsolution.htm file. Hand in the printout to your instructor.

## 2 Displaying a Message when a Web Page Is Opened

**Problem:** Not all Web pages are placed on the Internet. Many companies use in-house Intranets to provide employees with critical information and access to databases. The Little PC Company places all company information on an Intranet for their sales and technical support staff. As the Webmaster, the Human Resources department has asked you to display important employee messages when the Web page loads. They want the following message, *Please remember to update your employee benefit forms by the end of this month. Thank you. Human Resources.* You decide to accommodate the Human Resources department by writing a function that uses the built-in alert() function to display the message in a dialog box (Figure I-22). This approach allows you to change the message easily in the future.

**Instructions:** Insert the JavaScript Data Disk in drive A. Start Notepad. Open the littlepc.htm Web page, and add a function that is triggered by an onload event handler. Perform the following tasks.

1. Write a function, called HRMsg, which displays a message in a dialog box. Position the insertion point on line six in the SCRIPT section and enter the following code:

```
function HRMsg() {
   alert("Please remember to update your employee benefit forms by the end of this month.
Thank you. Human Resources.")
```

2. Locate the <BODY> tag (about line 14). Position the insertion point between the Y and the > symbol.
3. Type `onload="HRMsg()"` and do not press the ENTER key.
4. Save the Web page using the file name, littlepcsolution.htm, on the floppy disk in drive A.
5. Start your browser and then open the littlepcsolution.htm file to test the Web page.
6. Print the littlepcsolution.htm from Notepad. (*Note:* You will not be able to print the Web page while the dialog box is on the screen.) Hand in the printout to your instructor.

# In the Lab

**FIGURE I-22**

## 3 Correcting the Errors on a JavaScript Web Page

**Problem:** Paul's Painting estimate Web page has a form button that when clicked displays an Explorer User Prompt dialog box that asks for the number of square feet to be painted (Figure I-23a on the next page). When the user enters a value, however, and clicks the OK button, an error occurs. The regular Webmaster is sick today and your boss has asked you to fix the error. (*Hint*: The spelling of variables and function names is important.) The corrected Web page displays in Figure I-23b on the next page.

**Instructions:** Perform the following tasks to correct the errors.

1. Insert the JavaScript Data Disk in drive A. Start your browser. Click the Address text box and enter `a:\paulspaint.htm` to open the Web page.
2. Click the Paint Estimate button.
3. Use Notepad to correct the errors.
4. After correcting the errors, save the file using the file name, paulspaintsolution.htm, on the floppy disk in drive A.
5. Test the Web page by opening the paulspaintsolution.htm in your browser.

*(continued)*

*In the Lab*

## Correcting the Errors on a JavaScript Web Page *(continued)*

Explorer User Prompt dialog box

input text box

**FIGURE I-23a**

result displayed in text box

form button

**FIGURE I-23b**

6. If an error still exists, open paulspaintsolution.htm in Notepad and check the spelling and wording of all variables and functions. Repeat Steps 4 through 6 until all errors are corrected.
7. Print the Web page and the Notepad file. Hand in the printouts to your instructor.

JavaScript

P R O J E C T

**1**

# Integrating JavaScript and HTML

O B J E C T I V E S

You will have mastered the material in this project when you can:

- Discuss how to integrate JavaScript and HTML
- Insert SCRIPT tags on a Web page
- Write beginning and ending SCRIPT tags
- Define and use flickering to draw attention
- Describe the background color property of the document object
- Set the background color of a Web page using JavaScript
- Save the HTML file
- Test the Web page
- Discuss JavaScript variables
- Extract the system date
- Use several variables to construct a message
- Describe the write() method of the document object
- Write a user-defined function that displays a message and links viewers to a new site
- Describe how the setTimeout() method works
- Use the lastModified property to display the last modified document date
- Print an HTML Notepad file

# Ready, Set, Stop

## BMW's Driving School
## *Brakes* New Ground

W hile driving to class, you start thinking about your math test and weekend plans. Suddenly, a car pulls out in front of you. You jam on your brakes, swerve to the left, and narrowly avoid the collision.

Braking, cornering, and accident avoidance skills are required to face the rigors of sharing the road with today's aggressive drivers. BMW, the German carmaker known for its commitment to safety and performance, is driving home the need for driver training with its Ultimate Driving Experience.

The two-hour event held in major cities across the United States features an intensive, defensive driving course with classroom and racetrack components. Participants start the day by attending a *chalk talk* and learning driving dynamics. Then they divide into small groups and hit the road. With professional drivers at their sides, they maneuver BMW's 3 Series sedans through a winding track and learn the rudiments of accelerating, turning, and stopping.

After several trial runs, they are ready to put their split-second reactions to the test. Drivers are grouped into teams to face the ultimate challenge: using their newly honed skills to swerve through the track as quickly as possible. This timed auto-cross race allows drivers to gain confidence and compare their driving abilities.

For example, would you like to design your dream Z3 roadster? Just click Z3 roadster, then Build Your Own Z3, and let your creativity soar. How about a metallic fern green exterior with a two-tone sand leather interior? Or bright red with black upholstery? Do you prefer the 2.8 liter in-line six-cylinder or the 1.9 in-line four? Your configurations display in vivid detail in front of your eyes, complete with technical specifications, warranty and maintenance information, and features on BMW's engineering marvels.

The Web site's functionality is enhanced with JavaScript, the object-based language you will explore in this textbook. In each project in this book, you will use the Web page development cycle to define a problem, analyze the situation, and then develop the solution. Likewise, BMW's Web page developers used these design principles to create an effective interactive site. For example, their pages feature information on lease and financing options. You can obtain an estimated monthly payment for each car you design. If the figures look good, you can apply for credit online.

Just as BMW's Web site uses JavaScript to steer driving enthusiasts through its features effectively, its Ultimate Driving Experience uses defensive driving skills to help drivers navigate the roadways safely.

After competing in the race, drivers can wind down by test driving other BMW models, viewing historic BMW vehicles, or purchasing exclusive BMW accessories.

Realizing that teenagers have extraordinarily high accident records, the automaker developed a separate program for drivers ages 15 to 21. This four-hour segment motivates these inexperienced motorists to develop lifelong defensive driving skills.

While the Ultimate Driving Experience helps drivers maneuver successfully on today's highways, BMW has found a home on another highway – the information superhighway. Its Web site, www.bmwusa.com, features a multitude of interactive components.

# JavaScript

# Integrating JavaScript and HTML

P R O J E C T

**1**

C A S E   P E R S P E C T I V E

You are a summer intern in the Online Development Group at Fun with Phonics. At a general development group meeting, Mandy Senicott, the Webmaster, announces a contract has been signed with a new Internet service provider (ISP), which means the Web home page will be moved.

Mandy is concerned about the users who have links pointing to the old domain address in their bookmarks. The old ISP contract will not expire for two months, so Mandy asks you to create a Web page that announces the move and automatically forwards users to the new Web site.

Mandy informs you the Web page must meet the following criteria: the Web page must flicker to gain the reader's attention, then display a message about the move, and include a link to the new location. The page automatically displays a message that informs the reader they now will be linked to the new site after 15 seconds.

# Introduction

Many companies build and use Web sites, primarily to market and sell their products and services. Since 1996, many companies have developed and gained a substantial market edge using e-commerce (electronic commerce). **E-commerce** is business activity that takes place using networked computers and the Internet. For example, Auto-By-Tel, Dell Computers, Cisco Systems, and E-Trade all boast of market improvements because of their Web presence.

As a marketing tool, a good Web site must attract users and keep their attention. Marketing experts state that you have six to seven seconds to attract and retain someone's attention. This principle also applies to a well-designed Web page. You want a surfer to hit your page and stay, especially if you have a product or service to sell. Once users are on the page, you want them to stay and peruse it. If you are selling products or services, the page must convince them to make a purchase.

To gain a share of the cyber marketplace, many companies and individuals purchase their own domain names. In e-commerce, companies with easy to remember domain names are more likely to have repeat visitors to their Web sites. Because of the competition among Internet service providers, and the growth in users, many Web site locations are moved constantly. A Navigator bookmark or Internet Explorer favorite Web page a few months ago may no longer be valid now.

Unfortunately, when a Web site moves the user often encounters the error message: 404 Object not found. This error message does not tell you if the site has moved, has a new domain name, or if the site no longer exists on the Internet. Some organizations, however, leave a forwarding message at the old location or domain name when they move. This message informs you of the new domain name or address, and allows you to click a link to the new location. Unfortunately, HTML does not allow automatic links to domain addresses, the user must click a reference link.

One way Web developers solve this problem is to use JavaScript. JavaScript is an object-based language. An **object-based** language uses built-in objects, but is not capable of creating classes of objects or using inheritance features of object-oriented languages such as C++ or Java. In addition, JavaScript has predefined properties, methods, and event handlers.

As discussed in the Introduction to JavaScript Programming, an **object** is a person, place, or thing. **Properties** are attributes of objects and describe some aspect about the object.

You assign a property to an object by writing objectname.property=value. Spaces around the equal signs are optional.

**Methods** are actions, such as write, or function calls, such as Date("July 4, 2001"). You perform a method by writing objectname.method(parameters), where parameters are items or instructions the method uses.

Table 1-1 contains a short description of four commonly used objects with sample properties and methods.

**Table 1-1**

| OBJECT | SAMPLE PROPERTIES AND METHODS |
|---|---|
| window | The window object is the main object. Many of the window-object properties are objects in their own right (i.e., document, frame, and location). The window object is not needed in many statements because it is assumed. For example;<br>To link to a new site<br>    location = "www.scsite.com"<br>To open another window<br>    open("win1.htm", "window1", "toolbar = yes")<br>To cause a script to be executed after a specified period of time<br>    setTimeout("chngSite(s)", 15000) |
| document | The document object is one of the more often-used objects derived from the window object. A few of its properties and methods are fgColor, cookie, and write. For example;<br>To set a document foreground color use the fgColor property<br>    document.fgColor = "white"<br>To read the information stored in a cookie text file use the cookie property<br>    var cookieInfo = document.cookie<br>To display the date the Web page was last modified, combine with the write() method<br>    document.write("The date last modified"+document.lastmodified) |
| math | The math object provides the capability to perform calculations<br>PI is a property and represents the value of PI (3.14159).<br>pow() is a method, which means to raise to the power. For example;<br>    pow(value, exponent)<br>To calculate the area of a circle you would write<br>    var area = PI * pow(radius,2) |
| navigator | The navigator object determines which browser the user is running. For example;<br>appName is a property that contains the browser's code name<br>    var browser = navigator.appName<br>appVersion is a property that provides browser's release version<br>    var browserVer = navigator.appVersion |

**More About**

**E-commerce**

Internet technology enables companies to recap the benefits of electronic trading. In an *Information Week* survey on Internet usage, 81 percent of the companies deploy e-commerce systems to improve customer services, and 77 percent stated e-commerce improved business processes. For more information on e-commerce, visit www.scsite.com/js/p1.htm and then click e-commerce.

**More About**

**Auto-by-Tel, Dell, and E-trade**

Auto-by-Tel, Dell, and E-trade are very prominent Web sites. To find out how these companies incorporate graphics and interactivity to maintain a strong Web presence, visit www.scsite.com/js/p1.htm and then click Auto-by-Tel.

**More About**

**Domain Names**

To learn more about domain names, visit www.scsite.com/js/p1.htm and then click domain names.

**More About**

## Scripting Languages

Netscape's JavaScript and Microsoft's VBScript are the two main client side script languages used today. To read more about scripting languages and why many organizations want one common language platform, visit www.scsite.com/js/p1.htm and then click scripting languages.

An **event** is the result of a user's action. **Event handlers** are the way to associate that action with the set of JavaScript codes you want executed. The general form of an event handler is in Table 1-2.

| Table 1-2 – Event Handler | |
|---|---|
| **General form:** | `<TAG attribute eventhandler = "JavaScript code">` |
| **Comment:** | where TAG is the HTML tag; an attribute is a characteristic of a tag that can have a value assigned to it; eventhandler is the name of the JavaScript event handler; and JavaScript code is the instruction to execute. |
| **Example:** | `<SCRIPT LANGUAGE = "JavaScript">` |

The Introduction to JavaScript Programming has a complete list of event handlers shown in Tables I-8 on page J I.13.

# Project One — Fun with Phonics Web Page

You have determined the requirements for the Web page update and are ready to make the necessary changes. First, you will create a Web page (Figure 1-1a) that displays a message informing the user that the Web site location has been moved. Second, you will create a link to the new Web page location, so users may click the link and go directly to the Web site. The HTML code is in a file on the JavaScript Data Disk. Your job in this project is to add JavaScript code to the HTML file so the Web page displays as shown in Figures 1-1a and 1-1b. The HTML and JavaScript code is shown in Figure 1-1c.

**FIGURE 1-1a**

**FIGURE 1-1b**

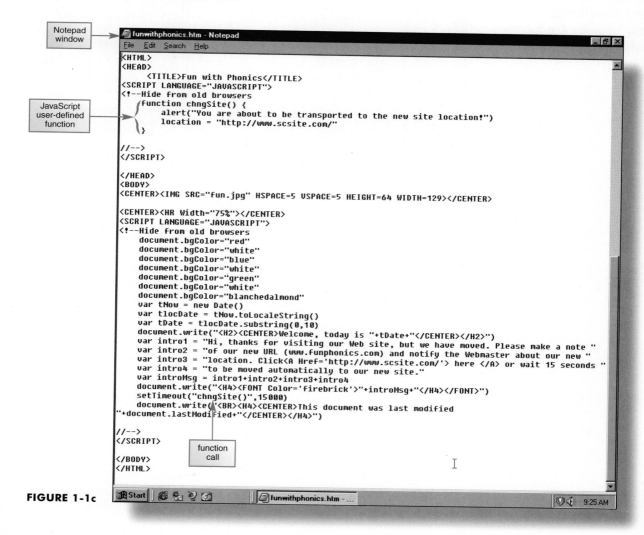

**FIGURE 1-1c**

## Starting Notepad

To start Notepad, Windows must be running. Perform the following steps to start Notepad.

**Steps**  **To Start Notepad**

**1** **Click the Start button on the taskbar and then point to Programs on the Start menu. Point to Accessories on the Programs submenu, and then point to Notepad.**

*Figure 1-2 shows the default menu structure for Accessories. Your system may have a different set of menus. Whenever you point to a menu name that has a right arrow following it, a submenu displays.*

FIGURE 1-2

**2** **Click Notepad. When the Notepad window displays, click the Maximize button.**

*The maximized blank Notepad window displays (Figure 1-3).*

FIGURE 1-3

---

The Notepad application is a text editor. If you are familiar with any word processing application, many of the same concepts apply. Notepad can cut, copy, and paste text, as well as search and find text. You do not need to format any text in this project. The Windows 98 version of Notepad automatically wordwraps. If you are using the Windows 95 version, however, you may have to check Word Wrap on the Edit menu. To begin, you must open the Fun with Phonics Web page. To open the fun.htm file in Notepad, perform the steps on the next page.

**To Open a Web Page Stored on the Data Disk**

**1** **Insert the JavaScript Data Disk in drive A.** If you do not have a copy of the JavaScript Data Disk, see the inside back cover for instructions for downloading the JavaScript Data Disk, or see your instructor. **Click File on the menu bar and then click Open. When the Open dialog box displays, type** `*.htm` **in the File name text box.**

*The Open dialog box displays (Figure 1-4). Text Documents is the default Files of type. The file name extension is changed to .htm.*

FIGURE 1-4

**2** **Click the Look in box arrow and then click 3½ Floppy (A:). Click fun.htm and then point to the Open button.**

*When you click the Look in box arrow, the Look in list displays (Figure 1-5). When you click 3½ Floppy (A:), a list of files displays with fun.htm highlighted.*

FIGURE 1-5

③ **Click the Open button.**

*The fun.htm document opens in the Notepad window. The fun.htm file name displays on the title bar (Figure 1-6).*

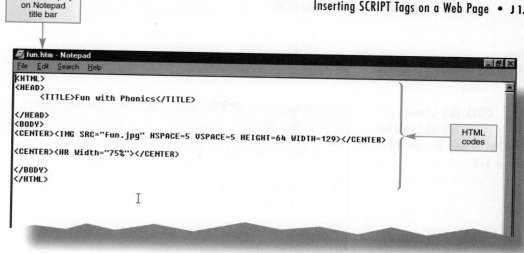

file name displays on Notepad title bar

```
fun.htm - Notepad
File   Edit   Search   Help
<HTML>
<HEAD>
      <TITLE>Fun with Phonics</TITLE>

</HEAD>
<BODY>
<CENTER><IMG SRC="fun.jpg" HSPACE=5 USPACE=5 HEIGHT=64 WIDTH=129></CENTER>

<CENTER><HR Width="75%"></CENTER>

</BODY>
</HTML>
```

HTML codes

FIGURE 1-6

**Other Ways**

1. Press ALT+F, press O

The fun.htm HTML code displays in Notepad. The next step is to insert the JavaScript code in the BODY section to make the Web page flicker.

# Inserting SCRIPT Tags on a Web Page

You can place JavaScript code anywhere in the HTML code. Most Web developers agree that the HEAD section should contain the user-defined JavaScript functions and the BODY section should contain the event handlers or other JavaScript code sections.

You always begin the JavaScript section with a SCRIPT tag, which indicates the language you are using. Similarly to other HTML tags, the JavaScript SCRIPT tag needs a beginning and ending tag. Some Web developers recommend inserting the beginning and ending tags immediately as you modify or construct the Web page. The important rule to remember is there must be a complete set of SCRIPT tags such as <SCRIPT> and </SCRIPT>.

## Writing the Beginning SCRIPT Tag

As discussed in the Introduction to JavaScript Programming, the SCRIPT tag has one attribute, which is LANGUAGE. You write the tag as <SCRIPT LANGUAGE = "JAVASCRIPT">. If you omit the LANGUAGE attribute, most browsers default to JavaScript.

Following the SCRIPT tag, Web developers commonly agree to add an HTML comment line. The HTML comment line hides any script language that a browser may not be able to interpret. As with all HTML tags, there must be a beginning and ending tag. To begin the JavaScript section you enter

```
<SCRIPT LANGUAGE="JAVASCRIPT">
<!--Hide from old browsers
```

In this project, you will use only JavaScript features that work in all versions of Internet Explorer or Netscape Navigator. To enter the beginning SCRIPT tag and comment to create a JavaScript section in the BODY section, perform the steps on the next page.

**More About**

**JavaScript**

To learn more about why JavaScript is used, visit www.scsite.com/js/p1.htm and then click JavaScript.

**More About**

**JavaScript Comment Lines**

An HTML comment is a tag that begins with <! and ends with >. If you fail to close the HTML comment with a bracket (>), all your HTML code will be ignored. In JavaScript, the double slash (//) is used to indicate comments.

**To Enter the Beginning SCRIPT Tag and Comment**

**1** **Click the blank line (line 10) above the </BODY> tag as shown in Figure 1-7.**

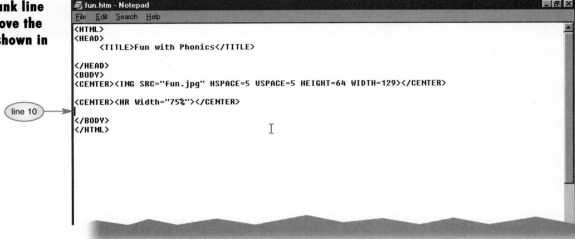

**FIGURE 1-7**

**2** **Type** <SCRIPT LANGUAGE="JAVASCRIPT"> **and then press the ENTER key. Type** <!--Hide from old browsers **and then press the ENTER key.**

*The beginning SCRIPT tag and comment display (Figure 1-8).*

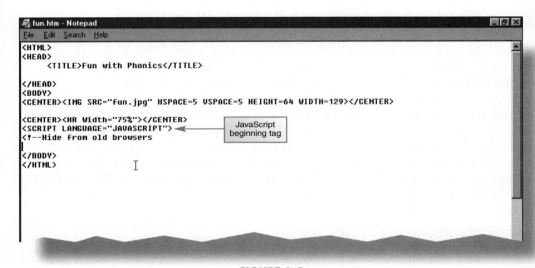

**FIGURE 1-8**

These lines begin the JavaScript section. Later, you will enter the ending tags before testing the Web page.

# Using a Flicker on a Web Page to Draw Attention

You probably have had some experience waiting for a Web page that takes too long to display. The number of users on a Web server, the speed of your connection, the amount of traffic on the Internet, the size of the Web page, and the number of graphics the Web page contains have an impact on how long it takes to display. Users begin to *wonder* and quit paying attention to their screens. One way to grab users' attention is to make the page flicker. You can make the page flicker using JavaScript code to change the background color in rapid succession.

With HTML, you set the background color once in the <BODY> tag with the BGCOLOR attribute. Because Web pages have one BODY section, the background color can be set only once. With JavaScript, you can change the background color anytime using the document object and BGCOLOR property. As described earlier, the general form of an object and property is objectname.propertyname = value.

To set the background color of your document to red, you write the following JavaScript code:

```
document.bgColor="red"
```

To create the flickering effect, place several of these statements in sequence, alternating between a color background and a white background. You may enter the property name using all lowercase, uppercase, or mixed-case letters as shown below.

```
document.bgColor="red"
document.bgColor="white"
document.bgColor="blue"
document.bgColor="white"
document.bgColor="green"
document.bgColor="white"
```

When a visitor references the Web page with the above code, the document background colors change immediately and flicker. Perform the following steps to create flicker on the Web page.

### More About

**The Document Object**

The document object is actually a property of the Window object. To learn more about the document object, visit www.scsite.com/js/p1.htm and then click document objects.

### More About

**Background Color Codes**

Color codes can be identified as either hex properties or the actual color name. A hex number 00FFFF indicates the amount of red, green, and blue to display, respectively. To see a complete list of colors and hex codes, visit www.scsite.com/js/p1.htm and click background colors.

 **To Create Flicker on the Web Page**

**1** **Position the insertion point on line 12. Type** document. bgColor="red" **and then press the ENTER key. Type** document.bgColor= "white" **and then press the ENTER key.**

*Each line is indented four spaces for readability purposes (Figure 1-9).*

**FIGURE 1-9**

**2** With the insertion point on line 14, enter the four lines of code as shown in Figure 1-10.

**FIGURE 1-10**

As you enter JavaScript code, be careful with the spelling and placement of quotation marks. The browser cannot interpret misspelled HTML tags and JavaScript commands. In addition, missing or unbalanced quotation marks cause the browser to misinterpret commands. These types of errors prevent the browser from loading and displaying the Web page properly. If users becomes confused or frustrated, they will abandon the Web page and look for another site.

## Setting the Background Color to a Static Color

After making the page flicker to gain the user's attention, set the background color to the final color. The background and text colors should be pleasing to the eye and provide ample contrast to make reading the text easy. Perform the following step to set the background color to blanched almond.

**Steps** To Set the Background Color to a Static Color

**1** **With the insertion point on line 18,** type document.bgColor= "blanchedalmond" **and then press the ENTER key.**

*This statement sets the background color to blanched almond (Figure 1-11).*

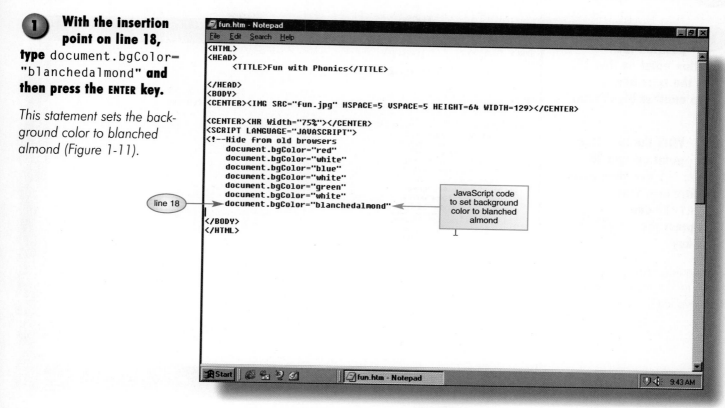

**FIGURE 1-11**

The six JavaScript statements entered on lines 12 to 17 make the page flicker. The last statement on line 18 sets the background color to a static blanched almond.

## Completing the JavaScript Section

As discussed earlier, all HTML tags must have beginning and ending tags to separate them from other page elements. To complete this set of JavaScript codes, you must add the ending SCRIPT tags. You must close the comment in line 11 and the beginning SCRIPT tag in line 10 as follows:

```
//-->
</SCRIPT>
```

The JavaScript //--> closes the beginning comment, and <!--Hide from old browsers, encloses the JavaScript code within the comments. If the user has an old browser, the JavaScript code is hidden from the user. In addition, if you do not close the comment, the Web page may display nothing when loaded. The </SCRIPT> tag closes the JavaScript section. This ending tag also prevents the HTML code that follows from being interpreted as JavaScript code. Perform the steps on the next page to enter the ending tags.

**Steps** To Enter the Ending SCRIPT Tag

**1** **If necessary, position the insertion point on line 19. Press the ENTER key to create another blank line.**

**2** **With the insertion point on line 20, type //--> and then press the ENTER key. Type </SCRIPT> and then press the ENTER key.**

*The ending //--> and </SCRIPT> tags complete the JavaScript section (Figure 1-12).*

```
fun.htm - Notepad
File  Edit  Search  Help
<HTML>
<HEAD>
      <TITLE>Fun with Phonics</TITLE>

</HEAD>
<BODY>
<CENTER><IMG SRC="fun.jpg" HSPACE=5 VSPACE=5 HEIGHT=64 WIDTH=129></CENTER>

<CENTER><HR Width="75%"></CENTER>
<SCRIPT LANGUAGE="JAVASCRIPT">
<!--Hide from old browsers
    document.bgColor="red"
    document.bgColor="white"
    document.bgColor="blue"
    document.bgColor="white"
    document.bgColor="green"
    document.bgColor="white"
    document.bgColor="blanchedalmond"

//-->
</SCRIPT>

</BODY>
</HTML>
```

line 19 → ending comment and SCRIPT tags

Start    fun.htm - Notepad                 9:44 AM

**FIGURE 1-12**

The JavaScript code to cause the Web page to flicker is complete. This is a good point to test the newly entered code. The HTML file must be saved on disk before it can be tested. You then can start your browser and display the saved file to check the flicker.

# Saving the HTML File

Save the file using the Save As command on the File menu. You are required to add the .htm extension to the file name, because Notepad automatically saves all files with the default .txt extension. Perform the following steps to save the HTML file on the floppy disk as funwithphonics.htm. The file name is not case sensitive and can be entered in uppercase or lowercase characters.

**To Save the File on the Floppy Disk**

**1** **Make sure the floppy disk is in drive A. Click File on the menu bar and then click Save As.**

*The Save As dialog box displays (Figure 1-13). The File name text box contains the highlighted entry of the previously opened file (a:\fun.htm).*

**FIGURE 1-13**

**2** **Type**

a:\funwithphonics.htm **in the File name text box (Figure 1-14).**

**FIGURE 1-14**

new file name
on title bar

**3** **Click the Save button.**

*The dialog box closes, the file is saved, and the new file name displays on the Notepad title bar (Figure 1-15).*

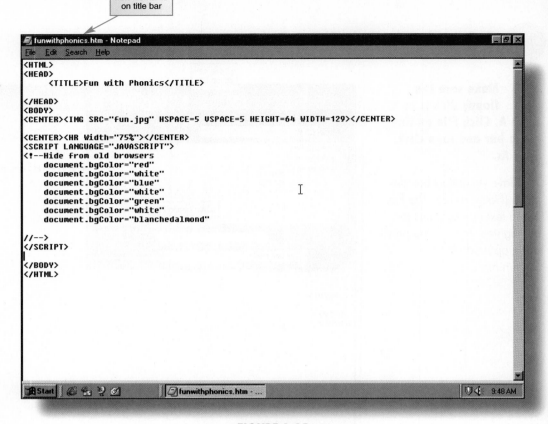

```
funwithphonics.htm - Notepad
File  Edit  Search  Help
<HTML>
<HEAD>
     <TITLE>Fun with Phonics</TITLE>

</HEAD>
<BODY>
<CENTER><IMG SRC="fun.jpg" HSPACE=5 VSPACE=5 HEIGHT=64 WIDTH=129></CENTER>

<CENTER><HR Width="75%"></CENTER>
<SCRIPT LANGUAGE="JAVASCRIPT">
<!--Hide from old browsers
    document.bgColor="red"
    document.bgColor="white"
    document.bgColor="blue"
    document.bgColor="white"
    document.bgColor="green"
    document.bgColor="white"
    document.bgColor="blanchedalmond"

//-->
</SCRIPT>

</BODY>
</HTML>
```

Start    funwithphonics.htm - ...    9:48 AM

**FIGURE 1-15**

*Other* **Ways**

1. Press ALT+F, A

You will need to remember the file name, funwithphonics.htm, when you test the file in the browser.

# Testing the Web Page

The next step is to test your funwithphonics.htm Web page. Missing periods, quotation marks, or misspelled words will cause errors. If an error occurs, a dialog box displays with a message and indicates where the browser could not interpret the JavaScript code. To continue loading your Web page, click the OK button in the dialog box if an error message displays. The browser will cease to process any more JavaScript code, and load what it can of the remaining Web page. Perform the following steps to test the Web page.

## To Test the Web Page

**1** **Start your browser.**

**2** **Click the Address box. Type** `a:\funwithphonics.htm` **and then press the ENTER key.**

*The Fun with Phonics web page displays in the browser window. The JavaScript code causes the Web page to flicker. The Web page then displays the background color blanched almond (Figure 1-16).*

**FIGURE 1-16**

If your browser does not display the Web page correctly, close any error message, and click the Notepad button on the taskbar. Check your JavaScript code according to Figure 1-15. Correct any errors, save the file, activate the browser, and then click the Refresh button.

# JavaScript Variables

As in other programming languages, JavaScript variables are used to store values temporarily. JavaScript variable naming conventions are similar to the naming conventions of variables in other programming languages such as C. For example, JavaScript variable names are case sensitive.
Table 1-3 shows the rules for naming JavaScript variables.

**More About**

## Variable Names

JavaScript variables are temporary places to store data. Visit www.scsite.com/js/p1.htm and then click variable names. At the Netscape site, scroll through the JavaScript Guide Contents frame on the left side until you find the section on Value, Variables, and Literals, and then click Variables.

### Table 1-3

| COMMENT | VALID NAMES EXAMPLE | INVALID NAMES EXAMPLE |
|---|---|---|
| Must begin with a letter or underscore | Months | 9Months |
| Rest of name must be letters or underscores | Last_Name | Last-Name |
| Do not use spaces or other punctuation | ZipCode | Zip.Code |
| Avoid JavaScript objects, properties, and reserved words | xNow | Date |

JavaScript variables are loosely typed. **Loosely typed** means you are not required to define the variable data types as either numeric or character in advance. JavaScript determines the data type from the data. This feature is an advantage, because variables are flexible and can store any data type. If you are not careful, however, you can change a variables' data type in the middle of JavaScript code and create an error. This type of error can be difficult to find.

String data types are variables that hold characters or a combination of letters, numbers, or symbols. Numeric data types hold numbers. Boolean data types contain logical data as *True* or *False*. To indicate the data type, define the variable by assigning the value to the variable. For example, assigning a string value to a variable as in

```
var LastName = "Simon"
```

makes the variable LastName a string data type. Assigning a numeric value to a variable as in

```
var pageCnt = 1
```

makes pageCnt a numeric data type. Assigning Boolean values to a variable as in

```
var Done = False
```

makes Done a Boolean data type. Conditional testing and loops use Boolean variables.

The var keyword is not required in the previous examples. Most Web developers and JavaScript programmers, however, recommend using the var keyword. If you display the value of a variable that you have not used previously in the program, JavaScript displays the term, undefined.

# Extracting the System Date

The next step is to display the date as shown in Figure 1-1a on page J 1.6. Web developers use the built-in Date() object to manipulate the current system date and time by creating a new object instance. The *new* keyword creates the new object instance

var variable = new object

where object is a JavaScript built-in object. A **built-in object** is a JavaScript object that is not dependent on nor belongs to another object, such as the document or window.

The parentheses after the Date() means you can obtain the current system date and time, or pass a specific date to the new object instance. By placing a specific date between the parentheses, the variable stores that date. For example,

```
var birthDay = Date("Jul, 13, 1975")
```

returns July 13, 1975 to birthDay.
Whereas, the statement

```
var curDate = new Date()
```

returns the current system date and time information as a string as follows:

Fri Jul 13 08:41:44 Central Daylight Time 2001

To extract just the date from the object instance (curDate), you use the toLocaleString and substring() methods as described in Table 1-4.

| Table 1-4 | |
|---|---|
| METHOD | EXPLANATION<br>*(In the examples below, assume the Date () object is nDate).* |
| toLocaleString() | Converts nDate to a string using the default display format used by the user's computer.<br>Use:     var tempDate = nDate.toLocaleString()<br>Result:   the date and time as MM/DD/YYYY HH:MM:SS (Windows format) assigned to tempDate |
| substring(x,y) | Any object may use the substring() method. The method extracts the date only from the Date() object.<br>Use:     var todaysDate = tempDate.substring(0,10)<br>Result:   the date as MM/DD/YYYY assigned to todaysDate |

To extract the current system date and use it in the format as MM/DD/YYYY, you write the following statements:

```
var tNow = new Date()
var tlocDate = tNow.toLocaleString()
var tDate = tlocDate.substring(0,10)
```

The first statement defines the new object for the date as tNow, which contains the day of the week, the month, day, time (in European time), the time zone, and the year as described earlier. The second statement uses the toLocaleString() method to extract the date and time and store it in tlocDate in the MM/DD/YYYY MM:HH:SS format. The third statement extracts only the date portion from the tlocDate variable.

The substring() method needs two parameters (x,y), where x is the starting point of the string and y is the location of the last character needed. Calculating these positions can be tricky because JavaScript uses relative addressing. **Relative addressing** means the location of any character in a string is calculated in relation to the first character in the string. Because the system identifies the first location address as zero (0), the first character position of a string is position 0. So in the string of data "MM/DD/YY  HH:MM:SS" the first M is position 0. The last character you want is the second Y, which is at relative position 7 (Table 1-5). The substring() method, however, requires you to state the last position as one character more than the actual last position. Thus, 7 + 1 equals 8. The substring() method parameters are (0,8) for the first digit of the date and the last digit of the date.

| Table 1-5 | | | | | | | | | | | | | | | | |
|---|---|---|---|---|---|---|---|---|---|---|---|---|---|---|---|---|
| M | M | / | D | D | / | Y | Y | | H | H | : | M | M | : | S | S |
| 0 | 1 | 2 | 3 | 4 | 5 | 6 | 7 | 8 | 9 | 10 | 11 | 12 | 13 | 14 | 15 | 16 |

Perform the steps on the next page to activate Notepad and enter the JavaScript code that will extract the current system date from the computer using the Date() object.

**More About**

**The System Date**

The way the system date displays in Netscape Navigator is different from the way the system date displays in Internet Explorer. Netscape extracts the date in the MM/DD/YY format. In Internet Explorer, the substring() method used to extract just the date is substring(0,8) not substring(0,10). The system date in Internet Explorer returns a string similar to Fri Jul 13 08:41:44 CDT 2001.

**More About**

**Extracting the System Date**

Because of the difference in how Netscape Navigator and Internet Explorer return the system date, you always must check your relative addressing used in the substring() method.

**To Extract the Current System Date Using the Date() Object**

**1** **Click the Notepad button on the taskbar to activate the Notepad window. Position the insertion point on line 19 beneath the document.bgColor= "blanchedalmond" statement.**

*The Notepad window and the funwithphonics.htm file display (Figure 1-17).*

```
funwithphonics.htm - Notepad
File  Edit  Search  Help
<HTML>
<HEAD>
      <TITLE>Fun with Phonics</TITLE>

</HEAD>
<BODY>
<CENTER><IMG SRC="fun.jpg" HSPACE=5 VSPACE=5 HEIGHT=64 WIDTH=129></CENTER>

<CENTER><HR Width="75%"></CENTER>
<SCRIPT LANGUAGE="JAVASCRIPT">
<!--Hide from old browsers
    document.bgColor="red"
    document.bgColor="white"
    document.bgColor="blue"
    document.bgColor="white"
    document.bgColor="green"
    document.bgColor="white"
    document.bgColor="blanchedalmond"

//-->
</SCRIPT>

</BODY>
</HTML>
```

line 19

depressed Notepad button

Start    funwithphonics.htm -...    9:55 AM

**FIGURE 1-17**

**2** **Type** var tNow = new Date() **and then press the ENTER key. Type** var tlocDate = tNow.toLocaleString() **and then press the ENTER key. Type** var tDate = tlocDate.substring (0,10) **and then press the ENTER key.**

*The three lines display (Figure 1-18).*

```
funwithphonics.htm - Notepad
File  Edit  Search  Help
<HTML>
<HEAD>
      <TITLE>Fun with Phonics</TITLE>

</HEAD>
<BODY>
<CENTER><IMG SRC="fun.jpg" HSPACE=5 VSPACE=5 HEIGHT=64 WIDTH=129></CENTER>

<CENTER><HR Width="75%"></CENTER>
<SCRIPT LANGUAGE="JAVASCRIPT">
<!--Hide from old browsers
    document.bgColor="red"
    document.bgColor="white"
    document.bgColor="blue"
    document.bgColor="white"
    document.bgColor="green"
    document.bgColor="white"
    document.bgColor="blanchedalmond"
    var tNow = new Date()
    var tlocDate = tNow.toLocaleString()
    var tDate = tlocDate.substring(0,10)

//-->
</SCRIPT>
```

extracts the current system date

**FIGURE 1-18**

The three statements extract the current system date in the desired format. For example, if the system date is Fri Jul 13 08:41:44 Central Daylight Time 2001, then the system assigns tDate the date 7/13/01.

## Displaying the Current System Date

You write directly to the Web page using the write() or writeln() methods. The general forms of the write() and writeln() methods are shown in Table 1-6.

| Table 1-6 – write() and writeln() Method | |
|---|---|
| **General form:** | document.write(message) |
| | document.writeln(message) |
| **Comment:** | where message is any combination of text variables, and HTML tags. |
| **Examples:** | document.write("<H1><CENTER>Welcome to our Web page</CENTER> </H1><BR>") |
| | document.writeln("Welcome to our Web page") |

The only difference between write() and writeln() is that writeln() displays each message parameter on a new line. To display the contents of a variable with a text string, you concatenate the text and the variable. **Concatenate** means to join or link together. The symbol for concatenate is the plus sign (+). In this project, to display a simple welcome message with the current date, you write

```
document.write("<H2><CENTER>Welcome, today is "+tDate+"</CENTER></H2>")
```

You enclose the HTML codes in quotation marks within the message text. The plus signs (+) concatenate the tDate variable with the message and the ending HTML codes. The message and HTML codes within parentheses are enclosed in quotation marks. The variable name is not enclosed in quotation marks.

Perform the following step to display the current system date in the initial greeting.

 **Steps** To Display the Current System Date in the Initial Greeting

**1 Position the insertion point on line 22. Type** document.write("<H2><CENTER>Welcome, today is "+tDate+"</CENTER></H2>") **and then press the ENTER key.**

Figure 1-19 shows the embedded HTML code, which writes the date in heading 2 style and centers it on the page. You concatenate the tDate variable with the message to display within the string.

> **More About**
>
> **writeln()**
>
> You can accomplish the same effect by inserting <P> or <BR> tags in the write() method.

```
funwithphonics.htm - Notepad
File  Edit  Search  Help
<HTML>
<HEAD>
      <TITLE>Fun with Phonics</TITLE>

</HEAD>
<BODY>
<CENTER><IMG SRC="fun.jpg" HSPACE=5 VSPACE=5 HEIGHT=64 WIDTH=129></CENTER>

<CENTER><HR Width="75%"></CENTER>
<SCRIPT LANGUAGE="JAVASCRIPT">
<!--Hide from old browsers
    document.bgColor="red"
    document.bgColor="white"
    document.bgColor="blue"
    document.bgColor="white"
    document.bgColor="green"
    document.bgColor="white"
    document.bgColor="blanchedalmond"
    var tNow = new Date()
    var tlocDate = tNow.toLocaleString()
    var tDate = tlocDate.substring(0,10)
    document.write("<H2><CENTER>Welcome, today is "+tDate+"</CENTER></H2>")

//-->
</SCRIPT>

</BODY>
```

line 22

displays greeting with date

**FIGURE 1-19**

# Using Several Variables to Construct a Message

The next step is to incorporate the message that displays following the date (Figure 1-1a on page J 1.6). Older browsers have a limit of 255 characters to a line. Thus, it is recommended that you break up large groups of text by using several variables to construct a message. Perform the following steps to construct a long message using several JavaScript variables.

## TO CONSTRUCT A MESSAGE USING SEVERAL VARIABLES

**1** Position the insertion point on line 23. Type `var intro1 = "Hi, thanks for visiting our Web site, but we have moved. Please make a note "` and then press the ENTER key.

**2** Type `var intro2 = "of our new URL (www.funphonics.com) and notify the Webmaster about our new "` and then press the ENTER key.

**3** Type `var intro3 = "location. Click<A Href='http://www.scsite.com/'> here </A> or wait 15 seconds "` and then press the ENTER key.

**4** Type `var intro4 = "to be moved automatically to our new site."` and then press the ENTER key.

**5** Type `var introMsg = intro1+intro2+intro3+intro4` and then press the ENTER key.

*The four variables store several lines of text. Make sure you place a space before the closing quotation mark in the first three lines. Note the embedded HTML codes in intro3 for the new Web site reference. Also, when placing quotation marks inside of quotation marks use single quotation marks as in the intro3 variable. The five lines of code display (Figure 1-20).*

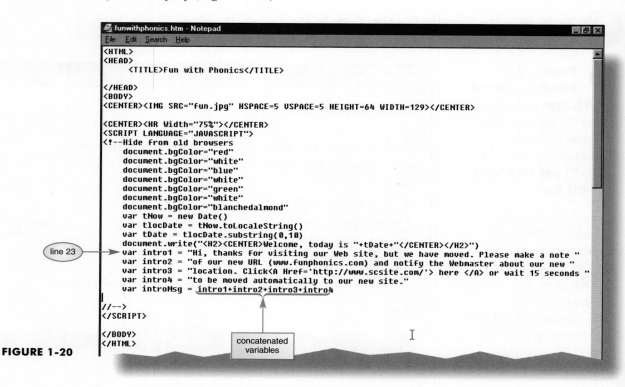

**FIGURE 1-20**

The last statement concatenates the four separate message variables into one message, which creates one continuous string of text. You need not worry about the length of the message.

## Writing the Message on the Web Page

To display the message as part of the Web page, you use the write() method. Use the heading 4 style and the font color firebrick to format the line. Perform the following step to write the message on the Web page.

 **To Write the Message on the Web Page**

**1** **Position the insertion point on line 28. Type** document. write("<H4><FONT Color='firebrick'> "+introMsg+"</H4> </FONT>") **and then press the ENTER key.**

*The document.write statement will display the combined message variable in a continuous sequence as if it was written as one long string of characters. Figure 1-21 shows the placement of the command and how the HTML codes are used.*

```
funwithphonics.htm - Notepad
File   Edit   Search   Help
<HTML>
<HEAD>
       <TITLE>Fun with Phonics</TITLE>

</HEAD>
<BODY>
<CENTER><IMG SRC="fun.jpg" HSPACE=5 VSPACE=5 HEIGHT=64 WIDTH=129></CENTER>

<CENTER><HR Width="75%"></CENTER>
<SCRIPT LANGUAGE="JAVASCRIPT">
<!--Hide from old browsers
    document.bgColor="red"
    document.bgColor="white"
    document.bgColor="blue"
    document.bgColor="white"
    document.bgColor="green"
    document.bgColor="white"
    document.bgColor="blanchedalmond"
    var tNow = new Date()
    var tlocDate = tNow.toLocaleString()
    var tDate = tlocDate.substring(0,10)
    document.write("<H2><CENTER>Welcome, today is "+tDate+"</CENTER></H2>")
    var intro1 = "Hi, thanks for visiting our Web site, but we have moved. Please make a note "
    var intro2 = "of our new URL (www.funphonics.com) and notify the Webmaster about our new "
    var intro3 = "location. Click<A Href='http://www.scsite.com/'> here </A> or wait 15 seconds "
    var intro4 = "to be moved automatically to our new site."
    var introMsg = intro1+intro2+intro3+intro4
document.write("<H4><FONT Color='firebrick'>"+introMsg+"</H4></FONT>")

//-->
</SCRIPT>

</BODY>
</HTML>
```

line 28

JavaScript code to display message

Start | funwithphonics.htm - ... | Fun with Phonics - Microso... | 9:57 AM

**FIGURE 1-21**

The one document.write() statement on line 28 displays a short paragraph formatted in the font size and color you desire. When displaying text on the Web page using this concatenation technique, you can use just one set of beginning and ending HTML formatting codes.

# Save and Test the Web Page

At this point, you should test the JavaScript code. Check your code for spelling errors, missing quotation marks, or parentheses. After you check for errors, save the file on the floppy disk in drive A, activate the browser, and then click the Refresh button. Perform the following steps to save the HTML file on the floppy disk in drive A.

## Steps To Save a File

**1** Make sure the JavaScript Data Disk is in drive A.

**2** Click File on the menu bar and then click the Save command.

*No dialog box displays (Figure 1-22). The file is saved using the same file name, funwithphonics.htm.*

**FIGURE 1-22**

## Other Ways

1. Press ALT+F, S

To test the Web page in the browser, perform the following step.

**Steps** ## To Test the Web Page in the Browser

**1** **Click the Fun with Phonics button on the taskbar to activate the browser. Click the Refresh button.**

*The Fun with Phonics Web page displays (Figure 1-23). The browser is the active window. Clicking the Refresh button, reloads the current Web page.*

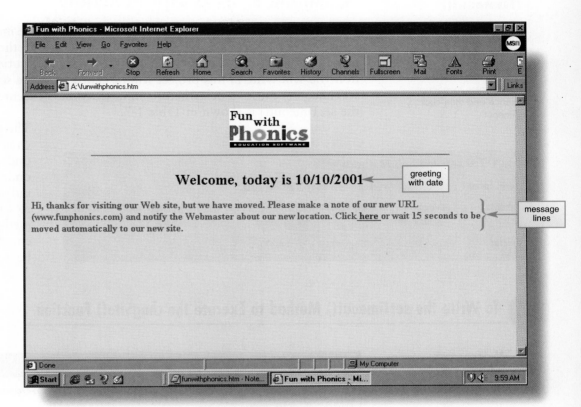

**FIGURE 1-23**

If the browser does not display the Web page correctly, close any error message, and then click the Notepad button on the taskbar. Check the JavaScript code against Figure 1-21 on page J 1.25. Correct any errors and save the file. Activate the browser and click the Refresh button.

After the test is complete, perform the following step to activate the Notepad window.

### TO ACTIVATE THE NOTEPAD WINDOW

**1** Click the Notepad button on the taskbar to activate the Notepad window.

*Notepad becomes the active window on the desktop. You can continue to edit the Notepad file.*

**More About**

**setTimeout()**

To learn more about the setTimeout() method, visit www.scsite.com/js/p1.htm and then click setTimeout. At the Netscape site, locate the Navigator JavaScript reference and then click setTimeout.

# Calling a JavaScript Function

JavaScript has two basic methods to call functions. One method to call functions is to use event handlers and object methods. The other method is to code the function name in a JavaScript section at the logical point of execution. The user-defined function you will write in this project will be called from the setTimeout() method. The setTimeout() causes a delay before an instruction is executed. The general form of the setTimeout() is shown in Table 1-7.

The user-defined function, chngSite(), executes in 15 seconds (time delay). Fifteen seconds is written as 15000 milliseconds. The next step is to write the setTimeout() method that will execute the chngSite() function, which will be written later.

| Table 1-7 – setTimeout() Method | |
| --- | --- |
| **General form:** | setTimeout("instruction", time delay in milliseconds) |
| **Comment:** | where instruction is any valid JavaScript statement, and time delay is expressed in number of milliseconds |
| **Example:** | setTimeout("chngSite()", 15000) |

 **Steps** To Write the setTimeout() Method to Execute the chngSite() Function

**1** If necessary, position the insertion point on line 29.

**2** Type setTimeout ("chngSite ()",15000) **and then press the ENTER key.**

*The setTimeout method waits 15 seconds (15 x 1000 milliseconds) and then calls the chngSite() function (Figure 1-24). The chngSite() function will be added to the HEAD section later.*

**FIGURE 1-24**

Be careful about the amount of time you give users to read a page that is transfering them to another page.

# Displaying the Last Modified Document Date

Most developers agree that you should display the date the Web page was last modified. The message displays at the bottom of the page, written with a small font to keep the message from distracting the user (Figure 1-1a on page J 1.6). JavaScript provides an easy way to display the date. The command is document.lastModified. You insert this command in a write() method with a message as follows:

```
document.write("<BR><H4><CENTER>This document was last modified
"+document.lastModified+"</CENTER></H4>")
```

Perform the following step to display the date last modified in a message.

 **To Display the Date Last Modified in a Message**

**1** **If necessary, position the insertion point on line 30, after the setTimeout() method. Type** document.write("<BR><H4><CENTER>This document was last modified "+document.lastModified+"</CENTER></H4>") **and then press the ENTER key.**

*The lastModified property displays the date and time the file was saved on disk (Figure 1-25).*

**FIGURE 1-25**

# Writing a JavaScript User-Defined Function

A **function** is JavaScript code that is written to perform certain tasks repeatedly. JavaScript comes with a number of built-in functions (Table 1-8 on the next page). Most of these functions actually belong to the Window object, but because the Window object is assumed, they are called built-in functions.

**Table 1-8**

| FUNCTION | EXPLANATION |
|---|---|
| close() | closes an open window |
| open() | opens a new window |
| print() | prints the contents of the window |
| setTimeout() | causes a script to be executed after a time delay |
| stop() | stops a download (same as clicking the Stop button) |

A **user-defined function** is one in which the Web developer writes the tasks to be performed. Functions replace large sets of JavaScript codes that are not able to fit within an HTML attribute. Most functions are associated with JavaScript event handlers, but can be written in any JavaScript section.

A function can have data passed to it, which is processed and a result is returned. This feature allows for flexibility in screen displays and interaction with the user. The code in the function is not executed until a JavaScript statement calls the function. To **call** a function means to have JavaScript execute the function.

The general form of a user-defined function is shown in Table 1-9.

 *About*

**Functions**

To learn more about JavaScript user-defined functions, visit ww.scsite.com/js/p1.htm and then click functions. At the Netscape site, scroll down the left frame until you find the section on Object Model and then click Functions.

**Table 1-9 – User-Defined Function**

| General form: | function FunctionName() { <br>    JavaScript code <br> } |
|---|---|
| Comment: | where FunctionName is the name of the user-defined function, and JavaScript code is the code you want executed when the function is called. |
| Example: | Function showBrowserName(){ <br>        alert("You are using" + navigator.appName) <br> } |

Naming conventions for functions are similar to those of variables. A function name must begin with a letter, may contain numerals and the underscore, but may not contain any spaces, punctuation (such as periods or commas), or reserved words. Table 1-10 shows valid and invalid user-defined function names. Values or parameters are passed to the function by placing a variable name between the parentheses.

**Table 1-10**

| VALID FUNCTION NAMES | INVALID FUNCTION NAMES | REASON |
|---|---|---|
| verifyForm() | 3Ddisplay() | starts with number |
| get_Cookie() | make.cookie | no periods allowed |
| calcPayment() | calc payment | space in middle of name |
| popWind() | pop-upWindow | no hyphens in name |

The function you need to write in this project is called chngSite() and is written as shown below:

```
function chngSite() {
      alert("You are about to be transported to the new site location!");
      location = "http://www.scsite.com/";
}
```

The built-in alert() function displays a message notifying the viewer of the link. The alert dialog box displays. The user must click a button in the dialog box to continue. Table 1-11 describes other functions that use dialog boxes. Following the alert() function, the location statement executes the link to the new Web site.

**Table 1-11**

| PROMPT AND CONFIRM DIALOG BOXES |
| --- |

**Prompt()**

| | |
| --- | --- |
| Purpose: | To prompt the user for input |
| Use: | var response = prompt("What is your name?") |
| Explanation: | A dialog box displays with a text box, and an OK and Cancel button. The prompt displays above the text box, the user types in the text box, and then clicks OK or Cancel. OK returns the value in the text box to the variable response. |

**Confirm**

| | |
| --- | --- |
| Purpose: | To prompt the user for a yes, no answer. |
| Use: | var makeItSo = confirm("Do you really want to open another window?") |
| Explanation: | A dialog box displays the prompt, and an OK and Cancel button. If the user clicks OK, then a True value is returned to makeItSo. If the user clicks the Cancel button, a False value is returned to makeItSo. |

## Placing User-Defined Functions in the HEAD Section

Where you place the user-defined functions is important. Most Web developers agree the HEAD section is where to place user-defined functions. The main reason functions are placed in the HEAD section of the HTML code is the function must be defined and loaded into memory before it can be called by the other JavaScript code or event handlers. If the user accidentally executes an event handler as the page is loaded, and the event handler is associated with a function not yet defined, the action will generate an error.

Complete the following steps to enter the chngSite() user-defined function in the HEAD section.

**Steps** To Enter the chngSite() User-Defined Function in the HEAD Section

**1** **Position the insertion point on the blank line (line 4) between the TITLE tags and the closing </HEAD> tag. Type** SCRIPT LANGUAGE= "JAVASCRIPT"> **and then press the ENTER key. Type** <!--Hide from old browsers **and then press the ENTER key (Figure 1-26).**

**FIGURE 1-26**

**2** **Type** function chngSite() { **and then press the ENTER key. Type** alert("You are about to be transported to the new site location!") **and then press the ENTER key. Type** location = "http://www. scsite.com/" **and then press the ENTER key. Type** } **and then press the ENTER key. Type** //--> **and then press the ENTER key. Type** </SCRIPT> **and then press the ENTER key.**

*The chngSite() user-defined function displays (Figure 1-27).*

```
funwithphonics.htm - Notepad                                    _ □ ×
File  Edit  Search  Help
<HTML>
<HEAD>
      <TITLE>Fun with Phonics</TITLE>
<SCRIPT LANGUAGE="JAVASCRIPT">
<!--Hide from old browsers
    function chngSite() {
         alert("You are about to be transported to the new site location!")
         location = "http://www.scsite.com/"
    }
//-->
</SCRIPT>

</HEAD>
<BODY>
<CENTER><IMG SRC="fun.jpg" HSPACE=5 VSPACE=5 HEIGHT=64 WIDTH=129></CENTER>

<CENTER><HR Width="75%"></CENTER>
<SCRIPT LANGUAGE="JAVASCRIPT">
<!--Hide from old browsers
    document.bgColor="red"
    document.bgColor="white"
    document.bgColor="blue"
    document.bgColor="white"
    document.bgColor="green"
    document.bgColor="white"
    document.bgColor="blanchedalmond"
    var tNow = new Date()
    var tlocDate = tNow.toLocaleString()
    var tDate = tlocDate.substring(0,10)
    document.write("<H2><CENTER>Welcome, today is "+tDate+"</CENTER></H2>")
    var intro1 = "Hi, thanks for visiting our Web site, but we have moved. Please make a note "
    var intro2 = "of our new URL (www.funphonics.com) and notify the Webmaster about our new "
    var intro3 = "location. Click<A Href='http://www.scsite.com/'> here </A> or wait 15 seconds "
    var intro4 = "to be moved automatically to our new site."
    var introMsg = intro1+intro2+intro3+intro4
```

> completed JavaScript code for chngSite() function

Start | funwithphonics.htm - ... | Fun with Phonics - Microso... | 10:05 AM

**FIGURE 1-27**

The HEAD section contains the user-defined functions, which are called by other JavaScript code or from the embedded event handlers in the HTML tags. This function is called by the setTimeout() method in the BODY section. At this point, save the HTML file and test the Web page.

### TO SAVE THE FILE ON THE FLOPPY DISK

**1** Make sure the JavaScript Data Disk is in drive A. Click File on the menu bar.

**2** Click Save on the File menu.

### TO TEST THE WEB PAGE

**1** Click the Fun with Phonics button on the taskbar.

**2** Click the Refresh button.

*The Web page displays (Figure 1-28a). After 15 seconds, a message displays (Figure 1-28b). You can click the OK button in the dialog box or wait 15 seconds. If you are connected to the Internet, you will be taken to the Shelly Cashman Series site (www.scsite.com). To return to the Web page in Figure 1-28a, click the Back button.*

**FIGURE 1-28a**

**FIGURE 1-28b**

If you encounter an error, make sure the variable and function names are consistent. Check the beginning and ending quotation marks on all strings, and the beginning and ending curly braces on the functions. Check that you have beginning and ending parentheses where needed.

# Printing the HTML File Using Notepad

After you have completed and tested the Web page, you may want to print it. You can print the HTML file using Notepad. Perform the following steps to print the funwithphonics.htm file.

 **To Print the HTML File Using Notepad**

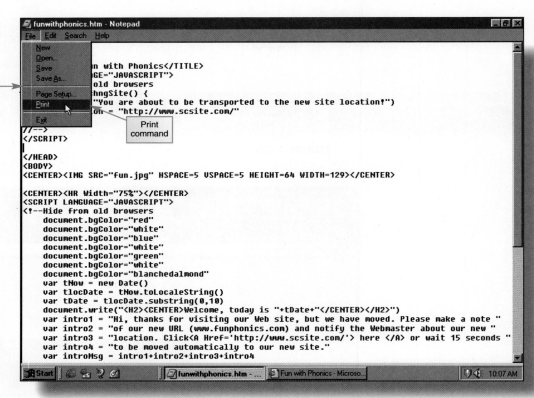

1 **If necessary, click the Notepad button on the taskbar. Click File on the menu bar and then point to Print (Figure 1-29).**

**FIGURE 1-29**

**2** **Click Print**

The HTML with the JavaScript
code prints (Figure 1-30).

funwithphonics.htm

```
<HTML>
<HEAD>
     <TITLE>Fun with Phonics</TITLE>
<SCRIPT LANGUAGE="JAVASCRIPT">
<!--Hide from old browsers
     function chngSite() {
          alert("You are about to be transported to the new site location!")
          location = "http://www.scsite.com/"
     }
//-->
</SCRIPT>

</HEAD>
<BODY>
<CENTER><IMG SRC="fun.jpg" HSPACE=5 VSPACE=5 HEIGHT=64 WIDTH=129></CENTER>

<CENTER><HR Width="75%"></CENTER>
<SCRIPT LANGUAGE="JAVASCRIPT">
<!--Hide from old browsers
     document.bgColor="red"
     document.bgColor="white"
     document.bgColor="blue"
     document.bgColor="white"
     document.bgColor="green"
     document.bgColor="white"
     document.bgColor="blanchedalmond"
     var tNow = new Date()
     var tlocDate = tNow.toLocaleString()
     var tDate = tlocDate.substring(0,10)
     document.write("<H2><CENTER>Welcome, today is "+tDate+"</CENTER></H2>")
     var intro1 = "Hi, thanks for visiting our Web site, but we have moved.
Please make a note "
     var intro2 = "of our new URL (www.funphonics.com) and notify the Webmaster
about our new "
     var intro3 = "location. Click<A Href='http://www.scsite.com/'> here </A> or
wait 15 seconds "
     var intro4 = "to be moved automatically to our new site."
     var introMsg = intro1+intro2+intro3+intro4
     document.write("<H4><FONT Color='firebrick'>"+introMsg+"</H4></FONT>")
     setTimeout("chngSite()",15000)
     document.write("<BR><H4><CENTER>This document was last modified
"+document.lastModified+"</CENTER></H4>")

//-->
</SCRIPT>

</BODY>
</HTML>
```

Page 1

**FIGURE 1-30**

**Printing with Notepad**

You can modify the header
and footer in Notepad. Click
File on the menu bar and then
click Page Setup. In the Page
Setup dialog box, type the
desired Header and Footer.
To learn more about Notepad
codes, search Notepad Help
for inserting headers and
footers.

# Project Summary

The Web page created in this project serves as a notice to Fun with Phonics customers indicating that the Web site has moved to a new location. The Web page meets the requirements of the Webmaster, Mandy Senicott. The Web page flickers to get the user's attention, sets the background color, displays a message, and allows the user to link manually to the new site if needed. After 15 seconds, a message notifies the user that the Web page will link automatically to the new site. The link executes when the user clicks the OK button in the message.

In creating this project, you learned how to modify a Web page using the Notepad text editor. You learned how and where to place JavaScript code in an HTML file. In adding the JavaScript code, you learned how to use the document object and write() method. The project introduced the concepts of creating new objects by defining variables. You learned the rules for naming variables. You learned about the Date() object and how to extract only the date from the user's computer system.

You learned how to write a user-defined function that calls the built-in alert function to display a message. You learned how to embed HTML codes within JavaScript code and to format displayed text. Using the setTimeout() method, you learned how to call the user-defined functions. Finally, you learned how to work with Notepad and test the Web page in your browser.

# What You Should Know

Having completed this project, you should be able to perform the following tasks:

▶ Activate the Notepad Window *(J 1.27)*

▶ Create Flicker on the Web Page *(J 1.13)*

▶ Construct a Message Using Several Variables *(J 1.24)*

▶ Display the Current System Date in the Initial Greeting *(J 1.23)*

▶ Display the Date Last Modified in a Message *(J 1.29)*

▶ Enter the Beginning SCRIPT Tag and Comment *(J 1.12)*

▶ Enter the chngSite() User-Defined Function in the HEAD Section *(J 1.31)*

▶ Enter the Ending SCRIPT Tag *(J 1.16)*

▶ Extract the Current System Date Using the Date() Object *(J 1.22)*

▶ Open a Web Page Stored on the Data Disk *(J 1.10)*

▶ Print the HTML File Using Notepad *(J 1.34)*

▶ Save a File *(J 1.26)*

▶ Save the File on the Floppy Disk *(J 1.17, J 1.32)*

▶ Set the Background Color to a Static Color *(J 1.15)*

▶ Start Notepad *(J 1.8)*

▶ Test the Web Page *(J 1.19, J 1.32)*

▶ Test the Web Page in the Browser *(J 1.27)*

▶ Write the Message on the Web Page *(J 1.25)*

▶ Write the setTimeout() Method to Execute the chngSite() Function *(J 1.28)*

# *Test Your Knowledge*

## 1 True/False

**Instructions:** Circle T if the statement is true or F if the statement is false.

T F 1. Since 1980, companies have developed and gained substantial marketing edge with e-commerce.

T F 2. Marketing experts will tell you that you have six to seven seconds to attract and retain someone's attention.

T F 3. One of the advantages to JavaScript is the capability to process data immediately on the user's machine.

T F 4. JavaScript cannot work with HTML codes.

T F 5. The SCRIPT tag can have three attributes.

T F 6. The exclamation point (!) is used to indicate HTML comments.

T F 7. To change Web page background colors dynamically, you use the BGCOLOR attribute in the <BODY> tag.

T F 8. You cannot view a Web page created and stored on a floppy disk. It must be posted to a Web server.

T F 9. To display text on the Web page with JavaScript, you use the document.write() object and method.

T F 10. In the setTimeout() method, the number of seconds that should lapse before a command is executed actually is stated in nanoseconds.

## 2 Multiple Choice

**Instructions:** Circle the correct response.

1. Marketing experts will tell you that you have _____ seconds to attract and retain someone's attention.
   a. 6 to 7
   b. 8 to 9
   c. 3 to 4
   d. 10 to 12

2. Notepad files have an automatic extension of _____.
   a. .DOC
   b. .HTM
   c. .TXT
   d. .HTML

3. You place JavaScript code in the _____ section(s) of a Web page.
   a. BODY
   b. HEAD and BODY
   c. HEAD
   d. TITLE

*(continued)*

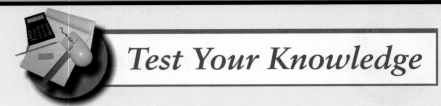

## Test Your Knowledge

**Multiple Choice** *(continued)*

4. The <SCRIPT> tag defaults automatically to which script language?
   a. VBScript
   b. DHTML
   c. Java
   d. JavaScript

5. What is the document property for changing the background color in JavaScript?
   a. backgroundColor
   b. bgColor
   c. bkColor
   d. pageColor

6. To test a Web page with your browser, click _____ on the menu bar, and then either click Open File or Open Page.
   a. File
   b. Edit
   c. Favorites
   d. View

7. Which of the following is *not* a data type for JavaScript variables?
   a. Boolean
   b. floating point
   c. string
   d. numeric

8. When defining a JavaScript variable it is best to use the _____ statement.
   a. define
   b. DIM
   c. var
   d. DIM var

9. Which of the following is *not* contained in the Date() object?
   a. the day of the week
   b. the time zone
   c. the GMT
   d. the year

10. When using the substring() method to extract a string of data, you need to supply the relative position of the first character to be extracted and _____.
    a. the relative position of the last character
    b. the relative length of the characters extracted
    c. the relative position of the last character plus one
    d. the number of characters in the entire string

# Test Your Knowledge

## 3 Understanding the Various Parts of a Web Page

**Instructions:** In Figure 1-31, arrows point to components of a Web page. Identify the various parts of the Web page in the spaces provided.

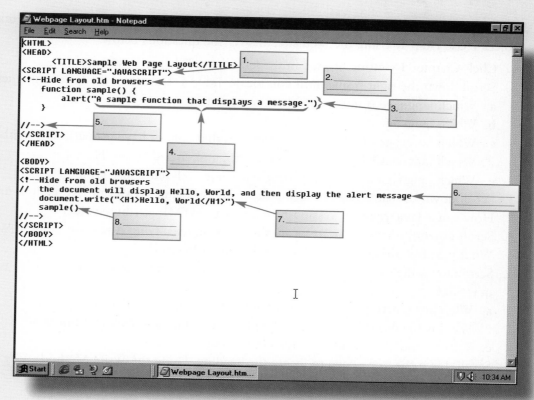

```
Webpage Layout.htm - Notepad
File  Edit  Search  Help
<HTML>
<HEAD>
        <TITLE>Sample Web Page Layout</TITLE>        1._____
<SCRIPT LANGUAGE="JAVASCRIPT">
<!--Hide from old browsers                           2._____
    function sample() {
        alert("A sample function that displays a message.")
    }                                                            3._____
//-->         5._____
</SCRIPT>
</HEAD>
                                                 4._____

<BODY>
<SCRIPT LANGUAGE="JAVASCRIPT">
<!--Hide from old browsers
//  the document will display Hello, World, and then display the alert message     6._____
    document.write("<H1>Hello, World</H1>")
    sample()
//-->
</SCRIPT>         8._____              7._____
</BODY>
</HTML>



                              I



Start    Webpage Layout.htm...                                    10:34 AM
```

**FIGURE 1-31**

## 4 Understanding Code Statements

**Instructions:** Carefully read each of the following descriptions. Write JavaScript code statements to accomplish these specific tasks. Number your answers to correspond to the code description. Record your answers on a separate sheet of paper. Hand in the answers to your instructor.

1. Write a JavaScript statement that will define a new variable object called OurTime. Assign it the Date() object.
2. Write a JavaScript statement that will define a new variable called LocOurTime. Assign it the toLocaleString() method with the new OurTime object described in Step 1.
3. Write a JavaScript statement that will set the background color to spring green.
4. Write a JavaScript statement that will concatenate three message variables (Msg1, Msg2, and Msg3) and assign to one variable called CompMsg.
5. Write a setTimeout method that calls a function newWindow() after 5 seconds.
6. Write the JavaScript statement that will display the following: This document was last changed on 10/31/01. (*Hint*: Assume the date has been extracted to a variable called curDate.)
7. Given the following: <Input Type="Button" Name="Continue" Value="Continue">, rewrite and add the event handler that executes a function called goNext() when the user clicks the button.

# *Use Help*

## 1 Exploring Online Documentation

**Instructions:** Start your browser. Type www.scsite.com/js/p1.htm in the Address text box and then click Project 1 Use Help 1. Using the Web site, answer the questions below.

1. Click Chapter 1 Getting Started in the left frame. What is JavaScript?
2. Scroll down the right frame until you locate Table 1-1. Answer the following questions:
   a. Which language is interpreted (not compiled)?
   b. Which language is object-oriented?
   c. Which language has classes and instances that cannot have properties or methods added dynamically?
   d. Which language's code is integrated with, and embedded in, HTML?
   e. Which language uses variable data types not declared (loose typing)?
3. Scroll down the same page to locate the heading, Using JavaScript Expressions as HTML Attribute Values. How can a JavaScript expression be used as an HTML attribute value?
4. Scroll down the same page to locate the heading, Specifying Alternate Content With the NOSCRIPT Tag. What purpose does the NOSCRIPT tag serve in JavaScript?
5. Scroll down the same page to locate the heading, Defining and Calling Functions. Answer the following questions:
   a. What are functions and list the basic parts?
   b. What is the difference between defining a function and calling a function?
   c. Why should you define functions in the HEAD section?
6. Scroll down the same page to locate the heading, Using the Write Method. Why is the write method one of the more often-used JavaScript methods?

## 2 Exploring Links to Other JavaScript Site Links

**Instructions:** Start your browser. Type www.scsite.com/js/p1.htm in the Address text box and then click Project 1 Use Help 2. Perform the following tasks.

1. Scroll down the left frame.
2. Click Chapter 1, The Message Box.
3. Read the entire section and click Let's Break it Down.
4. Read all the pages. After you have read the final page of Chapter 1, print the final page.
5. When you have completed Chapter 1, click On to Chapter 2, and then click the Red, Green, Blue, and White buttons to try the demonstration. Click Show me how to do it.
6. Read the Show me how to do it pages and print the last page. Hand in the printouts to your instructor.

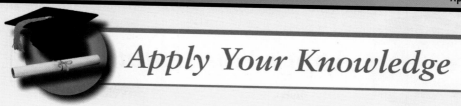

# Apply Your Knowledge

## 1 Changing the Message and Linking to a New Web Site for an Initial Screen

**Instructions:** Start Notepad. Open carrental.htm on the JavaScript Data Disk. If you did not download the Data Disk, see the inside back cover for instructions for downloading the JavaScript Data Disk or see your instructor. This Web page is an initial screen a viewer might encounter while doing a search for a car rental office. This Web page automatically links to a new Web site after 15 seconds. Figure 1-32 shows the completed Web page. The function, which executes the link to the new Web site, already has been coded. Perform the following tasks.

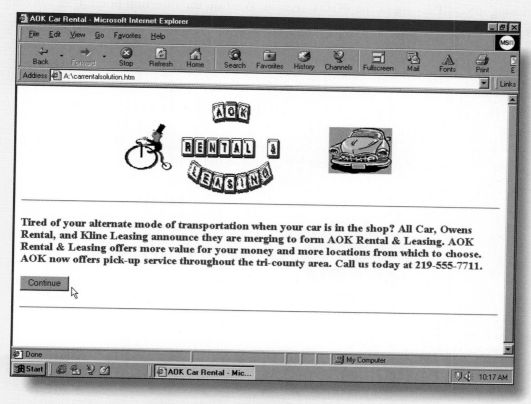

**FIGURE 1-32**

1. Locate the JavaScript tag after the images and horizontal line that contains the JavaScript comment, // build the message line & display.
2. Enter the following code:

```
var msgLine1="Tired of your alternate mode of transportation when your car is in the "
var msgLine2="shop? All Car, Owens Rental, and Kline Leasing announce they are merging "
var msgLine3="to form AOK Rental & Leasing. AOK Rental & Leasing offers more value for "
var msgLine4="your money and more locations from which to choose. AOK now offers pick-up "
var msgLine5="service throughout the tri-county area. Call us today at 219-555-7711."
```

3. Enter the following statement to concatenate the five variables into one variable called message:

```
var message = msgLine1+msgLine2+msgLine3+msgLine4+msgLine5
```

*(continued)*

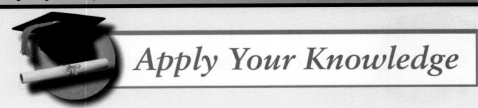

# Apply Your Knowledge

**Changing the Message and Linking to a New Web Site for an Initial Screen** *(continued)*

4. Display the message using the write() method as follows:
   document.write("<H3><FONT Color='darkgreen'><B>"+message+"</H3></FONT></B>").

5. Save the HTML file on the disk in drive A using the file name, carrentalsolution.htm.

6. Start your browser. Open the a:\carrentalsolution.htm Web page to test JavaScript code. If no errors occur, continue with Step 7. If an error occurs, activate Notepad and double-check your spelling in the HTML file. Save the file on the disk, and then click the Refresh button on the browser toolbar to retest.

7. Find the closing </SCRIPT> tag in the BODY section. Position the insertion point after the comment line that reads <!--Continue button>. Enter the following on separate lines:
   ```
   <FORM>
   <Input Type="Button" Name="Continue" Value="Continue" onClick="newSite()">
   </FORM>
   ```

8. Locate the setTimeout() method in the SCRIPT section and delete it.

9. Save the Notepad file, activate your browser, and click the Refresh button on your browser's toolbar to test the Web page.

10. Print the Web page.

11. Return to Notepad and print the HTML text file. Hand in the printouts to your instructor.

# In the Lab

## 1 Writing a Function that Changes Background Colors

**Problem:** You are teaching an introductory Web class at the local high school. You want to develop a Web page that allows your students to change the background color (Figure 1-33a) by clicking a button that is associated with a specific color. The Web page in Figure 1-33b has the azure background.

**FIGURE 1-33a**

# In the Lab

Web page after clicking Azure button

**FIGURE 1-33b**

**Instructions:** Start your browser and Notepad. Use Notepad to open jstutor.htm on the JavaScript Data Disk. If you did not download the Data Disk, see the inside back cover for instructions for downloading the JavaScript Data Disk or see your instructor. Perform the following tasks.

1. Locate the SCRIPT tag in the HEAD section.
2. On the line following the comment, // Change background color to color passed to function, enter the following:

```
function ChangeNow(color) {
    document.bgColor=color
}
```

3. Locate the form that creates the five input buttons with the color names in the BODY section.
4. For each button, insert the onclick event handler to call the ChangeNow() function and pass the associated color. Use the actual color name as the passed value that matches the button value as shown in the code for the Azure and Silver buttons.

   `<INPUT Type="button" Name="ChngRed" Value="Azure" onclick="ChangeNow('azure')">`
   `<INPUT Type="button" Name="ChngRed" Value="Silver" onclick="ChangeNow('silver')">`

5. Save the Notepad file on the disk in drive A using the file name, jstutorsolution.htm.
6. Activate the browser and open a:\jstutorsolution.htm in the browser to test your JavaScript code.
7. If any errors occur, double-check Steps 2 through 4 and test the file again. If no errors occur, print the Web page, activate Notepad, and print the HTML file. Hand in the printouts to your instructor.

# *In the Lab*

## 2 Adding Alert Messages to Display a Factoid before Executing a Link

**Problem:** You are an intern at Valley Recycling and the Webmaster, Juan Garcia, wants you to modify the current Welcome page (Figure 1-34a) to add a factoid to each of the four links. The factoid should display a message before the link is executed (Figure 1-34b). In addition, Juan requests that you add the date and time the document was last modified.

**FIGURE 1-34a**

**FIGURE 1-34b**

## In the Lab

**Instructions:** Start your browser and Notepad. Use Notepad to open valley.htm on the JavaScript Data Disk and then perform the following tasks.

1. Locate the first SCRIPT tag in the HEAD section of the Web page. The first function for the Paper button has been written. Using this function as a model, write three more functions, one for each of the remaining buttons (Glass, Plastic, Metal).

2. Type the remaining functions beneath the Paper() function. Press the SPACEBAR to indent in the same manner as the Paper() function.

3. The function for the Glass button is Glass().
   a. Assign the following factoid to a variable: Recycling glass containers saves 9 gallons of fuel oil for every ton of recycled glass.
   b. Display the variable with the factoid using the alert() function.
   c. Enter `location = "http://www.scsite.com/"` as the location command.
   d. Enter } (the closing brace).

4. The function for the Plastic button is Plastic().
   a. Assign the following factoid to one variable: Styrofoam is neither plastic nor recyclable.
   b. Assign the following factoid to another variable: Styrofoam still will be in your landfill 500 years from now. Is that what you want?
   c. Concatenate the two variables into one.
   d. Display the new variable with the factoid using the alert() function.
   e. Enter `location = "http://www.scsite.com/"` as the location command.
   f. Enter } (the closing brace).

5. The function for the Metal button is Metal().
   a. Assign the following factoid to one variable: For every ton of metal recycled, 2.5 tons of iron ore,
   b. Assign the following to another variable: .5 tons of coal, and 40 pounds of limestone are saved.
   c. Concatenate the two variables into one.
   d. Display the new variable with the factoid using the alert() function.
   e. Enter `location = "http://www.scsite.com/"` as the location command.
   f. Enter } (the closing brace).

6. Locate the HTML comment, <!--Date last modified>, towards the bottom of the document.

7. Display the date and time the document was last modified. Separate the two pieces of data using the substring() method as follows: `document.write("This document was last recycled on: "+document.lastModified.substring(0,8)+" at " + document.lastModified.substring(8,14))` and then add the HTML codes to center the message. Make the font color firebrick.

8. Save the HTML file on the disk in drive A using the file name, valleysolution.htm.

9. Activate the browser. Open the a:\valleysolution.htm Web page to test your JavaScript code.

10. If any errors occur, double-check Steps 2 through 7 and test again. If no errors occur, print the Web page, activate Notepad, and print the HTML file. Hand in the printouts to your instructor.

# In the Lab

## 3 Creating a Welcome Page that Displays Information in an Alert Message

**Problem:** You are the Webmaster at Rocky Mountain Steel Credit Union. The current Welcome page is very plain (Figure 1-35a). The credit union board chairperson, Terry Russell, wants you to add the day and time to the greeting and display an informative message when users click a link. The message informs users about specials relating to the linked page. For example, a message about the current loan rates displays when a user clicks the Loans link (Figure 1-35b). Terry suggests you add the date the document was last modified. Because you know that the message will change often, you decide to use the document.lastModified property to display the last modified date.

**FIGURE 1-35a**

**FIGURE 1-35b**

## In the Lab

**Instructions:** Start your browser and Notepad. Use Notepad to open Rocky.htm. Perform the following tasks.

1. Write the JavaScript code that will display a welcome message that includes the day of the week and the date. For example, Welcome, today is Fri Oct 5, 2001. Place this message beneath the credit union logo (Figure 1-35a). (*Hint*: use the Date() object and extract the day of the week, the date, and the year from the object. A sample output from the Date() object is

   Fri Oct 13 08:41:44 CDT 2001

   so you must count the position of the characters to use the substring() method to extract the day of the week, the date, and the year.

2. Write three functions that use the alert() function to display a message. Place them in the HEAD section (the SCRIPT section has been provided starting on the fourth line).

3. The first function name is showLoans(). It displays the message, Until the end of the month, new car loans are 6.8%.

4. The second function name is showSavings(). It displays the message, If you have more than $5,000 in savings, consider a CD.

5. The third function name is showEB(). It displays the message, Try our new BankAtHome software at the main branch.

6. Just before the </BODY> tag, insert another JavaScript section to display the date the document was last modified, but not the time. Include the HTML code <H6> to make the text small and centered between margins.

7. Save the Notepad file on the disk in drive A using the file name, rockysolution.htm.

8. Activate the browser. Open the a:\rockysolution.htm Web page to test your JavaScript code.

9. If any errors occur double-check Steps 1 through 6 and test again. If no errors occur, print the Web page, activate Notepad, and print the HTML file. Hand in the printouts to your instructor.

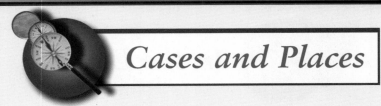

# Cases and Places

The difficulty of these case studies varies:
▶ are the least difficult; ▶▶ are more difficult; and ▶▶▶ are the most difficult.

**1** ▶ You have taken a summer job with Ace Carpet and Furniture Cleaning. The owner asks you to create a Web site for them. Because you have just finished your course in Web page design, you tell the owner it is important to have a first page that captures the viewer's attention. You suggest this page be simple in design, but direct in content information. After a few seconds, the page automatically transfers to the Web site main page. Use the concepts and techniques presented in this project to create the greeting page.

**2** ▶ As part of your course credit in your marketing class, you must volunteer to work for a not-for-profit organization one hour a week. Because you like working with children, you volunteer for Kids Club. Kids Club has a Web page created by the Internet service provider they use. The provider, however, has informed Kids Club that the domain address will be changed. Kids Club will have use of the old domain address for three months before it is disabled. The director of Kids Club is aware of your computer skills and asks you to create a greeting page for the old domain address to notify viewers of the address change and automatically link users to the new domain address. Use the concepts and techniques presented in this project to create the greeting page.

**3** ▶ Your father owns a heating and cooling business. He has a Web page with a local Internet service provider. The business will be carrying a new furnace and air conditioning unit starting in the fall. American Furnace and Air Conditioning (AFAC) only recognizes top heating and cooling businesses as distributors. Because this manufacturer is recognized nationally as one of the best, your father wants current viewers to be aware of the new line now. He asks you to create a new greeting page that has a link to the current Web page and a link to the AFAC Web page. Use the concepts and techniques presented in this project to create the greeting page.

**4** ▶▶ You have a summer internship with the local ad and sales paper (*The Community Shopper*). At a general meeting, you suggest they start a Web site that contains ads, local announcements, community news, and other features. The editor is very impressed with your suggestion and states she was thinking about signing a contract with the local Internet service provider. You are instructed to create a greeting page with links to each of the shopper's features. The editor would like an input box that would prompt users for the name of their community. Once the user enters the name of the community, the user is linked automatically to Web ads and news associated with their community. Use the concepts and techniques presented in this project to create the greeting page.

**5** ▶▶ Your sister recently graduated from Chiropractic College and is ready to open an office. She would like to start a Web site, but wants it to be more than an advertisement page. You suggest that she have a greeting page that has a list containing the top ten ailments treated by chiropractors. The viewer selects one of the ailments and then is linked to a page that explains the ailment, common causes, and common treatments. Use the concepts and techniques presented in this project to create the greeting page.

JavaScript

PROJECT

**2**

# Creating Pop-up Windows, Adding Scrolling Messages, and Validating Forms

O B J E C T I V E S

You will have mastered the material in this project when you can:

- Explain the four basic components of a scrolling message
- Write a user-defined function to display a scrolling message in a form text box
- Describe the If statement
- Define conditionals and discuss the conditional operands
- Define recursion
- Describe the focus() method
- Write a user-defined function to calculate mortgage payments
- Validate data entry using a nested If...Else statement
- Describe the parseInt(), parseFloat(), and isNaN() built-in functions
- Describe the math pow() method
- Write a user-defined function to format output in currency format
- Discuss For and While loops
- Use the open() method to display another Web page in a pop-up window
- Use the lastModified property to display the date a Web page was last modified

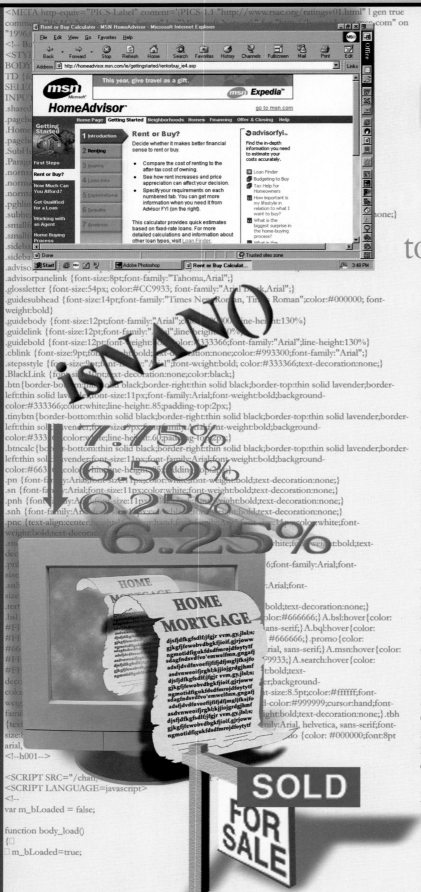

# It Figures!

## Mortgage Sites Are Keys to Home Ownership

**T**he *American Dream* is owning a home. The dream can be yours once you save for the down payment and earn sufficient income. But how much do you need to save? And how much do you need to earn? Now you can find the answers easily by navigating the Internet.

Do you need to know how much house fits your budget? Various sites help you determine how much house you can afford, the amount you can borrow, and the amount of your monthly payments.

At these sites, you follow step-by-step instructions that prompt you to make choices, such as the number of years you plan to live in the house and input numbers, such as the amount you plan to borrow.

The Web page you will build in this project estimates a monthly payment based on the amount borrowed, the interest rate, and the length of the loan. As users enter each amount, JavaScript uses the isNaN() — Is Not a Number — function to evaluate the figures and ensure they are numeric.

Likewise, Microsoft's MSN HomeAdvisor Web site (homeadvisor.msn.com) offers a finance page using JavaScript that prompts you for figures and then uses the isNaN() function to validate each amount. The program performs calculations and finds 50 lenders offering products that fit your needs. You can sort these products according to criteria such as the lowest interest rate or the smallest monthly payment.

If these monthly figures make you uncomfortable, the various sites offer options with calculators that work like gigantic spreadsheets and let you fiddle with the numbers. For example, you often can obtain a lower interest rate if you pay points, which are one percent of the loan amount. Or you can try another type of mortgage, such as an adjustable rate loan, that has a low interest rate for the first year or so.

Once you determine the right mortgage for your budget, the sites allow you to check current mortgage rates in your area. Some help you prequalify for a loan, which strengthens negotiating power when discussing prices with home sellers.

Others send e-mail messages alerting you when national mortgage rates move upward or downward by at least one-tenth of one percent, which can happen daily.

When you find the ideal property, you can apply for the cybermortgage online. Banks and various financial institutions in the United States lend $725 billion each year; online mortgage approvals are expected to cut into at least five percent of that amount in the next few years as more than 2,000 lenders with Web sites vie for mortgage dollars. By eliminating loan officers, you often can save money and add that sum to your down payment. Some sites promise approval in less than five minutes.

Various pages offer online appraisals. Others estimate the costs of homeowner's insurance, property taxes, closing costs, and private mortgage insurance, which often is needed if your down payment is less than 20 percent of the purchase price.

Using the Internet to explore the multitude of mortgage options can save time and money. Your efforts can open the door to financial flexibility, and to your new home. It figures!

# JavaScript

# Creating Pop-up Windows, Adding Scrolling Messages, and Validating Forms

PROJECT 2

**CASE PERSPECTIVE**

You have taken a part-time job with Home Finders Nationwide Realty to work on their Web site. Carrie Rayburn, the owner, dislikes their current Web page and wants the page to be more interesting. You suggest adding a simple, but eye-catching scrolling message box. Carrie likes the idea and suggests that the first message remind site visitors of current, low interest rates.

Carrie mentions that customers have asked for mortgage payment information. She suggests a page with a large table that lists various mortgage amounts, interest rates, the number of years for the mortgage, and the associated monthly payment. You recommend making the Web page more interactive by adding a mortgage payment calculator form. The form would allow customers to enter the mortgage loan amount, interest rate, and number of years, and then click a button to display the monthly mortgage payment. You also suggest that a notice about the mortgage payment calculator display in a pop-up window that opens each time a customer hits the Home Finders Nationwide Realty Web page. Carrie asks you to implement your suggestions.

## Introduction

In Project 1, you learned how to integrate JavaScript and HTML. You learned how to use variables and objects to extract the current system date from the computer and to use several variables to construct a message. You further learned how to write a user-defined function that calls the built-in alert() function.

This project reinforces these topics and introduces new ones, including creating a scrolling message that uses the string length property and the If statement. You also will learn how to validate form text boxes using the If…Else statement and parseInt(), parseFloat(), and IsNaN() built-in functions. You will learn how to use the math object's pow() method in a formula, and how to format results as currency. Finally, you will learn to use the open() method to display messages in a pop-up window. These JavaScript techniques and statements allow you to improve the functionality of your Web pages.

## Project Two — Home Finders Nationwide Realty

Before starting on the project, you meet with Carrie to summarize your planned modifications to the Web site. You state that you determine the following needs, data validation requirements, and calculations based on your discussion.

**Needs:** When the Web page first loads, a pop-up window displays a message informing users of the new mortgage payment calculator (Figure 2-1a). The Web page also includes a scrolling message that constantly displays, to remind visitors of the current low mortgage rates (Figure 2-1b). The mortgage payment form allows users to calculate their monthly payment based on the amount of mortgage, interest rate, and number of years for the mortgage (Figure 2-1c). Separate functions validate the data

pop-up
window

FIGURE 2-1b

**TRY OUR NEW LOAN ESTIMATOR**

Click the Estimate Mortgage Payment link. Enter the data needed for each text box. Then click the Calculate button. Try it as often as you wish by clicking the Reset button.

Close Window

FIGURE 2-1a

link to
Mortgage Payment
Calculator

scrolling
message

Estimate Mortgage Payment

are at their LOWEST!— —M

entered in the form, calculate the monthly payment, and display the result in currency format. To give the user confidence that the data is current, the date the page was last modified will display at the bottom of the page.

**Estimate Mortgage Payments**

Amount of Mortgage:

Interest Rate as % (e.g. 7.9):

Number of Years:

Monthly Payment:

form

form text
boxes

Calculate    Reset

Reset
button

Calculate
button

This document was last modified 10/30/01 14:41:42

date Web
page last
modified

FIGURE 2-1c

**Data validation requirements:** The user enters the data (used in the mathematical calculation for the monthly payment) in the form text boxes (Figure 2-1c on the previous page). The data must not be blank and must be numeric. If the data is not valid, an alert message box notifies the user and positions the insertion point in the appropriate text box. Until all entries are valid, the formula will not attempt to calculate the monthly payment.

**Calculations:** The formula for calculating a monthly payment is

$$\text{monthly payment} = \text{loan} * \text{rate} / (1 - (1 / (1 + \text{rate})^{\text{payments}}))$$

where loan is the total amount of the mortgage, rate is the interest rate, and payments is the number of payments to be made. Because the interest rate is a percent, the function must convert the annual rate to a monthly rate. The formula also must convert the number of years into the total number of payments.

### Starting Notepad and Opening the Home.htm File

Your first step is to open the HTML file to which you will add JavaScript code using Notepad. The HTML file for the Home Finders Nationwide Realty Web page is stored on the JavaScript Data Disk as a file named home.htm. See the inside back cover for instructions for downloading the JavaScript Data Disk or see your instructor for information on accessing the files required in this book. To start Notepad and open the home.htm file, perform the following steps.

**TO START NOTEPAD AND OPEN A WEB PAGE STORED ON THE DATA DISK**

1. Click the Start button on the taskbar. Click Programs on the Start menu. Click Accessories on the Programs submenu.

2. Click Notepad on the Programs submenu.

3. Insert the JavaScript Data Disk in drive A.

4. Click Open on the File menu.

5. Click 3½ Floppy (A:) in the Look in list box. Type *.htm in the File name text box and then press the ENTER key.

6. Double-click the document, home.htm.

*The home.htm document displays in the Notepad window (Figure 2-2).*

FIGURE 2-2

With the home.htm HTML file open, the next step is to create the text box in the BODY section that will contain the scrolling message.

# Inserting a Scrolling Message on a Web Page

A simple way to attract the attention of a site visitor is to add a scrolling message to your Web page. Companies often use scrolling messages on their Web sites to highlight breaking news, key products, or special promotions. The scrolling message displays either in a text box within the Web page or on the status bar in the browser window.

To make it easier to build scrolling messages, Microsoft developed the MARQUEE HTML tag. While Internet Explorer recognizes the MARQUEE tag, Netscape Navigator does not. By writing your own user-defined function, however, can you create a scrolling message that works with virtually any browser.

A scrolling message has four basic components: (1) the display object; (2) the message; (3) the position; and (4) the delay. The **display object** defines where the scrolling message displays, which is either on the status bar or in a form text box. The **message** is a text string assigned to a variable. The text string is what the user sees when the message displays. Netscape warns Web developers that large messages use memory inefficiently. In addition, large text strings may cause older Netscape browsers to crash. The **position** is the starting location in which the message first displays in the display object. The starting location can be either the left or right side of the display object. The **delay** is the length of time between when a message ends and when it starts to appear again.

## Scrolling Messages

Another reason to avoid assigning a scrolling message to the status bar is that the message can hide information the user needs to see relating the current or next page being loaded.

## The MARQUEE Tag

The MARQUEE tag is one of Microsoft's JScript statements. For more information on the MARQUEE tag, visit www.scsite.com/js/p2.htm and then click Marquee.

The Web page you create in this project includes a scrolling message in a form text box (Figure 2-1b on page J 2.5). The form you construct is a single text box. When creating the form text box, you must name the form and the text box objects. Later, the function you write uses these names to assign the text to the text box. Figure 2-3 shows the code for the form containing the single text box. The name of the form is msgForm, and the name of the text box is scrollingMsg.

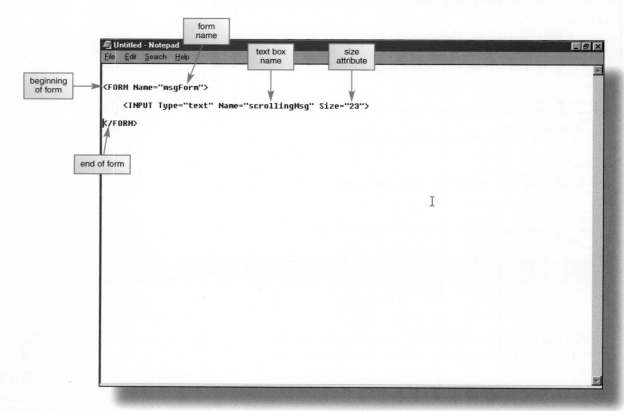

**FIGURE 2-3**

These names serve as variables in the JavaScript code when assigning the message string to the text box. The size attribute indicates the display width of the text box.

## Creating a Form Text Box to Display a Scrolling Message

With JavaScript, you can assign a scrolling message to either the status bar or a text box. Because visitors to a Web page often do not look at the status bar, most Web developers agree that a scrolling message in a text box on the Web page is the better location.

The Web page for Home Finders Nationwide Realty uses a table to arrange and organize the graphics, links, and scrolling message (Figure 2-4). The center cell of the table contains a link to the mortgage payment form. You will place the form text box for the scrolling message in the same cell as this link. Perform the following steps to create a form text box to display a scrolling message.

**Steps** ## To Create a Form Text Box to Display a Scrolling Message

**1** **Scroll down to the BODY section and position the insertion point on line 25 (beneath the paragraph </P> tag).**

*Place the insertion point as shown in Figure 2-4.*

```
home.htm - Notepad                                                    _ □ ×
File  Edit  Search  Help
<HTML>
<HEAD>
        <TITLE>Home Finders Nationwide Realty</TITLE>

</HEAD>
<BODY>

<P ALIGN="CENTER"><IMG SRC="homelogo.jpg">
</P>
<DIV ALIGN="CENTER"><CENTER>

<TABLE BORDER="0" WIDTH="75%">            ◄———  beginning
  <TR>                                            of table
    <TD></TD>
    <TD><P ALIGN="CENTER"><IMG SRC="calculator.jpg" WIDTH="100" HEIGHT="106"></A></TD>
    <TD></TD>
  </TR>
  <TR>
    <TD><P ALIGN="CENTER">
    <IMG SRC="house1.gif" WIDTH="180" HEIGHT="144"></TD>
    <TD>
        <P ALIGN="CENTER">
        <A HREF="#LoanCalc">Estimate Mortgage Payment</A>
        </P>

    </TD>
    <TD><P ALIGN="CENTER">
    <IMG SRC="house2.gif" WIDTH="180" HEIGHT="144"></TD>
  </TR>
  <TR>
    <TD></TD>
    <TD>
    <IMG SRC="house3.gif" WIDTH="180" HEIGHT="144"></TD>
    <TD></TD>
  </TR>
```

*center cell of table* · *line 25* · *end of cell*

*link to Mortgage Payment Calculator*

Start · home.htm - Notepad · 8:46 AM

**FIGURE 2-4**

**2** **Type <FORM Name= "msgForm"> and then press the ENTER key. Type <INPUT Type="text" Name="scrollingMsg" Size="23"> and then press the ENTER key. Type </FORM> and then press the ENTER key.**

*The HTML code for the form and the input text box displays. Each line of the code is indented for readability purposes (Figure 2-5).*

```
HEAD>
        <TITLE>Home Finders Nationwide Realty</TITLE>

</HEAD>
<BODY>

<P ALIGN="CENTER"><IMG SRC="homelogo.jpg">
</P>
<DIV ALIGN="CENTER"><CENTER>

<TABLE BORDER="0" WIDTH="75%">
  <TR>
    <TD></TD>
    <TD><P ALIGN="CENTER"><IMG SRC="calculator.jpg" WIDTH="100" HEIGHT="106"></A></TD>
    <TD></TD>              form
  </TR>                     name
  <TR>
    <TD><P ALIGN="CENTER">
    <IMG SRC="house1.gif" WIDTH="180" HEIGHT="144"></TD>
    <TD>
        <P ALIGN="CENTER">
        <A HREF="#LoanCalc">Estimate Mortgage Payment</A>
        </P>
        <FORM Name="msgForm">
            <INPUT Type="text" Name="scrollingMsg" Size="23">
        </FORM>

    </TD>
    <TD><P ALIGN="CENTER">
    <IMG SRC="house2.gif" WIDTH="180" HEIGHT="144"></TD>
  </TR>
  <TR>
    <TD></TD>
    <TD>
```

*code to create text box in cell* · *text box name*

Start · home.htm - Notepad · 8:49 AM

**FIGURE 2-5**

The form text box created by the HTML code serves as the display object for the scrolling message. The name of the form is msgForm, and the name of the text box is scrollingMsg. The Name attributes in the FORM tag and the INPUT tag become properties of the msgForm object in the user-defined function, scrollingMsg().

The next section describes the statements you need to write a user-defined function, scrollingMsg(), to display the scrolling message in the form text box.

## Creating a User-Defined Function for a Scrolling Message

The **scrollingMsg() function** performs three tasks: (1) it assigns the message and a space to the display object (which, in this project, is the form text box); (2) it checks for the end of the message, and (3) it assigns the next character in the message to the text box, starting with the beginning of the message, in order to make the message scroll.

The scrollingMsg() function requires three variables: the message; a spacer; and the initialization of the beginning position of the message in the form text box. The variables are assigned initial values before the function statements, as follows:

```
var scrollMsg = "Mortgage Rates are at their LOWEST!"
var msgSpace = "---    ---"
var beginPos = 0
```

You assign the message text to the scrollMsg variable. Using the msgSpace variable, you define a space to place a break after a message. In this instance, the msgSpace variable contains three hyphens, three spaces, and three hyphens. The beginPos initial value is zero, which indicates that the message starts at the leftmost position in the text box. Recall from Project 1 that JavaScript uses relative addressing to determine locations, meaning that the first character position of a string is position 0.

The scrollMsg and msgSpace values are concatenated and assigned to the scrollingMsg text box using the statement

```
document.msgForm.scrollingMsg.value = scrollMsg.substring(beginPos,
scrollMsg.length)+msgSpace+scrollMsg.substring(0,beginPos)
```

The object, document.msgForm.scrollingMsg.value, is derived from the form object and the input object. Figure 2-6 illustrates the relationship between these objects and how the statement is derived.

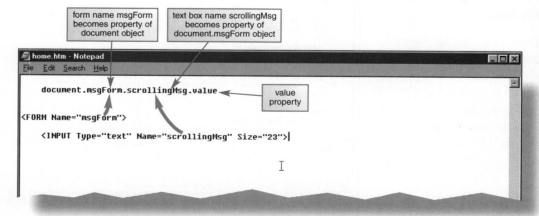

**FIGURE 2-6**

In this statement, the form object (msgForm) becomes an attribute of the document object, and the input text box object (scrollingMsg) becomes an attribute of the msgForm object. JavaScript assigns a value (the message) to the text box object, scrollingMsg, using the value attribute.

The remainder of the assignment statement concatenates the scrollMsg variable, the msgSpace variable, and the beginning of the scrollMsg. Recall that the scrollingMsg() function assigns the next character in the message to the text box, starting with the beginning of the message. The substring() method is used to return the beginning of the message. As you learned in Project 1, the substring() method needs two parameters (x,y), where x is the starting point of the string and y is the location of last character needed. To create the scrollingMsg() user-defined function and define its variables, perform the following steps.

## Steps: To Create the scrollingMsg() User-Defined Function

**1** **Position the insertion point on line 4.**

*Line 4 is located in the HEAD section of the HTML code (Figure 2-7).*

```
home.htm - Notepad
File  Edit  Search  Help
<HTML>
<HEAD>
        <TITLE>Home Finders Nationwide Realty</TITLE>
|
</HEAD>
<BODY>

<P ALIGN="CENTER"><IMG SRC="homelogo.jpg">
</P>
<DIV ALIGN="CENTER"><CENTER>

<TABLE BORDER="0" WIDTH="7
```
line 4

**FIGURE 2-7**

**2** **Type** `<SCRIPT LANGUAGE= "JAVASCRIPT">` **and then press the ENTER key. Type** `<!-- Hide from old browsers` **and then press the ENTER key. Type** `var scrollMsg = "Mortgage rates are at their LOWEST!"` **and then press the ENTER key. Type** `var msgSpace = "---    ---"` **and then press the ENTER key. Type** `var beginPos = 0` **and then press the ENTER key.**

*Figure 2-8 shows the three variables and their assigned initial values.*

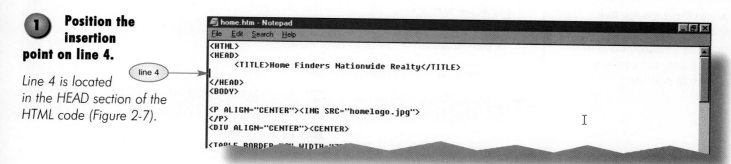

```
home.htm - Notepad
File  Edit  Search  Help
<HTML>
<HEAD>
        <TITLE>Home Finders Nationwide Realty</TITLE>
<SCRIPT LANGUAGE="JAVASCRIPT">
<!--Hide from old browsers
   var scrollMsg = "Mortgage rates are at their LOWEST!"
   var msgSpace = "---    ---"
   var beginPos = 0
|
</HEAD>
<BODY>

<P ALIGN="CENTER"><IMG SRC="homelogo.jpg">
</P>
<DIV ALIGN="CENTER"><CENTER>

<TABLE BORDER="0" WIDTH="75%">
  <TR>
    <TD></TD>
    <TD><P ALIGN="CENTER"><IMG SRC="calculator.jpg" WIDTH="100" HEIGHT="106"></A></TD>
    <TD></TD>
  </TR>
  <TR>
    <TD><P ALIGN="CENTER">
    <IMG SRC="house1.gif" WIDTH="180" HEIGHT="144"></TD>
    <TD>
      <P ALIGN="CENTER">
      <A HREF="#LoanCalc">Estimate Mortgage Payment</A>
      </P>
      <FORM Name="msgForm">
        <INPUT Type="text" Name="scrollingMsg" Size="23">
      </FORM>
    </TD>
    <TD><P ALIGN="CENTER">
    <IMG SRC="house2.gif" WIDTH="180" HEIGHT="144"></TD>
```

text of scrolling message

initialized variables for function

spacer

Start          home.htm - Notepad                    8:50 AM

**FIGURE 2-8**

**3** **Type** function scrollingMsg() { **and then press the** **ENTER key. Type** document.msgForm.scrollingMsg.value = scrollMsg.substring (beginPos,scrollMsg.length)+msgSpace+ scrollMsg.substring (0,beginPos) **and then press the ENTER key.**

*Figure 2-9 shows the function name and the statement to assign the message to the text box. The assignment statement wraps around to a second line, but consider this statement one line.*

```
home.htm - Notepad
File  Edit  Search  Help
<HTML>
<HEAD>
     <TITLE>Home Finders Nationwide Realty</TITLE>
<SCRIPT LANGUAGE="JAVASCRIPT">
<!--Hide from old browsers
     var scrollMsg = "Mortgage rates are at their LOWEST!"
     var msgSpace = "---    ---"
     var beginPos = 0
     function scrollingMsg() {
         document.msgForm.scrollingMsg.value =
scrollMsg.substring(beginPos,scrollMsg.length)+msgSpace+scrollMsg.substring(0,beginPos)

</HEAD>
<BODY>

<P ALIGN="CENTER"><IMG SRC="homelogo.jpg">
</P>
<DIV ALIGN="CENTER"><CENTER>

<TABLE BORDER="0" WIDTH="75%">
  <TR>
     <TD></TD>
     <TD><P ALIGN="CENTER"><IMG SRC="calculator.jpg" WIDTH="100" HEIGHT="106"></A></TD>
     <TD></TD>
  </TR>
  <TR>
     <TD><P ALIGN="CENTER">
     <IMG SRC="house1.gif" WIDTH="180" HEIGHT="144"></TD>
     <TD>
        <P ALIGN="CENTER">
        <A HREF="#LoanCalc">Estimate Mortgage Payment</A>
        </P>
        <FORM Name="msgForm">
           <INPUT Type="text" Name="scrollingMsg" Size="23">
        </FORM>
```

beginning of scrollingMsg() function

message text assigned to text box

line wraps as code is entered

Start | home.htm - Notepad | 8:51 AM

**FIGURE 2-9**

The JavaScript statements assign the message to the text box, append the spacer value, and start the message display with the first character. Be sure to count the assignment statement on line 10 as one line. The next steps are to increment the beginPos variable, and append the next character from the message string to the text box.

## Incrementing the Position Locator Variable

To cause the message to scroll in the text box, you must increment the position locator variable by one. As discussed in the Introduction and shown in Table 2-1, JavaScript provides several ways to increment variables.

| Table 2-1 – Incrementing a Variable | |
|---|---|
| STATEMENT | EXPLANATION |
| variable++ | adds 1 to variable |
| variable = + 1 | adds number after plus sign to variable |
| variable = variable + 1 | executes expression on right side of equal sign, and assigns the result to variable on left side |

A good programming practice is to use statements easily understood by programmers familiar with other languages. To increment the beginPos locator, you write

```
beginPos = beginPos + 1
```

Once incremented, this new value of the position locator allows the substring() method to extract the next character in the message string and append it to the end of the message in the text box.

# Entering an If Statement

After incrementing the position location variable (beginPos) by one, you must determine if the current value of beginPos exceeds the length of the message. To determine if the current value of the beginPos variable is greater than the length of the message, use the If statement. The general form of the If statement is shown in Table 2-2. The first part of the If statement is written as if (condition). You place the JavaScript code to be executed if the result of the conditional test is True within a set of curly braces. Figure 2-10 shows the flowchart that corresponds to an If statement.

| Table 2-2 – If Statement | |
|---|---|
| **General form:** | if (condition) {<br>        JavaScript statements if condition true<br>} |
| **Comment:** | The condition is the comparison of values. If the result of the comparison is true, JavaScript executes the statements between the curly braces. |
| **Example:** | if (beginPos > scrollMsg.length) {<br>    beginPos = 0<br>} |

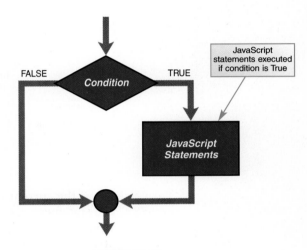

**FIGURE 2-10**

A **condition** is any expression that evaluates to True or False. When writing an If statement, you must place parentheses around the condition, but leave a space after the If statement so that JavaScript does not interpret the If statement as a function. Table 2-3 shows the conditional operands used for comparisons. For more information on conditionals, refer to page J I.10 of the Introduction.

| Table 2-3 – Conditional Operands | | |
|---|---|---|
| *OPERAND* | *EXAMPLE* | *RESULTS* |
| = = | (a == b) | True if a equals b |
| != | (a != b) | True if a does not equal b |
| > | (a > b) | True if a is greater than b |
| < | (a < b) | True if a is less than b |
| >= | (a >= b) | True if a is greater than or equal to b |
| <= | (a <= b) | True if a is less than or equal to b |
| && | (a == b) && (x < y) | True if both conditions are true (a equals b and x is less than y) |
| \|\| | (a != b) \|\| (x >= a) | True if either condition is true (a does not equal b or x is greater than or equal to a) |

**More About**

**The If Statement**

If statements are an integral part of script languages and Web pages. For more information on If statements, visit www.scsite.com/js/p2.htm and then click If statement.

**More About**

**Conditional Operators**

Conditional operators in JavaScript are similar to the operators used by other programming languages. For more information on conditional operators, visit www.scsite.com/js/p2.htm and then click conditional operators.

The flowchart shown in Figure 2-11 illustrates how the If statement compares the beginning position variable (beginPos) with the overall length of the message (scrollMsg.length).

**FIGURE 2-11**

If the current value of beginPos variable exceeds the scrollMsg.length variable, the statement assigns the value zero to the beginPos variable. When you set the beginPos to zero, it sets the variable back to the first character position of the text string. Perform the following steps to enter an If statement.

*Steps* **To Enter an If Statement**

**1** **Position the insertion point on line 11. Type** beginPos = beginPos + 1 **and then press the ENTER key.**

*The expression used to increment the beginning position variable displays (Figure 2-12).*

```
home.htm - Notepad
File  Edit  Search  Help
<HTML>
<HEAD>
    <TITLE>Home Finders Nationwide Realty</TITLE>
<SCRIPT LANGUAGE="JAVASCRIPT">
<!--Hide from old browsers
    var scrollMsg = "Mortgage rates are at their LOWEST!"
    var msgSpace = "---    ---"
    var beginPos = 0
    function scrollingMsg() {
        document.msgForm.scrollingMsg.value =
scrollMsg.substring(beginPos,scrollMsg.length)+msgSpace+scrollMsg.substring(0,beginPos)
        beginPos = beginPos + 1

</HEAD>
<BODY>

<P ALIGN="CENTER"><IMG SRC="homelogo.jpg">
</P>
<DIV ALIGN="CENTER"><CENTER>

<TABLE BORDER="0" WIDTH="75%">
  <TR>
    <TD></TD>
      <TD><P ALIGN="CENTER"><IMG SRC="calculator.jpg" WIDTH="100" HEIGHT="106"></A></TD>
    <TD></TD>
  </TR>
  <TR>
```

line 11

increments position variable by 1

**FIGURE 2-12**

**2** **Type** if
(beginPos >
scrollMsg.length) {
**and then press the ENTER
key. Type** beginPos = 0
**and then press the ENTER
key. Type** } **and then press
the ENTER key.**

*The If statement
displays (Figure 2-13).*

If statement

FIGURE 2-13

# Using the setTimeout() Method to Create a Recursive Function Call

Recall from Project 1, the **setTimeout()** method calls a function or evaluates an expression after a specified amount of time has elapsed, which is measured in milliseconds. To complete the scrollingMsg() function, you need to add a setTimeout() method that pauses before calling the scrollingMsg() function again. This programming technique, called **recursion**, is used to call the same function from within the function. In this project, the recursive call to the scrollingMsg() function is what makes the message scroll in the text box continuously. Perform the steps on the next page to add the setTimeout() method to create a recursive call to the scrollingMsg() function.

**More** *About*

**Recursion**

Recursive functions generally have a condition that eventually stops the function. For more information on recursion, visit www.scsite.com/js/ p2.htm and then click recursion.

**To Add the setTimeout() Method to Create a Recursive Function Call**

 **With the insertion point on line 15,** type `window.setTimeout ("scrollingMsg()", 200)` **and then press the ENTER key. Type** `}` **and then press the ENTER key three times.**

*The setTimeout() method pauses the scrolling message for 200 milliseconds and then again calls the scrollingMsg function.*

FIGURE 2-14

 **Type** `//-->` **and then press the ENTER key. Type** `</SCRIPT>` **and then press the ENTER key.**

*The end //--> and </SCRIPT> tags complete the JavaScript section (Figure 2-14).*

**More About**

**Event Handlers**

Event handlers are the primary technique for calling functions. To learn more about event handlers, visit www.scsite.com/js/p2.htm and then click event handlers.

The setTimeout() method calls the function scrollingMsg() every 200 milliseconds, which allows the message to scroll continuously through the text box. Web developers warn that recursive calls can create undesired results, such as infinite loops or stack overflows. You should use recursive functions carefully to avoid Web page failures.

## Adding an Event Handler

The next step is to add an event handler to start the scrolling message when the Web page loads. Recall that an event is a user action. When the user performs an action, such as clicking a button, an event handler triggers associated JavaScript code. In this project, the onload() event handler is used to start the scrollingMsg() function. To have the function called when the page is loaded, you place the onload() event handler in the <BODY> tag. When you insert an event handler within an HTML tag, the statement takes the general form, as shown in Table 2-4.

| Table 2-4 – Event Handler | |
|---|---|
| **General form:** | <TAG tag attributes eventhandlername = "JavaScript instruction"> |
| **Comment:** | where TAG is the HTML tag; tag attributes are any HTML attributes; eventhandlername is any of the event handlers; and JavaScript instruction is any JavaScript code or function name. |
| **Examples:** | <A HREF = "#LoanCalc" onclick = "doMort()")> <br> <INPUT Type = "Button" Name = "Calc" Value = "Calculate" onclick = "Calc()"> |

Event handler names are not case sensitive. The Netscape documentation warns that mixed case spellings may not work and strongly recommends Web developers to use all lowercase spellings. In addition, you cannot use all of the event handlers with all HTML tags and attributes. Table 2-5 shows some of the event handlers and the associated HTML attributes. For example, the onclick event handler triggers JavaScript code when used with buttons and links, while the onload event handler is used generally with BODY, FRAMESET, and IMG tags.

The onload event handler is used to trigger an action when a document is loaded into the browser window. In this project, the onload event handler calls the scrollingMsg() function, using the following statement:

```
onload="scrollingMsg()"
```

| Table 2-5 | |
|---|---|
| OBJECT | EVENT HANDLER |
| button | onclick |
| document | onload, onunload |
| form | onsubmit, onreset |
| hyperlink | onclick, onmouseover, onmouseout |
| image | onload, onabort |
| input box | onblur, onchange, onfocus |
| submit button | onclick |
| window | onload, onunload, onblur, onfocus |

where onload is the event handler and scrollingMsg is the handler text. The statement is entered directly after the beginning BODY tag. To enter the onload event handler to call the scrollingMsg() function, perform the following steps.

### Steps: To Enter the Event Handler to Call the scrollingMsg() Function

**1** **Locate the <BODY> tag on line 24. Position the insertion point directly between the word, BODY, and the > symbol. Press the SPACEBAR once.**

**2** **Type** onload= "scrollingMsg()" **and do not press the ENTER key.**

*The onload() event handler displays within the BODY tag. The onload() event handler will call the user-defined function, scrollingMsg(), when the Web page loads (Figure 2-15).*

**FIGURE 2-15**

# Saving the HTML File and Testing the Web Page

As you work on a document, you periodically should save your file. Save this file using the file name, homefinders.htm. As in Project 1, you must be sure to add the .htm extension to the file name when you save the file, because Notepad automatically saves all files with a .txt extension. Perform the following steps to save the HTML file on your JavaScript Data Disk using Notepad.

### TO SAVE THE FILE ON THE DATA DISK

**1** With your JavaScript Data Disk in drive A, click Save As on the File menu.

**2** Type a:\homefinders.htm in the File name text box and then click the Save button in the Save As dialog box.

*The file is saved to the JavaScript Data Disk in drive A. The new file name displays on the Notepad title bar.*

While working on a project, save your file several times. After you have saved a file the first time, subsequent Save commands use the same file name. In addition, every time you need to test your Web page you also must save the HTML file by viewing it with your browser. In general, it is a good development practice to test the Web page several times during its development and a final time before posting it to your Web site. When site visitors encounter errors on a Web site, they often leave the Web site — meaning a potential customer is lost. To view and test your Web page using your browser, perform the following steps.

### TO TEST THE WEB PAGE

**1** Start your browser. If necessary, click the Maximize button.

**2** Click the Address text box. Type a:\homefinders.htm and then press the ENTER key.

*The Home Finders Nationwide Realty Web page displays with the scrolling message in the text box (Figure 2-16).*

**FIGURE 2-16**

If your browser does not display the Web page correctly, close any error messages and then click the Notepad button on the taskbar. Check your JavaScript code according to Figures 2-7 through 2-15 on pages J 2.11 through J 2.17. Correct any errors, save the file, activate the browser, and then click the Refresh button. The next section discusses the mortgage payment calculator form.

# The Mortgage Payment Calculator Form

The mortgage payment calculator form shown in Figure 2-17 allows user input. The form is created using HTML and JavaScript code that displays the form and the results (Figure 2-17). To assign a value to a text box object within a form, you must use the form name, the text box name, and the value attribute. Table 2-6 shows the general form of the JavaScript statement used to assign a value to a text box object within a form.

**FIGURE 2-17**

| Table 2-6 – Assign Statement | |
|---|---|
| **General form:** | document.formname.textboxname.value = variable_or_literal |
| **Comment:** | where formname is the name of the form; textboxname is the name of a text box in the form; value is the attribute; and the variable_or_literal is the value assigned to the text box. |
| **Examples:** | document.MortCalc.Amount.value = LoanAmt<br>document.MortCalc.Amount.value = "12500" |

### Inserting an Event Handler in an Anchor Tag

In this project, you insert an onclick event handler in an anchor tag to trigger a user-defined function when a user clicks the Estimate Mortgage Payment link. The **anchor** tag defines a target link. The Estimate Mortgage Payment link, for example, refers to an anchor located within the Home Finders page, directly above the mortgage payment calculator (Figure 2-16). When the user clicks the link, the browser scrolls to the anchor reference within the page to display the form used for the mortgage payment calculator.

An anchor tag begins with <A> within the HTML code. The onclick() event handler inside the anchor tag triggers the user-defined function called doMort() when the Estimate Mortgage Payment link is clicked. The doMort() user-defined function contains statements that clear the text boxes and then display the insertion point in the Amount of Mortgage text box. To insert an event handler in the anchor tag for the Estimate Mortgage Payment link, perform the following steps.

 **To Insert an Event Handler in an Anchor Tag**

**1** **Make sure Notepad is the active window. Scroll down to the BODY section. Position the insertion point on line 41 between the last quotation mark and the > symbol of the <A HREF= "#LoanCalc"> anchor tag.**

*Figure 2-18 shows the position of the insertion point.*

**FIGURE 2-18**

**2** Type `onclick="doMort()"` **and do not press the ENTER key.**

The onclick() event handler is entered within the anchor tag (Figure 2-19).

```
homefinders.htm - Notepad
File  Edit  Search  Help
<BODY onload="scrollingMsg()">

<P ALIGN="CENTER"><IMG SRC="homelogo.jpg">
</P>
<DIV ALIGN="CENTER"><CENTER>

<TABLE BORDER="0" WIDTH="75%">
  <TR>
    <TD></TD>
    <TD><P ALIGN="CENTER"><IMG SRC="calculator.jpg" WIDTH="100" HEIGHT="106"></A></TD>
    <TD></TD>
  </TR>
  <TR>
    <TD><P ALIGN="CENTER">
    <IMG SRC="house1.gif" WIDTH="180" HEIGHT="144"></TD>
    <TD>
      <P ALIGN="CENTER">
      <A HREF="#LoanCalc" onclick="doMort()">Estimate Mortgage Payment</A>
      </P>
      <FORM Name="msgForm">
          <INPUT Type="text" Name="scrollingMsg" Size="23">
      </FORM>
    </TD>
    <TD><P ALIGN="CENTER">
    <IMG SRC="house2.gif" WIDTH=      ="144"></TD>
  </TR>
  <TR>
    <TD></TD>
    <TD>
```

text that displays as link

anchor tag

location of event handler

**FIGURE 2-19**

When the viewer clicks the Estimate Mortgage Payment link, the onclick() event handler will execute the doMort() function. The next step is to code the doMort() user-defined function in the HEAD section, below the scrollingMsg() user-defined function.

# Writing the doMort() User-Defined Function

The doMort() function shown in Table 2-7 will clear all the text boxes in the form and set the focus to the Amount of Mortgage text box.

**Setting the focus** means giving attention to an object. When you set focus to a text box, the JavaScript statement automatically positions the insertion point in the text box. The general form of the focus() method is shown in Table 2-8.

The user sees only the insertion point in the Amount of Mortgage text box and is not aware of the other commands. To clear each text box, you assign a blank to the value property of each object, as shown in lines 20 through 23 in Table 2-7. Line 24 shows setting the focus to the Amount text box. The spacing shown in the tables is for readability purposes. A good programming practice is to indent lines of code under functions, If, If...Else, and Loop statements. To enter the doMort() function to clear the text boxes and set focus to the Amount of Mortgage text box, perform the steps on the next page.

**Table 2-7**

| LINE | CODE |
|------|------|
| 19 | `function doMort() {` |
| 20 | `    document.MortCalc.Amount.value=" "` |
| 21 | `    document.MortCalc.Rate.value=" "` |
| 22 | `    document.MortCalc.Years.value=" "` |
| 23 | `    document.MortCalc.Payment.value=" "` |
| 24 | `    document.MortCalc.Amount.focus()` |
| 25 | `}` |

**Table 2-8 – focus() Method**

| | |
|---|---|
| **General form:** | document.formname.objectname.focus() |
| **Comment:** | where formname is the name of the form that contains the object; and objectname identifies the object to which focus should be set. |
| **Example:** | `document.MortCalc.Amount.focus()` |

## Steps To Enter the doMort() Function

**1** Position the insertion point in the HEAD section on line 18.

**2** Enter the JavaScript code as shown in Table 2-7 on the previous page.

*These statements cause the Web page to scroll down to the form when the user clicks the Estimate Mortgage Payment link. The doMort() function clears the text boxes and places the insertion point in the Amount of Mortgage text box (Figure 2-20).*

**FIGURE 2-20**

The focus() method in line 23 causes the Web page to scroll down and position the insertion point in the desired text box when the user clicks the Estimate Mortgage Payment link (Figure 2-16 on page J 2.18).

### Saving and Testing the Web Page

Before continuing, you should double-check the spelling, special characters, and quotation marks in the code. The next steps are to save your file and test the Web page.

#### TO SAVE AND TEST THE WEB PAGE

**1** With your JavaScript Data Disk in drive A, click File on the menu bar and then click Save on the File menu.

**2** Click the browser button on the taskbar.

**3** Click the Refresh button on the browser toolbar.

**4** Click the Estimate Mortgage Payment link.

*The Web page should display the mortgage payment calculator form with the insertion point in the Amount of Mortgage text box (Figure 2-21).*

**FIGURE 2-21**

If your browser does not display the Web page correctly, close any error messages and then click the Notepad button on the taskbar. Check your JavaScript code against Figures 2-18 through 2-20 on pages J 2.20 through J 2.22. Correct any errors and save the file. Activate the browser and then click the Refresh button.

# Validating the Mortgage Payment Calculator Form

Form validation is one of the most important features of JavaScript. With JavaScript, the validation procedure is completed on the user's computer instead of the Web server on which the Web page is stored. Along with form validation, JavaScript's math features allow immediate processing of the data. Form validation uses the If...Else statement, which is an extension of the If statement as shown in the flowchart in Figure 2-22.

### Validating Data Using the If...Else Statement

Much like the If statement, an If...Else statement tests a condition. If the condition is true, the statements between the curly braces after the If (condition) statement execute. The statements between the curly braces after the Else statement execute if the condition is false.

In this form, you will use the Calc() validation function to convert and store the text box values in temporary variables for validation. The Calc() validation function is placed within an If...Else statement, so that, if the value of a text box is invalid (a True condition), a message displays, the text box clears, and the insertion point is placed back in the text box. This occurs until the user enters valid data in the text box. If the value is valid (a False condition), the next text box is examined until all text boxes are validated. The validation process is shown in the flowchart in Figure 2-23 on the next page.

**More About**

## Validation

Programmers also should write JavaScript code to test data for values that are negative or zero, and reject them as invalid. To keep things simple, the validation presented in this project only tests to ensure that all entered values are numeric. For more information, visit www.scsite.com/js/p2.htm and then click validation.

**FIGURE 2-22**

**FIGURE 2-23**

This validation design is necessary because of the event-driven nature of JavaScript. When a user triggers an event that calls a function, processing stays within that function until all statements execute. Because all the statements execute in a function, the form validation routine uses nested If...Else statements to ensure each text box is validated correctly. By nesting If...Else statements, you can place another If...Else statement inside of another as shown in Figure 2-24. Using nested If...Else statements is one method to test multiple conditions.

Attempting to place separate If statements to validate a series of text boxes will not work with event driven programming logic as desired. Each If statement executes until all the statements in the function are complete. Processing continues through the entire set of If statements without terminating as may be desired; thus, the need for the nested If...Else statements. In addition, the placement of the curly braces is important to the logical processing and validation of the text boxes. The curly braces must enclose a complete block of If or Else statements. As shown in Figure 2-24, if the first condition is false, no other statements execute in this block of code. Most Web developers recommend writing nested If...Else statements with the indentation shown in Figure 2-24 for readability purposes.

**More About**

**Validating Forms**

JavaScript programmers have developed several ways to validate forms. For more information about validating forms, visit www.scsite.com/js/p2.htm and then click validating forms.

**More About**

**The parseInt() Function**

The parseInt() function is one of the built-in functions of JavaScript. You can use the parseInt() function to convert integer numbers to binary, decimal, and hexadecimal form. For more information, visit www.scsite.com/js/p2.htm and then click parseInt().

**FIGURE 2-24**

## Validating Data Criteria Using Built-in Functions

When validating data, you may have to evaluate several criteria. You may want, for example, to ensure that a text box is not blank or that it contains numeric data (not text or characters). JavaScript accepts data entered into a text box as string data. You must convert the string values to a number before they can be tested or validated. Table 2-9 describes the built-in functions used for converting values.

**Table 2-9**

| BUILT-IN FUNCTION | SAMPLE AND EXPLANATION |
|---|---|
| answer = eval(expression) | **Sample:** `answer = eval("1"+"2"+"3")` <br> **Explanation:** converts string values to numbers and executes the expression |
| variable = parseInt(value, base) | **Sample:** `parseInt(mortAmount, 10)` <br> **Explanation:** value is any string; base is the number base to which you want the string converted. A 2 means binary base number, an 8 means octal, and a 10 means decimal. Returns an integer value, stripping the value after the decimal point. |
| variable = parseFloat(value) | **Sample:** `parseFloat(mortAmount)` <br> **Explanation:** returns the value as a floating-point number. A floating-point number is a number with a fractional or decimal value. |
| isNaN(value) | **Sample:** `isNaN(mortAmount)` <br> **Explanation:** returns a Boolean condition of true or false. isNaN means is Not a Number. |

## The parseFloat() Function

The parseFloat() function is one built-in function. The parseFloat function parses a string argument and returns a floating-point number. If the first character cannot be converted to a number, it returns "NaN" (not a number). For more information on the parseFloat() function, visit www.scsite.com/js/p2.htm and then click parseFloat().

## The isNaN() Function

The isNaN() built-in function is the only function that tests for numeric values. The test uses the NOT operator. For more information on the isNaN() function, visit www.scsite.com/js/p2.htm and then click isNaN().

In this project you create the Calc() user-defined function that converts and stores the text box values as integer or floating-point numbers in temporary variables. The function passes the value of the text box to a variable, uses the parseInt() function to convert the variable to a number, and then uses the isNaN() function to verify the value is a number. To pass the text box values to the function, you must place the name of the form (in this case, myform) in the parentheses of the user-defined function Calc() as shown in Figure 2-25.

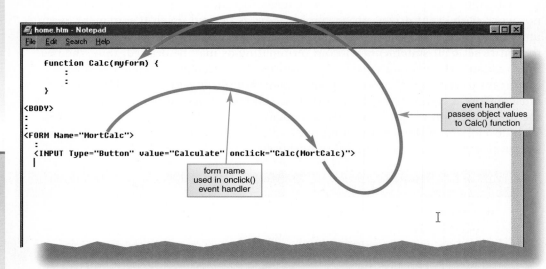

**FIGURE 2-25**

The If statement beginning in line 29 in Table 2-10 checks the condition to see if the value for the variable mortAmount is not a number. If the result of the condition is true (it is not a number) the function performs the following steps. It notifies the user with an alert message (line 30); it clears the text box entry (line 31); and then it sets the focus back to the Amount of Mortgage text box (line 32). The final curly brace in line 33 closes the If statement.

| Table 2-10 | |
|---|---|
| LINE | CODE |
| 26 | `function Calc(myform) {` |
| 27 | `var mortAmount=document.MortCalc.Amount.value` |
| 28 | `var mortAmount=parseInt(mortAmount,10)` |
| 29 | `if (isNaN(mortAmount)) {` |
| 30 | `alert("The loan amount is not a number!")` |
| 31 | `document.MortCalc.Amount.value=" "` |
| 32 | `document.MortCalc.Amount.focus()` |
| 33 | `}` |

To enter the Calc() user-defined function that validates the value in the Amount of Mortgage text box, perform the following steps.

### Steps: To Enter a Calc() User-Defined Function

**1** If necessary, activate Notepad. Scroll up to the HEAD section. Position the insertion point on line 26.

**2** Enter the JavaScript code as shown in Table 2-10.

*The JavaScript statement passes the text box values to the Calc() function, which converts the Amount of Mortgage value to an integer. If the value is not a number, an alert message displays and the focus is reset to the Amount of Mortgage text box (Figure 2-26).*

**FIGURE 2-26**

Because you have two more text boxes to validate in this form, you want the function to continue checking the text box values. The If...Else statement provides the control needed to test the remaining text boxes. Table 2-11 shows the code to validate the data entered in the Interest Rate as % text box. The interest rate validation is similar to that of the mortgage amount, except that you will use the parseFloat() function (line 36 in Table 2-11). Because the interest rate is a floating point number, it requires the parseFloat() function to keep the interest rate a floating number. Table 2-12 on the next page shows the code used to validate the data entered in the Number of Years text box.

**Table 2-11**

| LINE | CODE |
|------|------|
| 34 | else { |
| 35 | var mortRate=document.MortCalc.Rate.value |
| 36 | var mortRate=parseFloat(mortRate) |
| 37 | if (isNaN(mortRate)) { |
| 38 | alert("The interest rate is not a number! ) |
| 39 | document.MortCalc.Rate.value=" " |
| 40 | document.MortCalc.Rate.focus() |
| 41 | } |

**Table 2-12**

| LINE | CODE |
|------|------|
| 42 | else { |
| 43 | var mortYears=document.MortCalc.Years.value |
| 44 | var mortYears=parseInt(mortYears,10) |
| 45 | if (isNaN(mortYears)) { |
| 46 | alert("The number of years is not a number!") |
| 47 | document.MortCalc.Years.value=" " |
| 48 | document.MortCalc.Years.focus() |
| 49 | } |
| 50 | } |
| 51 | } |
| 52 | } |

Perform the following steps to enter the Else portion of the nested If…Else statement that validates the data entered in the Interest Rate as % and Number of Years text boxes.

 **To Enter the Else Portion of the Nested If…Else Statement**

**1** **Position the insertion point on line 34.**

**2** **Enter the JavaScript code as shown in Table 2-11 on the previous page.**

*The first Else statement displays (Figure 2-27).*

```
homefinders.htm - Notepad
File  Edit  Search  Help
    function doMort() {
        document.MortCalc.Amount.value=" "
        document.MortCalc.Rate.value=" "
        document.MortCalc.Years.value=" "
        document.MortCalc.Payment.value=" "
        document.MortCalc.Amount.focus()
    }

    function Calc(myform) {
        var mortAmount=document.MortCalc.Amount.value
        var mortAmount=parseInt(mortAmount,10)
        if (isNaN(mortAmount)) {
            alert("The loan amount is not a number!")
            document.MortCalc.Amount.value=" "
            document.MortCalc.Amount.focus()
        }
        else {
            var mortRate=document.MortCalc.Rate.value
            var mortRate=parseFloat(mortRate)
            if (isNaN(mortRate)) {
                alert("The interest rate is not a number!")
                document.MortCalc.Rate.value=" "
                document.MortCalc.Rate.focus()
            }

//-->
</SCRIPT>

</HEAD>
<BODY onload="scrollingMsg()">

<P ALIGN="CENTER"><IMG SRC="homelogo.jpg">
</P>
<DIV ALIGN="CENTER"><CENTER>
```

line 34

beginning of nested If statement

**FIGURE 2-27**

**3** Position the insertion point on line 42.

**4** Enter the JavaScript code as shown in Table 2-12.

*The second Else statement displays (Figure 2-28).*

JavaScript statements to validate data entered in the Amount of Mortgage text box

JavaScript statements to validate data entered in the Interest Rate text box

line 42

JavaScript statements to validate data entered in the Number of Years text box

```
function Calc(myform) {
    var mortAmount=document.MortCalc.Amount.value
    var mortAmount=parseInt(mortAmount,10)
    if (isNaN(mortAmount)) {
        alert("The loan amount is not a number!")
        document.MortCalc.Amount.value=" "
        document.MortCalc.Amount.focus()
    }
    else {
        var mortRate=document.MortCalc.Rate.value
        var mortRate=parseFloat(mortRate)
        if (isNaN(mortRate)) {
            alert("The interest rate is not a number!")
            document.MortCalc.Rate.value=" "
            document.MortCalc.Rate.focus()
        }
        else {
            var mortYears=document.MortCalc.Years.value
            var mortYears=parseInt(mortYears,10)
            if (isNaN(mortYears)) {
                alert("The number of years is not a number!")
                document.MortCalc.Years.value=" "
                document.MortCalc.Years.focus()
            }
        }
    }
}
//-->
</SCRIPT>

</HEAD>
<BODY onload="scrollingMsg()">
```

**FIGURE 2-28**

Placing the If...Else statement within the Calc() function allows you to validate the three text boxes as the user enters data. If the user enters a non-numeric value in any text box, the validation will notify the user and place the insertion point back in that text box.

## Adding an Event Handler to Call a Function

Once the user enters valid data in the three form text boxes, he or she can click the Calculate button to calculate the monthly payment. To calculate the monthly payment requires calling the Calc() function. To call the Calc() function by clicking the Calculate button, you must associate an event handler with the Calculate button. Perform the steps on the next page to enter the event handler to call the Calc() function.

## Steps  To Enter the onclick Event Handler to Call the Calc() Function

**1** Scroll down to the BODY section inside the table. Position the insertion point on line 120, directly before the rightmost > bracket.

**2** Press the SPACEBAR. Type onclick= "Calc(MortCalc)" and do not press the ENTER key.

*The event handler associates the function Calc() and the Calculate button that is part of the mortgage payment calculator form (MortCalc) (Figure 2-29).*

FIGURE 2-29

## Saving and Testing the Web Page

The function will not yet calculate the monthly payment, but you can test your validation statements. Before continuing, double-check the spelling, special characters, and quotation marks. The next step is to save your file and test the JavaScript code using your Web browser. To save and test your Web page, perform the following steps.

### TO SAVE AND TEST THE WEB PAGE

**1** With your JavaScript Data Disk in drive A, click File on the menu bar and then click Save on the File menu.

**2** Click the browser button on the taskbar.

**3** Click the Refresh button on the browser toolbar.

**4** When the Web page displays, click Estimate Mortgage Payment to display and set the focus to the Amount of Mortgage text box.

**5** Enter test data set 1, as shown in Table 2-13. Press the TAB key to move the insertion point to the next text box.

**6** When you have entered test data set 1, click the Calculate button.

**7** When the message box displays, click the OK button.

**8** Click the Reset button on the Web page.

**9** Repeat steps 5 through 8, using test data sets 2, 3, and 4 (Table 2-13).

**Table 2-13**

| TEST DATA SET | AMOUNT OF MORTGAGE | INTEREST RATE AS % | NUMBER OF YEARS | COMMENT |
|---|---|---|---|---|
| 1 | | 7.9 | 30 | Amount of Mortgage blank |
| 2 | 10000 | A | | Interest Rate invalid |
| 3 | 25000 | 1 | 5 | Valid |
| 4 | 69000 | 7.9 | | Number of Years blank |

*The Web page displays the mortgage payment calculator with the insertion point in the Amount of Mortgage text box. When you enter test data set 4, an alert message displays to notify you that the data entered for Number of Years is invalid (Figure 2-30).*

**FIGURE 2-30**

If your browser does not display the Web page correctly, close any error message windows, and click the Notepad button on the taskbar. Check your JavaScript code against Figures 2-26 through 2-29 on pages J 2.27 through J 2.30. Correct any errors and save the file. Activate the browser and then click the Refresh button.

# Determining the Monthly Payment

The next statement in the Calc() function calls a user-defined function, named monthly(), that you will create to calculate the monthly payment. The monthly() function requires that valid data is entered in the Amount of Mortgage, Interest Rate as %, and Number of Years text boxes before it can calculate the monthly payment. Once the monthly() function calculates the monthly payment, it returns the result to the Monthly Payment text box.

The function call is inserted on line 52, before the last curly brace of the Calc() function. The function call is written as follows

```
document.MortCalc.Payment.value=monthly(mortAmount,mortRate,mortYears)
```

In this statement, MortCalc is the name of the form; Payment is the name of the Monthly Payment text box; and value is the value returned by the monthly() user-defined function. The variables mortAmount, mortRate, and mortYears are the values entered in the Amount of Mortgage, Interest Rate as %, and Number of Years text boxes.

Perform the following steps to enter a function call that passes the required values to the monthly() user-defined function.

 **To Pass Values to the monthly() User-Defined Function**

**1** **Scroll up to the HEAD section.** Position the insertion point on line 52. Press the ENTER key to insert a blank line. Position the insertion point on the blank line.

*The insertion point displays on the blank line (Figure 2-31).*

**FIGURE 2-31**

2  **Type** document.
MortCalc.
Payment.value=monthly
(mortAmount,mortRate,
mortYears) **and then
press the ENTER key.**

*The function call statement
displays (Figure 2-32).*

```
homefinders.htm - Notepad
File  Edit  Search  Help
    function Calc(myform) {
        var mortAmount=document.MortCalc.Amount.value
        var mortAmount=parseInt(mortAmount,10)
        if (isNaN(mortAmount)) {
            alert("The loan amount is not a number!")
            document.MortCalc.Amount.value=" "
            document.MortCalc.Amount.focus()
        }
        else {
            var mortRate=document.MortCalc.Rate.value
            var mortRate=parseFloat(mortRate)
            if (isNaN(mortRate)) {
                alert("The interest rate is not a number!")
                document.MortCalc.Rate.value=" "
                document.MortCalc.Rate.focus()
            }
            else {
                var mortYears=document.MortCalc.Years.value
                var mortYears=parseInt(mortYears,10)
                if (isNaN(mortYears)) {
                    alert("The number of years is not a number!")
                    document.MortCalc.Years.value=" "
                    document.MortCalc.Years.focus()
                }
            }
        }
        document.MortCalc.Payment.value=monthly(mortAmount,mortRate,mortYears)   ← call to monthly()
                                                                                    function
    }

//-->
</SCRIPT>

</HEAD>
<BODY onload="scrollingMsg()">
```

Start  | homefinders.htm - No... | Home Finders Nationwide ...                9:25 AM

**FIGURE 2-32**

If you were to test the Web page at this point, an error message would display
because you have not yet entered the monthly() function into the HTML file.

## Creating the monthly() Function

The monthly() function, which is used to calculate the monthly payment amount,
requires three parameters: the mortgage amount (mortAmount), the interest rate
(mortRate), and the number of years that the payments will be made (mortYears).
The call statement entered in the previous set of steps passes the three variables —
mortAmount, mortRate, and mortYears — to the monthly() function. The JavaScript
code for the function is shown in Table 2-14.

**Table 2-14**

| LINE | CODE |
|------|------|
| 56 | function monthly(mortAmount,mortRate,mortYears) { |
| 57 |     var Irate=mortRate/1200 |
| 58 |     var Pmts=mortYears*12 |
| 59 |     var Loan=mortAmount |
| 60 |     return Loan * (Irate / (1 - (1 / Math.pow(1+Irate,Pmts)))) |
| 61 |  } |

You use the validated values in a mathematical expression or formula that calculates the monthly payment. The formula for calculating a monthly payment is shown in line 60. JavaScript does not use typical programming language symbols to represent exponentiation. To calculate the expression $(1 + Irate)^{payment}$, JavaScript uses the pow() method associated with the Math object. Table 2-15 shows the general form of the pow() method.

## More About

### Math Object Methods

The Math object has a number of helpful methods, including pow(). For more information on the Math object, visit www.scsite.com/js/p2.htm and then click Math object methods.

| Table 2-15 – Math.pow() Method | |
|---|---|
| **General form:** | Math.pow(number, exponent) |
| **Comment:** | where number is the value raised to the power of the exponent value. The pow() method accepts variables (X, n), constants (2, 3), or both (Sidelength, 2). |
| **Example:** | Math.pow(2,3) <br> Math.pow(X,n) <br> Math.pow(Sidelength,2) |

Before the formula executes, however, you must convert two of the values. In line 57, the annual rate of interest must be converted to a monthly rate. In line 58, the number of years must be converted to the number of payments. To convert the monthly interest and shift the decimal point to the right two places, divide the annual rate by 1200 and store it in the variable Irate. To convert the total number of payments multiply the years by 12 and store it in Pmts. The following statements show how to convert the interest and years. To prevent the mortAmount from being changed accidentally, assign it to a temporary variable (Loan) as shown in line 59.

The return statement (line 60) tells the function to send the results of the expression back to the calling function. The value then displays in the Monthly Payment text box. Perform the following steps to enter the monthly() function.

## Steps To Enter the monthly() Function

**1** Position the insertion point on line 56, the line directly above the //--> tag.

**2** Enter the JavaScript code as shown in Table 2-14 on the previous page and then press the ENTER key.

*The monthly() function displays (Figure 2-33).*

```
        document.MortCalc.Rate.focus()
    }
    else {
        var mortYears=document.MortCalc.Years.value
        var mortYears=parseInt(mortYears,10)
        if (isNaN(mortYears)) {
            alert("The number of years is not a number!")
            document.MortCalc.Years.value=" "
            document.MortCalc.Years.focus()
        }
    }
    document.MortCalc.Payment.value=monthly(mortAmount,mortRate,mortYears)
}

function monthly(mortAmount,mortRate,mortYears) {
    var Irate=mortRate/1200
    var Pmts=mortYears*12
    var Loan=mortAmount
    return Loan * (Irate / (1 - (1 / Math.pow(1+Irate,Pmts))))
}

//-->
</SCRIPT>

</HEAD>
```

line 56

JavaScript statements to execute monthly() function

converts number of years to number of payments

converts annual percentage to monthly decimal

homefinders.htm - Notepad

File    Edit    Search    Help

**FIGURE 2-33**

Before continuing, you should double-check the spelling, symbols, parentheses, curly braces, and quotation marks in the code. The next steps are to save your file and test the Web page using test data.

## TO SAVE AND TEST THE WEB PAGE

**1** With your JavaScript Data Disk in drive A, click File on the menu bar and then click Save on the File menu.

**2** Click the browser button on the taskbar.

**3** Click the Refresh button on the browser toolbar.

**4** If necessary, click the Amount of Mortgage text box to place the insertion point in the text box.

**5** Type 69000 in the Amount of Mortgage text box and then press the TAB key.

**6** Type 7.9 in the Interest Rate as % text box and then press the TAB key.

**7** Type 30 in the Number of Years text box and then click the Calculate button.

*The amount of the monthly payment, 501.4957296230, displays (Figure 2-34).*

**FIGURE 2-34**

If your browser does not display the Web page correctly, close any error messages and then click the Notepad button on the taskbar. Check your JavaScript code against Figures 2-31 through 2-33 on pages J 2.32 through J 2.34. Correct any errors and save the file. Activate the browser, click the Refresh button, and then reenter the data listed in the previous steps.

# Formatting the Monthly Payment Output as Currency

In the previous steps, the monthly payment amount calculated using the test data displayed as the value, 501.4957296230. To set the form to display the monthly payment amount in a currency format with two decimal places and a dollar sign, you need to enter a new function called dollarFormat(). First, you must enter a statement that passes the resulting string object of the monthly payment Calc() function to the dollarFormat() function. The dollarFormat() function then analyzes the string and adds commas and displays the number with a dollar sign and two decimal places.

To format the result, the dollarFormat() function performs these five basic steps. The function: (1) takes the string value and separates the dollars from the cents based on the position of the decimal point; (2) determines the location of the decimal point using the indexOf() method; (3) separates the value to the left of the decimal point as the dollar amount and the value to the right of the decimal point as the cents amount; (4) inserts commas every three positions in dollar amounts exceeding 999; and (5) reconstructs the string value with two decimal places, inserts a dollar sign immediately to left of the first digit without spaces, and then returns the completed formatted value.

## More About

### The indexOf() Method

The indexOf() method often is used in conjunction with other string methods to subdivide string values. For more information on the indexOf() method, visit www.scsite.com/js/p2.htm and then click indexOf().

## Using the indexOf() Method

The indexOf() method is used to search a string for a particular value and returns the relative location of that value within the string. The indexOf() method searches the string object for the desired value, which is enclosed within the quotation marks. Table 2-16 shows the general form of the indexOf() method.

| Table 2-16 – indexOf() Method | |
|---|---|
| **General form:** | var position = stringname.indexOf("c") |
| **Comment:** | where position is a variable; stringname is any string object; and "c" is the value for which the function searches. |
| **Example:** | `var decipos = valuein.indexOf(".")` |

If the search value is found in the string object, the indexOf() method returns the relative position of the value within the string object. If the search value is not found, the indexOf() method returns a negative one (-1). In this project, the indexOf() method is used to search for a decimal point in the monthly payment amount. Figure 2-35 provides an example of how the indexOf() method works.

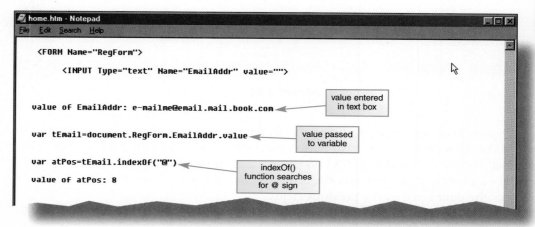

**FIGURE 2-35**

## Determining the Dollars Portion

The dollarFormat() function initializes the variable that will return the formatted value and the variable used to manipulate the unformatted value. Most programmers agree it is a good programming practice to clear and initialize variables to ensure the data is valid. Table 2-17 shows the JavaScript code used to initialize the variables.

Lines 64 and 65 clear the variables used to assemble the formatted output. The indexOf() method in line 66 returns a value indicating the location of the decimal point – a value stored as the decipos. The decipos value indicates at what position to concatenate the decimal values. Lines 67 and 68 test the decipos variable for a value greater than zero. If the value of decipos is zero, then the input value (valuein) is an integer. If the value of decipos is negative one, then decipos is set equal to the length of the string, as shown in line 68.

Perform the following steps to enter the dollarFormat() function and initialize the variables.

**Table 2-17**

| LINE | CODE |
|------|------|
| 63 | `function dollarFormat(valuein) {` |
| 64 | `    var formatStr=""` |
| 65 | `    var Outdollars=""` |
| 66 | `    var decipos=valuein.indexOf(".")` |
| 67 | `    if (decipos==-1)` |
| 68 | `        decipos=valuein.length` |

### Steps) To Enter the dollarFormat() Function

**1** Position the insertion point on line 63.

**2** Enter the JavaScript code as shown in Table 2-17 and then press the ENTER key.

*The dollarFormat() function and the statements to initialize the variables display (Figure 2-36).*

**FIGURE 2-36**

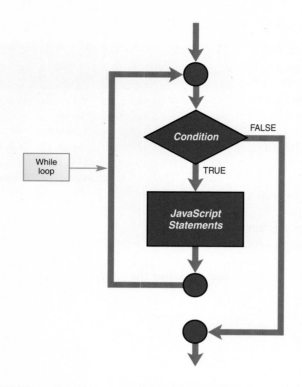

**FIGURE 2-37**

The first three statements initialize the variables that temporarily hold data during the formatting process. The indexOf() method determines the position of the decimal point and stores it in the variable decipos. The If statement verifies if a decimal point exists; if not, it sets the position to the length of the string.

Next, you enter statements that will format any dollar values greater than three digits with commas. To accomplish this task, you will use a While loop.

## Using For Loops and While Loops

A **loop** is a series of statements that executes repeatedly until it satisfies a condition. JavaScript has two types of loops, the For loop and the While loop. Both the For loop and the While loop use the logic illustrated by the flowchart in Figure 2-37. Both loops first test a condition to determine if the instructions in the loop are to be executed.

The **For loop** relies on a conditional statement using numeric values and thus often is referred to as a counter-controlled loop. Table 2-18 shows the general form of the For loop.

| Table 2-18 – For Loop | |
|---|---|
| **General form:** | for (start; stop; counter-control) {<br>    JavaScript statements<br>} |
| **Comment:** | where start is a variable initialized to a beginning value; stop is an expression indicating the condition at which the loop should terminate; and the counter-control is an expression indicating how to increment or decrement the counter. Semicolons separate the three variables. |
| **Examples:** | for (j=1; j=5; j++) {<br>for (ctr = 6; ctr < 0; ctr--) {<br>for (item = 1; item = 100; item=+2) { |

The **While loop** relies on a conditional statement that can use either a numeric value or a string. Table 2-19 shows the general form of the While loop.

| Table 2-19 – While Loop | |
|---|---|
| **General form:** | while (condition) {<br>    JavaScript statements<br>} |
| **Comment:** | where condition is either a numeric value or a string; and the JavaScript statements execute while the result of the condition is true. |
| **Examples:** | while (ctr < 6) {<br>while (isNaN(temp)) {<br>while (Response != "Done") { |

## Extracting the Dollars Portion and Inserting Commas

In this project, the While loop is used in formatting the dollar value of the Monthly Payment value. The dollars portion is represented by the digits to the left of the decimal point. If the dollars portion of the mortgage payment contains more than three digits, you need to insert commas. To determine how many digits are in the dollar portion of the monthly payment amount, you use an If...Else statement. Table 2-20 shows the JavaScript statements used to determine the length of the dollar value and placement of the commas.

**Table 2-20**

| LINE | CODE |
|------|------|
| 69 | `var dollars=valuein.substring(0,decipos)` |
| 70 | `var dollen=dollars.length` |
| 71 | `if (dollen>3) {` |
| 72 | `   while (dollen>0) {` |
| 73 | `      tDollars=dollars.substring(dollen-3,dollen)` |
| 74 | `      if (tDollars.length==3) {` |
| 75 | `         Outdollars=","+tDollars+Outdollars` |
| 76 | `         dollen=dollen-3` |
| 77 | `      } else {` |
| 78 | `         Outdollars=tDollars+Outdollars` |
| 79 | `         dollen=0` |
| 80 | `      }` |
| 81 | `   }` |
| 82 | `if (Outdollars.substring(0,1)==",")` |
| 83 | `   dollars=Outdollars.substring(1,Outdollars.length)` |
| 84 | `else` |
| 85 | `   dollars=Outdollars` |
| 86 | `}` |

The substring() method on line 69 uses the decipos value (the location of the decimal point) to extract the dollar value (the variable dollars). Next, a series of statements determine the length of the dollar value and then assign the length to the variable, dollen (line 70). Line 71 begins the If statement. Lines 72 through 81 use a While loop that places a comma every three digits, as needed. The statements insert a comma every three digits, while the length of the dollar value is greater than three digits. Line 73 extracts three digits starting from the right by subtracting 3 from the length of the dollar value (dollen). Line 74 verifies three digits and line 75 inserts a comma in the output string. Line 76 decrements the length of the dollar value to look for the next group of three digits. When no more groups of three digits exist, the length of dollen is set to zero (line 79) and the loop terminates at line 81. The statements in lines 82 through 86 prevent the code from inserting a comma if only three digits are to the left of the decimal point. Perform the steps on the next page to extract the dollar portion of the output and insert commas into the output, if needed.

## To Extract the Dollar Portion of the Output and Insert Commas

**1** Position the insertion point at line 69, the line directly below the statement, **decipos=valuein. length.**

**2** Enter the JavaScript code as shown in Table 2-20 on the previous page and then press the ENTER key.

*The code displays (Figure 2-38).*

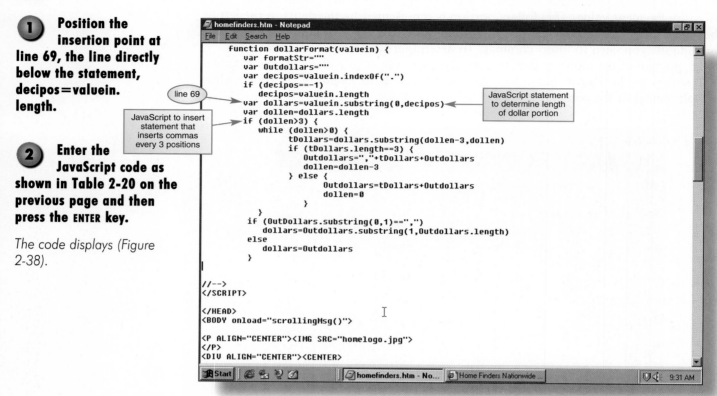

**FIGURE 2-38**

Before continuing, you should double-check the spelling, special characters, and quotation marks in the code.

### Extracting the Cents Portion and Defining the Decimal Amount

Recall that the mortgage payment amount should display with two decimal places to the right of the decimal point. After you have written JavaScript to extract the dollar portion of the string and place commas, as needed, you must write a statement to extract the cents portion from the valuein string. Table 2-21 shows the statement used to complete this task.

| Table 2-21 | |
|---|---|
| *LINE* | *CODE* |
| 87 | `var cents=valuein.substring(decipos+1, decipos+3)` |
| 88 | `if (cents=="")` |
| 89 | `cents="00"` |

The statement at line 87 extracts two digits from the valuein string, starting at the calculated monthly payment decimal point position plus one. The value returned is tested to see if it is an integer (line 88). If it is — meaning the monthly payment is a dollar value like $432.00 or $51.00 — line 89 assigns two zeros to the cents string. If it is not, the statements in line 87 extract and store the first two decimal places as the cents portion of the monthly payment. Perform the following steps to enter the statements to extract the cents portion of the monthly payment and define the decimal amount.

 **Steps** **To Extract the Cents Portion and Define the Decimal Amount**

**1** **Position the insertion point on line 87.**

**2** **Enter the JavaScript code as shown in Table 2-21 and then press the ENTER key.**

*The code displays (Figure 2-39).*

```
homefinders.htm - Notepad
File  Edit  Search  Help
     function dollarFormat(valuein) {
        var formatStr=""
        var Outdollars=""
        var decipos=valuein.indexOf(".")
        if (decipos==-1)
           decipos=valuein.length
        var dollars=valuein.substring(0,decipos)
        var dollen=dollars.length
        if (dollen>3) {
           while (dollen>0) {
                tDollars=dollars.substring(dollen-3,dollen)
                if (tDollars.length==3) {
                    Outdollars=","+tDollars+Outdollars
                    dollen=dollen-3
                } else {
                        Outdollars=tDollars+Outdollars
                        dollen=0
                }
           }
           if (OutDollars.substring(0,1)==",")
              dollars=Outdollars.substring(1,Outdollars.length)
           else
              dollars=Outdollars
        }
        var cents=valuein.substring(decipos+1,decipos+3)
        if (cents=="")
           cents="00"


//-->
</SCRIPT>

</HEAD>
<BODY onload="scrollingMsg()">
```

line 87

JavaScript statements to add zeroes to right of decimal point if no decimal value

**FIGURE 2-39**

The JavaScript statements extract the first two digits to right of the decimal point and store them as the cents portion. For values that are blank or null, the JavaScript statements add two zeroes for the decimal amount. JavaScript does not have a function that rounds decimal values up or down to the next cent. Because the monthly payment is only an estimate, however, the mortgage payment calculator does not need to round the cents values.

### Reconstructing the Formatted Output and Returning the Formatted Value

Next, you must write JavaScript statements to reconstruct (concatenate) the formatted dollars and cents output into a payment amount value, store the payment amount value in the formatStr variable, and return the formatStr value. Table 2-22 shows the statements needed to complete this task.

When you enter the JavaScript code as shown in Table 2-22, make sure you place a period between the quotation marks in line 90, as this represents the decimal point. Also be sure not to forget the final brace (line 92). Perform the following steps to reconstruct the formatted output and return the formatted value.

**Table 2-22**

| LINE | CODE |
|------|------|
| 90 | `var formatStr="$"+dollars+"."+cents` |
| 91 | `return formatStr` |
| 92 | `}` |

 **Steps** **To Reconstruct the Formatted Output and Return the Formatted Value**

**①** **Position the insertion point on line 90.**

**②** **Enter the JavaScript code as shown in Table 2-22.**

*The code displays (Figure 2-40).*

```
function dollarFormat(valuein) {
    var formatStr=""
    var Outdollars=""
    var decipos=valuein.indexOf(".")
    if (decipos==-1)
        decipos=valuein.length
    var dollars=valuein.substring(0,decipos)
    var dollen=dollars.length
    if (dollen>3) {
        while (dollen>0) {
            tDollars=dollars.substring(dollen-3,dollen)
            if (tDollars.length==3) {
                Outdollars=","+tDollars+Outdollars
                dollen=dollen-3
            } else {
                Outdollars=tDollars+Outdollars
                dollen=0
            }
        }
        if (OutDollars.substring(0,1)==",")
            dollars=Outdollars.substring(1,Outdollars.length)
        else
            dollars=Outdollars
    }
    var cents=valuein.substring(decipos+1,decipos+3)
    if (cents=="")
        cents="00"
    var formatStr="$"+dollars+"."+cents
    return formatStr
}

//-->
</SCRIPT>
```

line 90 → JavaScript statement to reconstruct payment amount value

**FIGURE 2-40**

The JavaScript statements add the dollar sign and decimal point to the variable formatStr and display the monthly payment value in the currency format.

## Passing the Monthly Payment Value to the dollarFormat() Function

To pass the monthly payment value to the function, you first must call the dollarFormat() function. The JavaScript statements used to call the dollarFormat() function use the same general form as the call to the monthly() function (see Figure 2-32 on page J 2.33). Perform the following steps to enter the JavaScript statements needed to pass the monthly payment as a string object to the dollarFormat() function.

### Steps: To Pass the Monthly Payment Value to the dollarFormat() Function

**1** **Position the insertion point line 53 (Figure 2-41).**

```
          alert("The interest rate is not a number!")
          document.MortCalc.Rate.value=" "
          document.MortCalc.Rate.focus()
     }
     else {
          var mortYears=document.MortCalc.Years.value
          var mortYears=parseInt(mortYears,10)
          if (isNaN(mortYears)) {
             alert("The number of years is not a number!")
             document.MortCalc.Years.value=" "
             document.MortCalc.Years.focus()
          }
     }
     document.MortCalc.Payment.value=monthly(mortAmount,mortRate,mortYears)
}

  function monthly(mortAmount,mortRate,mortYears) {
     var Irate=mortRate/1200
     var Pmts=mortYears*12
     var Loan=mortAmount
     return Loan * (Irate / (1 - (1 / Math.pow(1+Irate,Pmts))))
  }

  function dollarFormat(valuein) {
     var formatStr=""
     var Outdollars=""
     var decipos=valuein.indexOf(".")
     if (decipos==-1)
        decipos=valuein.length
     var dollars=valuein substring(0,dec
```

line 53

**FIGURE 2-41**

**2** **Type** document. MortCalc. Payment.value= dollarFormat(document .MortCalc.Payment. value) **as the statement.**

*The statement displays directly below the statement that calls the monthly() function before the closing brace (Figure 2-42).*

```
          alert("The interest rate is not a number!")
          document.MortCalc.Rate.value=" "
          document.MortCalc.Rate.focus()
     }
     else {
          var mortYears=document.MortCalc.Years.value
          var mortYears=parseInt(mortYears,10)
          if (isNaN(mortYears)) {
             alert("The number of years is not a number!")
             document.MortCalc.Years.value=" "
             document.MortCalc.Years.focus()
          }
     }
     document.MortCalc.Payment.value=monthly(mortAmount,mortRate,mortYears)
     document.MortCalc.Payment.value=dollarFormat(document.MortCalc.Payment.value)
}

  function monthly(mortAmount,mortRate,mortYears) {
     var Irate=mortRate/1200
     var Pmts=mortYears*12
     var Loan=mortAmount
```

JavaScript statement to call to dollarFormat() function

**FIGURE 2-42**

This statement passes the unformatted monthly result as a string object to the dollarFormat() function, which then formats the result. Finally, the result displays in the Monthly Payment text box formatted as currency with the dollar sign and two decimal points.

Before continuing, you should double-check the spelling, special characters, and quotation marks in the code. The next steps are to save your file and test the Web page.

### TO SAVE AND TEST THE WEB PAGE

1. With your JavaScript Data Disk in drive A, click File on the menu bar and then click Save on the File menu.

2. Click the browser button on the taskbar.

3. Click the Refresh button on the browser toolbar.

4. Enter the same test data in the text boxes: Mortgage Amount – 69000; Interest Rate as % – 7.9; and Number of Years – 30.

5. Click the Calculate button.

*The formatted result displays in the currency format, as $501.49 (Figure 2-43).*

**FIGURE 2-43**

If your browser does not display the Web page correctly, close any error messages and then click the Notepad button on the taskbar. Check your JavaScript code against Figures 2-36 through 2-42 on pages J 2.37 through J 2.43. Correct any errors and save the file. Activate the browser and then click the Refresh button.

# Adding a Pop-up Window

Recall from Project 1 that one way to display messages on a Web page is to use alert and confirm message boxes. These message boxes, however, only display text on a gray background. To create more visually interesting messages, you can use JavaScript to open and display another HTML file in a separate window that displays colors, graphics, animations, and other media. Such a window is called a **pop-up window**, because it displays over the previously opened browser window.

To create a pop-up window, you use the open() method. Table 2-23 shows the general form of the open() method. Table 2-24 describes the more commonly used pop-up window features.

| Table 2-23 – open() Method | |
|---|---|
| **General form:** | var windowname=open("window file name(URL)", "object name", "window features") |
| **Comment:** | where windowname is an optional name of a window object (required only if you need to refer to the pop-up window in any other Web page); window file name is the name of the HTML file; and window features describe how the window should display. |
| **Examples:** | open("Adwindow.htm", "AdWin", "RESIZE=Off, TITLEBAR=False") |

| Table 2-24 | | | |
|---|---|---|---|
| FEATURE | WRITTEN AS | DESCRIPTION | COMMENTS |
| LOCATION | "LOCATION" | includes URL bar | |
| MENUBAR | "MENUBAR" | includes menu bar | default is on; if off, pop-up window is a fixed size |
| RESIZE | "RESIZE=Off" | allows user to resize | |
| SCROLLBARS | "SCROLLBARS" | includes scrollbars | |
| STATUS | "STATUS" | includes status bar | |
| TITLEBAR | "TITLEBAR=False" | removes title bar | default is true |
| TOOLBAR | "TOOLBAR=Yes" | includes toolbar | |
| WIDTH | "WIDTH=220" | states width in pixels | being replaced by innerWidth and outerWidth |
| HEIGHT | "HEIGHT=450" | states height in pixels | being replaced by innerHeight and outerHeight |

### More About

## Creating Pop-up Windows

In addition to using alert() message boxes, Web developers use pop-up windows to display messages. For more information on pop-up windows, visit www.scsite. com/js/p2.htm and then click pop-up windows.

When adding the statement for a pop-up window, you should enclose all of the pop-up window features within one set of quotation marks. In this project, for example, to open the notice.htm file in a pop-up window, you enter

```
open("notice.htm", "noticeWin", "WIDTH=400, HEIGHT=220")
```

The statement opens the notice.htm file in a pop-up window that is 400 pixels wide and 220 pixels high. Web developers usually enter the open() method in a user-defined function and call it with an onload event handler placed in the BODY section of the HTML file. Another way to execute JavaScript statements when a Web page loads is to place the user-defined function in the HEAD section.

Because this page already has an onload event handler for the scrolling message bar in the BODY section, you must insert the open() method statement in the HEAD section of the HTML file. To enter the open() method to open the notice.htm file in a pop-up window, perform the steps on the next page.

**To Enter the open() method to Open a Pop-up Window**

**1** **Position the insertion point on line 94, the line directly above the //--> tag (Figure 2-44).**

```
            if (dollen>3) {
                while (dollen>0) {
                    tDollars=dollars.substring(dollen-3,dollen)
                    if (tDollars.length==3) {
                        Outdollars=","+tDollars+Outdollars
                        dollen=dollen-3
                    } else {
                        Outdollars=tDollars+Outdollars
                        dollen=0
                    }
                }
                if (OutDollars.substring(0,1)==",")
                    dollars=Outdollars.substring(1,Outdollars.length)
                else
                    dollars=Outdollars
            }
            var cents=valuein.substring(decipos+1,decipos+3)
            if (cents=="")
                cents="00"
            var formatStr="$"+dollars+"."+cents
            return formatStr
        }

line 94 ──→ |
//-->
</SCRIPT>

</HEAD>
<BODY onload="scrollingMsg()">

<P ALIGN="CENTER"><IMG SRC="homelogo.jpg">
</P>
<DIV ALIGN="CENTER"><CENTER>

<TABLE BORDER="0" WIDTH="75%">
```

**FIGURE 2-44**

**2** **Type** open ("notice.htm", "noticeWin", "WIDTH=400, height=220") **and then press the ENTER key.**

*Entering the open() method on the last line in the HEAD section means that it will execute as soon as the HEAD section of the Web page loads (Figure 2-45).*

```
                while (dollen>0) {
                    tDollars=dollars.substring(dollen-3,dollen)
                    if (tDollars.length==3) {
                        Outdollars=","+tDollars+Outdollars
                        dollen=dollen-3
                    } else {
                        Outdollars=tDollars+Outdollars
                        dollen=0
                    }
                }
                if (OutDollars.substring(0,1)==",")
                    dollars=Outdollars.substring(1,Outdollars.length)
                else
                    dollars=Outdollars
            }
            var cents=valuein.substring(decipos+1,decipos+3)
            if (cents=="")
                cents="00"
            var formatStr="$"+dollars+"."+cents
            return formatStr
        }

    open("notice.htm","noticeWin","WIDTH=400,HEIGHT=220")   ←── JavaScript
//-->                                                            statement to open
</SCRIPT>                                                        notice.htm file in a
                                                                pop-up window
</HEAD>
<BODY onload="scrollingMsg()">

<P ALIGN="CENTER"><IMG SRC="homelogo.jpg">
</P>
<DIV ALIGN="CENTER"><CENTER>
```

**FIGURE 2-45**

The WIDTH and HEIGHT features supplied in the open() method allow you to determine the size at which the pop-up window initially displays. Because the default value for the RESIZE feature is on, a user also can resize the pop-up window once it opens. The notice.htm file that opens in the pop-up window already has been created and is stored on the JavaScript Data Disk. Figure 2-46 shows the HTML and JavaScript code used in the notice.htm file.

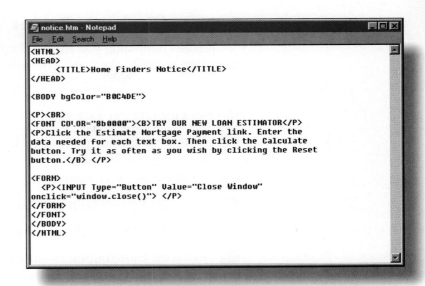

FIGURE 2-46

## Adding the Date Last Modified

As in the Fun with Phonics Web page in Project 1, you want to display the date the file was last modified at the bottom of the Home Finders Nationwide Realty Web page. To place this message at the bottom of the page, you will need to add a complete JavaScript section. To enter the JavaScript code to display the date the file was last modified, perform the following steps.

### TO DISPLAY THE DATE LAST MODIFIED

**1** Position the insertion point on line 171, the line directly above the closing </BODY> tag.

**2** Type <SCRIPT LANGUAGE="JAVASCRIPT"> and then press the ENTER key.

**3** Type <!-- Hide from old browsers and then press the ENTER key.

**4** Type document.write("<CENTER><FONT COLOR='maroon'><H5>This document was last modified "+document.lastModified+"</H5></FONT></CENTER>") and then press the ENTER key.

**5** Type //--> and then press the ENTER key.

**6** Type </SCRIPT> and then press the ENTER key.

*This completes the JavaScript section. The H5 tag makes the font small, so that the message is unobtrusive (Figure 2-47).*

line 171

```
         ...hly            </TD>
        <TD><INPUT Type="text" Name="Payment" value=" " Size="12"></TD>
     </TR>
     <TR>
        <TD><INPUT Type="Button" value="Calculate" onclick="Calc(MortCalc)">
            <INPUT Type="Reset"></TD>
     </TR>
   </TABLE>
</FORM>
</CENTER>
<HR>
<BR>
<BR>
<SCRIPT LANGUAGE="JAVASCRIPT">
<!--Hide from old browsers
    document.write("<CENTER><FONT COLOR='maroon'><H5>This document was last modified
"+document.lastModified+"</H5></FONT></CENTER>")
//-->
</SCRIPT>

</BODY>
</HTML>
```

JavaScript statements to display date last modified

FIGURE 2-47

### Saving and Testing the Finished Web Page

Before continuing, you should double-check the spelling, special characters, and quotation marks in the code. The next steps are to save your file and test the Web page.

### TO SAVE AND TEST THE WEB PAGE

**(1)** With your JavaScript Data Disk in drive A, click File on the menu bar and then click Save on the File menu.

**(2)** Click the browser button on the taskbar.

**(3)** Click the Refresh button on the browser toolbar.

**(4)** Click the Close Window button to close the pop-up window.

**(5)** Click the Close button to close the browser window.

*The pop-up window displays. If necessary, scroll down to verify that the last line displays the date the page was last modified (the date and time the file was saved on disk) (Figure 2-48).*

**FIGURE 2-48**

If your browser does not display the Web page correctly, close any error messages and then click the Notepad button on the taskbar. Check your JavaScript code against Figures 2-44 through 2-47 on pages J 2.46 through J 2.47. Correct any errors and save the file. Activate the browser and then click the Refresh button.

## Printing the HTML File Using Notepad

After you have completed and tested your Web page, you may want to print it. You can print the HTML file with Notepad. Perform the following steps to print the homefinders.htm Notepad file.

### TO PRINT THE HTML FILE USING NOTEPAD

**(1)** If necessary, click the Notepad button on the taskbar to activate the Notepad window.

**(2)** Click Print on the File menu.

*A Notepad Print dialog box briefly displays with a message that indicates the homefinders.htm file is being printed. The dialog box closes after the file has been sent to the printer. The HTML file with the JavaScript code prints (Figure 2-49).*

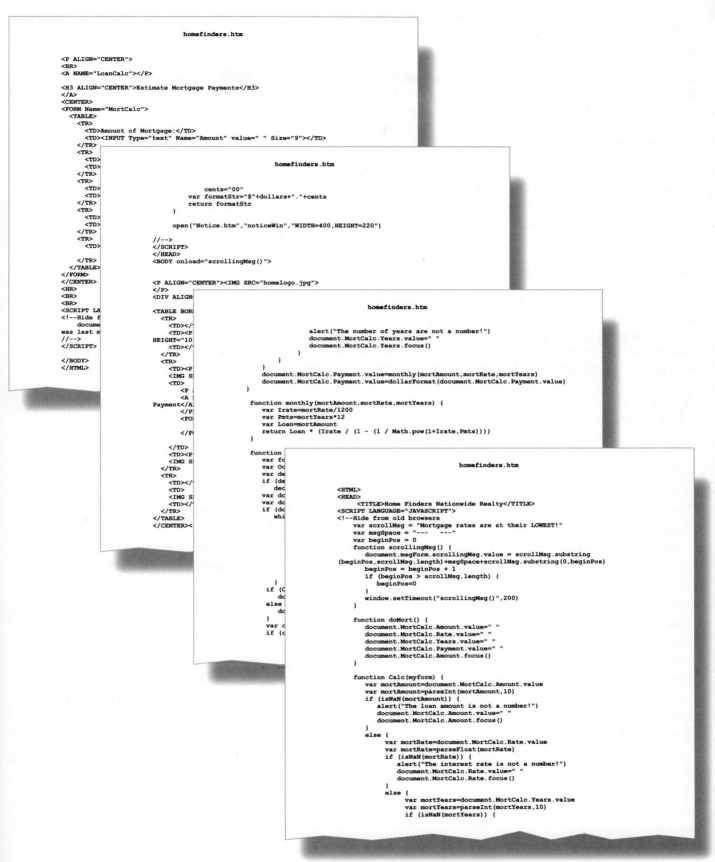

```
homefinders.htm

<P ALIGN="CENTER">
<BR>
<A NAME="LoanCalc"></P>

<H3 ALIGN="CENTER">Estimate Mortgage Payments</H3>
</A>
<CENTER>
<FORM Name="MortCalc">
  <TABLE>
    <TR>
      <TD>Amount of Mortgage:</TD>
      <TD><INPUT Type="text" Name="Amount" value=" " Size="9"></TD>
    </TR>
    <TR>
      <TD>
      <TD>
    </TR>
    <TR>
      <TD>
      <TD>
    </TR>
    <TR>
      <TD>
      <TD>
    </TR>
    <TR>
      <TD>
    </TR>
  </TABLE>
</FORM>
</CENTER>
<HR>
<BR>
<BR>
<SCRIPT LA
<!--Hide f
    docume
was last m
//-->
</SCRIPT>

</BODY>
</HTML>
```

```
homefinders.htm

        cents="00"
    var formatStr="$"+dollars+"."+cents
    return formatStr
}

    open("Notice.htm","noticeWin","WIDTH=400,HEIGHT=220")

//-->
</SCRIPT>
</HEAD>
<BODY onload="scrollingMsg()">

<P ALIGN="CENTER"><IMG SRC="homelogo.jpg">
</P>
<DIV ALIGN

<TABLE BOR
  <TR>
    <TD></
    <TD><P
HEIGHT="10
    <TD><
  </TR>
  <TR>
    <TD><P
    <IMG S
    <TD>
      <P
      <A
Payment</A
      </P
      <FO

      </F

    </TD>
    <TD><P
    <IMG S
  </TR>
  <TR>
    <TD></
    <TD>
    <IMG S
    <TD></
  </TR>
</TABLE>
</CENTER><
```

```
homefinders.htm

        alert("The number of years are not a number!")
        document.MortCalc.Years.value=" "
        document.MortCalc.Years.focus()
      }
    }
    document.MortCalc.Payment.value=monthly(mortAmount,mortRate,mortYears)
    document.MortCalc.Payment.value=dollarFormat(document.MortCalc.Payment.value)
}

function monthly(mortAmount,mortRate,mortYears) {
    var Irate=mortRate/1200
    var Pmts=mortYears*12
    var Loan=mortAmount
    return Loan * (Irate / (1 - (1 / Math.pow(1+Irate,Pmts))))
}

function
    var fo
    var Ou
    var de
    if (de
        dec
    var dc
    var dc
    if (dc
        whi
```

```
homefinders.htm

<HTML>
<HEAD>
    <TITLE>Home Finders Nationwide Realty</TITLE>
<SCRIPT LANGUAGE="JAVASCRIPT">
<!--Hide from old browsers
    var scrollMsg = "Mortgage rates are at their LOWEST!"
    var msgSpace = "---   ---"
    var beginPos = 0
    function scrollingMsg() {
        document.msgForm.scrollingMsg.value = scrollMsg.substring
(beginPos,scrollMsg.length)+msgSpace+scrollMsg.substring(0,beginPos)
        beginPos = beginPos + 1
        if (beginPos > scrollMsg.length) {
            beginPos=0
        }
        window.setTimeout("scrollingMsg()",200)
    }

    function doMort() {
        document.MortCalc.Amount.value=" "
        document.MortCalc.Rate.value=" "
        document.MortCalc.Years.value=" "
        document.MortCalc.Payment.value=" "
        document.MortCalc.Amount.focus()
    }

    function Calc(myform) {
        var mortAmount=document.MortCalc.Amount.value
        var mortAmount=parseInt(mortAmount,10)
        if (isNaN(mortAmount)) {
            alert("The loan amount is not a number!")
            document.MortCalc.Amount.value=" "
            document.MortCalc.Amount.focus()
        }
        else {
            var mortRate=document.MortCalc.Rate.value
            var mortRate=parseFloat(mortRate)
            if (isNaN(mortRate)) {
                alert("The interest rate is not a number!")
                document.MortCalc.Rate.value=" "
                document.MortCalc.Rate.focus()
            }
            else {
                var mortYears=document.MortCalc.Years.value
                var mortYears=parseInt(mortYears,10)
                if (isNaN(mortYears)) {
```

**FIGURE 2-49**

# Project Summary

In this project, you created a Web page that will allow Home Finders Nationwide Realty customers to calculate the amount of their monthly mortgage payment, based on the amount of mortgage, interest rate, and the number of years. The form validates the data as the user enters it and displays the resulting monthly payment amount using the currency format. Per the request of Home Finders owner, Carrie Rayburn, you also added a scrolling message to remind customers of low interest rates; you also added a pop-up window to display information on using the mortgage payment calculator.

In creating this Web page, you used and expanded on the JavaScript commands you learned in Project 1. To begin, you wrote a scrollingMsg() user-defined function to create a scrolling message that displays in the text box. The scrolling message used the substring() method and introduced the string length property. In addition, this function introduced the If statement and showed how to create a recursive call to the scrollingMsg() function.

You learned how to set the focus on a form text box; pass the form text box values to a function; and use the If...Else statement to validate data in a text box. The project introduces the concepts of validating data using the parseInt(), parseFloat(), and isNaN() built-in functions, as well as using the pow() method in the user-defined function Calc() to calculate the mortgage payment amount. You learned how to return values from a user-defined function and format string output results to appear as currency.

In creating a pop-up window on the Web page, you learned how to use the open() method to open a pop-up window and to set the features of this window. You then used the lastModified property to display the date the Web page was last modified. Finally, you saved the file and tested the Web page in your browser.

# What You Should Know

Having completed this project, you now should be able to perform the following tasks:

▶ Add the setTimeout() Method to Create a Recursive Function Call *(J 2.16)*

▶ Create a Form Text Box to Display a Scrolling Message *(J 2.9)*

▶ Create the scrollingMsg() User-Defined Function *(J 2.11)*

▶ Display the Date Last Modified *(J 2.47)*

▶ Enter a Calc() User-Defined Function *(J 2.27)*

▶ Enter an If Statement *(J 2.14)*

▶ Enter the dollarFormat() Function *(J 2.37)*

▶ Enter the doMort() Function *(J 2.22)*

▶ Enter the Else Portion of the Nested If...Else Statement *(J 2.28)*

▶ Enter the onclick() Event Handler to Call the Calc() Function *(J 2.30)*

▶ Enter the monthly() Function *(J 2.34)*

▶ Enter the Event Handler to Call the scrollingMsg() Function *(J 2.17)*

▶ Enter the open() method to Open a Pop-up Window *(J 2.46)*

▶ Extract the Cents Portion and Define the Decimal Amount *(J 2.41)*

▶ Extract the Dollar Portion of the Output and Insert Commas *(J 2.40)*

▶ Insert an Event Handler in an Anchor Tag *(J 2.20)*

▶ Pass the Monthly Payment Value to the dollarFormat() Function *(J 2.43)*

▶ Pass Values to the monthly() User-Defined Function *(J 2.32)*

▶ Print the HTML File Using Notepad *(J 2.49)*

▶ Reconstruct the Formatted Output and Return the Formatted Value *(J 2.42)*

▶ Save and Test the Web Page *(J 2.22, J 2.30, J 2.35, J 2.44, J 2.48)*

▶ Save the File on the Data Disk *(J 2.18)*

▶ Start Notepad and Open a Web Page Stored on the Data Disk *(J 2.6)*

▶ Test the Web Page *(J 2.18)*

# Test Your Knowledge

## 1 True/False

**Instructions:** Circle T if the statement is true or F if the statement is false.

T F 1. Microsoft's MARQUEE HTML tag also works with other browsers.

T F 2. A scrolling message has four basic components: the message, position, display object, and delay.

T F 3. To assign a value, such as a scrolling message, to a text box, you must name both the form and the text box.

T F 4. Web developers agree that the status bar is the best place for a scrolling message.

T F 5. A condition is any expression that evaluates to true or false.

T F 6. Recursion is a programming technique used to have a function call another function from within itself.

T F 7. When a JavaScript statement automatically positions the insertion point in the text box, the text box is considered "onfocus."

T F 8. The parseInt() method has two properties: the string value and base.

T F 9. The Math.pow() method returns the exponent power of a square root.

T F 10. The indexOf() method is used to search a string for a particular character and return the relative location of that character within the string.

## 2 Multiple Choice

**Instructions:** Circle the correct response.

1. Which of the following is not a basic component for a scrolling message?
   a. the message
   b. the position
   c. the window object
   d. the time delay

2. Programmers call placing attention on an object _____.
   a. setting the focus
   b. giving the focus
   c. losing the focus
   d. out of focus

3. In an If statement, the _____ is placed in parentheses directly after the word, If.
   a. function
   b. JavaScript command
   c. condition
   d. event handler

*(continued)*

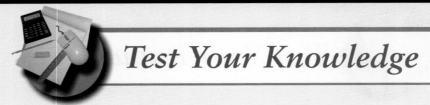

## Test Your Knowledge

**Multiple Choice** *(continued)*

4. In JavaScript, which of the following symbols represents the operand, equal to?
   a. =
   b. !=
   c. *=
   d. = =
5. Which event handler performs an action when users click an associated button or link?
   a. onclick
   b. onsubmit
   c. onmouseover
   d. onload
6. Which event handler performs an action when a document is loaded?
   a. onclick
   b. onload
   c. onsubmit
   d. onfocus
7. In an If...Else statement, what statements are executed if the condition is true?
   a. the statements after the condition
   b. the statements after the else
   c. both statements
   d. neither; control is passed to whatever statements follow the last }
8. The parseFloat() built-in function returns a(n) _____ number.
   a. integer
   b. floating point
   c. absolute
   d. negative
9. The pow() method executes mathematical _____.
   a. exponents
   b. square roots
   c. rounding
   d. string conversions
10. Which window feature, in the open() window method, includes the URL bar?
    a. status
    b. title bar
    c. toolbar
    d. location

# Test Your Knowledge

## 3 Understanding Event Handlers

**Instructions:** Fill in the blanks with the missing object or event handler names.

| OBJECT | EVENT HANDLER |
|--------|---------------|
| _____ | onclick |
| _____ | onload, onunload |
| form | _____, _____ |
| hyperlink | onclick, _____, onmouseout |
| _____ | onload, onabort |
| input box | onblur, _____, _____ |
| submit button | _____ |
| _____ | _____, _____, onblur, onfocus |

## 4 Understanding Code Statements

**Instructions:** Carefully read each of the following descriptions. Write JavaScript code statements to accomplish these specific tasks. Record your answers on a separate sheet of paper. Number your answers to correspond to the code description.

1. Given the following form code, write the JavaScript statement to set focus on the Email text box.

```
<FORM Name="Form1">
        <INPUT Type="text" Name="BillingHours " value=" ">
        <INPUT Type="text" Name="Email" value=" ">
</FORM>
```

_____

2. Using the same form as in question 1, write a JavaScript statement to assign the Email text box to a variable called TempEmail.

_____

3. Using the same form as in question 1, write a JavaScript statement to assign the BillingHours text box to a variable and convert it to a floating-point number.

_____

4. Given the following assignment statement: `var tempString="Test#12,Fall1999"`
write a JavaScript statement to extract the data before the comma and store it in tempTest and to extract the data after the comma and store it in tempDate.

_____

5. Given the following geometry formulas, write the equivalent JavaScript statements.

   area = $s^2$ _____

   area = $\pi r^2$ _____

JavaScript

*Use Help*

# 1 Exploring Online Documentation

**Instructions:** Start your browser. Type the following in the Address text box: www.scsite.com/js/p2.htm and then click Project 2 Use Help 1. Using the Web site, answer the questions below.

1. Click Chapter 9, Events and Event Handlers in the left frame. Read about event handlers and answer the following: describe the onabort, onchange, onkeydown, and onmouseover event handlers.
2. Click Chapter 2, Capturing Event Handlers, in the left frame. Read about capturing events and answer the following questions:
   a. What does it mean to capture an event?
   b. What are the steps for capturing an event?
3. Return to the Project 2 Use Help 1 Web page. Click Frequently Asked Questions. Scroll down the page to find sections 2.4, 2.5, 4.6, 4.9, and 4.10 and then answer the following questions:
   a. How do you use the different substring functions to extract part of a string?
   b. How do you round numbers off to a certain number of decimal places?
   c. Why does a call to window.open() not display the window type and size specified?
   d. How do you create a modal window (one that cannot be minimized) using JavaScript?
   e. How do you control the placement of a new window using window.open()?
   f. How do you close a window without causing a confirm prompt to appear?
4. Hand in the answers to your instructor.

# 2 Exploring Links to Other JavaScript Sites

**Instructions:** Start your browser. Type the following URL in the Address text box: www.scsite.com/js/p2.htm and then click Project 2 Use Help 2. Perform the following tasks.

1. Click Microsoft's Marquee Statement. Read about the MARQUEE tag. Print the Web page.
2. Return to the Project 2 Use Help 2 Web page. Click JavaScript Statements. Click Chapter 3, Statements, in the left frame. Locate information on the If...Else discussion. Read and print this section.
3. Return to the Chapter 3, Statements, Web page. Locate information on the While statement. Read and print this section.
4. Click Chapter 4, Core, in the left frame. Click the Math link. Locate and click the pow link. Read and print this section.
5. Return to the left frame. Click Chapter 13, Global Functions, in the left frame. Locate information on the isNaN(), parseInt(), and parseFloat() functions. Read and print these sections.
6. Return to the Project 2 Use Help 2 Web page. Click Forms. Click Chapter 7, Form, and then click Form. Read and print this section.
7. Return to the Project 2 Use Help 2 Web page. Click Tutor. Scroll down to find Chapter 3 IF-THEN statements, in the left frame. Read the entire section and print the fourth page. Scroll down and click Chapter 4, While Loops and Text methods, in the left frame. Read the entire section. Print the fifth page.
8. Hand in the printouts to your instructor.

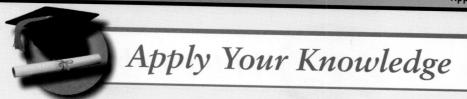

# Apply Your Knowledge

## 1 Validating a Simple Registration Form

**Instructions:** Start Notepad. Open the Web page midwestrest.htm on the JavaScript Data Disk. If you did not download the Data Disk, see the inside back cover for instructions for downloading the JavaScript Data Disk or see your instructor. This Web page contains a simple registration form with three text boxes and one text area (Figure 2-50). The JavaScript code to validate the guest name and location already has been entered. You are to write the JavaScript code to validate the e-mail entered in the Your E-mail Address text box. Where appropriate, indent the lines of code. Perform the following tasks.

**FIGURE 2-50**

1. Locate the JavaScript tags and the validate() function in the HEAD section. Position the insertion point after the comment // validate the e-mail.
2. Enter `var RegeMail=document.Register.eMail.value`
3. Use the indexOf() function to determine if the e-mail address contains an @ sign. Enter `var atSign = RegeMail.indexOf("@")`
4. Enter `if (RegeMail == " " || atSign == -1) {`
5. Enter the following JavaScript statements under the If statement, indenting the statements where appropriate:
   ```
   alert("Please enter your e-mail address")
   document.Register.eMail.value=""
   document.Register.eMail.focus()
   ```
6. Save the HTML file using the file name, midwestrestsolution.htm, on the Data Disk.
7. Start your browser. Open the a:\midwestrestsolution.htm Web page to test your JavaScript code. If any errors occur activate Notepad and double-check steps 1 through 6, save, and test again. If no errors occur, print the Web page, and activate Notepad and print the HTML file. Hand in the printouts to your instructor.

## *In the Lab*

# 1 Calculating the Wind Chill Factor for a Ski Resort

**Problem:** You have a summer job as an assistant to the Webmaster at the Pine Peaks Ski Lodge. The Webmaster, Marian Shilling, asks you create a Web page that will allow guests and visitors to calculate the wind chill. Because the data is not fed directly to the computer, users must input the temperature and the wind speed in a form as shown in Figure 2-51. You then validate the data entered is numeric so it can be used in the wind chill conversion formula.

**FIGURE 2-51**

**Instructions:** Start your browser and Notepad. Using Notepad, open the pinepeaks.htm file from the JavaScript Data Disk. If you did not download the Data Disk, see the inside back cover for instructions for downloading the JavaScript Data Disk or see your instructor. Write a function called windChill() that accepts outside temperature and wind speed data from the user and displays the estimated wind chill by performing the following tasks.

1. Locate the SCRIPT tag in the HEAD section. Position the insertion point on line 6.
2. Enter the following code, indenting the lines of code, where appropriate:

```
function windChill(myform) {
        var Temp=document.Chill.OutTemp.value
        var Temp=parseInt(Temp,10)
```

3. Test that Temp is a number. If Temp is not a number, the statement will display a message, clear the OutTemp text box, and set focus to the OutTemp text box.
4. With the insertion point on line 8, enter the following code to test Temp and process for the True condition:

```
        if (isNaN(Temp)) {
                alert("Enter the outdoor temperature")
                document.Chill.OutTemp.value=" "
                document.Chill.OutTemp.focus()
        } else {
```

# In the Lab

5. With the insertion point on line 13, enter the following code to validate the value entered as the wind speed:

```
var Wind=document.Chill.windSpeed.value
var Wind=parseInt(Wind,10)
if (isNaN(Wind)) {
    alert("Enter the average wind speed")
    document.Chill.windSpeed.value=" "
    document.Chill.windSpeed.focus()
} else {
```

6. With the insertion point on line 20, enter the following code to calculate the wind chill temperature using the formula Temp-(1.5 * Wind) and assign the result to The wind chill is text box.

```
windChillTemp=Temp-(1.5 * Wind)
document.Chill.WindChill.value=windChillTemp
        }
    }
}
```

7. Locate the INPUT tag for the How Cold button. Insert the onclick event handler to call the windChill() function.

8. Save the HTML file using the file name, pinepeakssolution.htm, on the Data Disk.

9. Activate the browser and open pinepeakssolution.htm to test your JavaScript code. Use the following test data: Temp 22 and wind speed 7. The result 11.5 should display in The wind chill is text box.

10. If any errors occur, double-check steps 2 through 6 and test again. If no errors occur, print the Web page, activate Notepad, and print the HTML file. Hand in the printouts to your instructor.

## 2 Calculating a Percentage and Formatting the Result as a Percentage

**Problem:** You work part-time in the Online Development Group at Tri-County Community Hospital. The registered dietician, Tasha Barnes, requests that you develop a Nutrition Facts Web page that allows users to enter in the number of fat grams and total number of calories for a meal. Your Web page calculates the number of calories from fat alone and the percentage of the total calories. The results display in the text boxes. The nutritionist asks that you display the percentage of calories from fat as a percent value, not as a decimal value (Figure 2-52).

**FIGURE 2-52**

*(continued)*

## *In the Lab*

### Calculating a Percentage and Formatting the Result as a Percentage *(continued)*

**Instructions:** Start your browser and Notepad. Using Notepad, open the nutritionfacts.htm file on the JavaScript Data Disk. Perform the following tasks.

1. Locate the JavaScript section in the HEAD section and the comment, // calculate fat calories, on line 24. Position the insertion point directly beneath the first slash (/).

2. Complete the FatCal() user-defined function by entering the following JavaScript code. The JavaScript code calculates the total fat calories, assigns the TotalFatCal value to a text box, calculates the percentage of fat, and formats the result to display as a percentage.

```
var TotalFatCal = FatGrams * 9
document.Fat.Total.value = TotalFatCal
```

3. Enter the following after the // calculate percentage of fat comment and before the closing brace.

```
var TotalFatPerc = TotalFatCal/FatNumbCal
var TotalFatPerc = new String(TotalFatPerc)
document.Fat.FatPerc.value = makePerc(TotalFatPerc)
```

4. Write a function, called makePerc, which formats the result in the FatPerc text box as a percent. Position the insertion point on line 32 after the comment line, // Start makePerc function here, and enter the following code:

```
function makePerc(TotalFatPerc) {
        var valuein = TotalFatPerc
        strPercent = ""
        tPercent = valuein
        decimal = tPercent.indexOf(".")
        Percent = parseInt(tPercent.substring(decimal+1,decimal+3),10)
        strPercent = Percent+"%"
        return strPercent
        }
```

5. Locate the INPUT tag for the Calculate button. Insert the onclick event handler to call the FatCal() user-defined function.

6. Save the HTML file using the file name, nutritionfactssolution.htm, on the Data Disk.

7. Activate your browser. Open the nutritionfactssolution.htm Web page in the browser to test your JavaScript code. Use the following test data: fat grams – 19, total number of calories – 1259. The calories from fat are 171 and the percentage is 13%.

8. If any errors occur double-check steps 2 and 3 and test again. If no errors occur, print the Web page, activate Notepad, and print the HTML file. Hand in the printouts to your instructor.

## 3 Calculating Retirement Savings

**Problem:** You are an intern at Tri Star Investing. Jennifer Casey, the Webmaster, wants to develop a Web page that calculates this present value problem: Given an average annual interest rate, how much money should an individual save each month to be worth a certain amount, in a certain number of years? Jennifer's idea is that customers can use the page to enter in the years until retirement, the average annual interest expected, and their retirement amount goal. Jennifer wants you to create a form that will validate each text box and display the result as currency (Figure 2-53b). In addition, when you open the Web page, a pop-up window displays an advertising message (Figure 2-53a).

**Instructions:** Start your browser and Notepad. Use Notepad to open tristar.htm on the JavaScript Data Disk.

# In the Lab

**FIGURE 2-53a**

**FIGURE 2-53b**

Perform the following tasks.

1. Locate the form and text box names.
2. Using the form and text box names provided, write a function to validate the years, interest rate, and goal text boxes using the techniques described in this project.
3. Write a function to determine the monthly investment. To calculate the monthly investment, use the formula:

    monthly = goal * rate / (1 - (1 / (1 + rate)$^{deposits}$ ) )

    where goal is the retirement goal, rate is the estimated annual rate of interest, and deposit is the number of monthly deposits. Enter the rate as a percent and convert to a monthly amount using the following formula: rate = rate/1200

    Enter the monthly deposit and convert it to an annual amount as follows: deposits = years * 12
4. Pass the goal, years, and rate to this function.
5. Write a function that formats the result as currency, use the function developed in this project as a guide.
6. Add JavaScript statements that will open the file, tristarad.htm, on the JavaScript Data Disk as a pop-up window when the Tri Star Web page is opened.
7. Save the HTML file using the file name, tristarsolution.htm, on the JavaScript Data Disk.
8. Activate the browser. Open the tristarsolution.htm file to test your JavaScript code. Use the test data shown in Figure 2-53b.
9. If any errors occur, double-check steps 1 through 6 and test again. Look for matching variable names, missing quotation marks, parentheses, or braces. If no errors occur, print the Web page, activate Notepad, and print the HTML file.

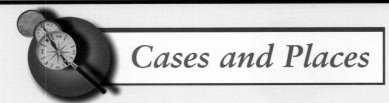

# Cases and Places

The difficulty of these case studies varies:
▶ are the least difficult; ▶▶ are more difficult; and ▶▶▶ are the most difficult.

**1** ▶ Your sister owns a travel agency, for which she has a Web page that features trips to 10 European nations. She wants you to add a pop-up window with a currency exchange form on the Web page. On the form, the user should enter the exchange rate and the number of dollars to be exchanged. To display the exchange rate in dollars in a text box, the user can click a button named "Exchange." Use the concepts and techniques presented in this project to create the Web page.

**2** ▶▶ As captain of your fraternity bowling team, you have decided to create a Web page that displays the team standings. One of your teammates suggests that you add a pop-up window with a form that allows bowlers to enter game scores and calculate their bowling average. The form should accept input in a While loop that counts the number of scores. Use the concepts and techniques presented in this project to create the Web page.

**3** ▶▶ As treasurer of your investment club, you are asked to create a Web page that calculates stock dividend reinvestments. The Web page should allow users to enter the current price of a stock; the number of shares owned; the amount of dividends the company pays on each share; and how often the company pays dividends. After validating the fields, the page should display the amount of time it will take to earn a new share of stock by investing the dividends. Use the concepts and techniques presented in this project to create the Web page.

**4** ▶▶▶ To help entice moviegoers, the manager of the local movie theater wants to create a Web page to display a listing of currently running movies and show times. In addition, the manager wants to have a form that allows customers to order tickets online. The form should use option buttons or check boxes for data entry of the number of tickets, matinee discounts, and credit card number; and validate the data. Once they have ordered, users can pay for tickets at the window or via credit card online. Use the concepts and techniques presented in this project to create a form for the theater Web page (you do not have to build a form to transfer the data to, and store it in, a database).

**5** ▶▶▶ A new subdivision developer has staked out an area for 4,500 homes and would like to have a Web page that displays a map with each lot numbered. In addition, he wants customers to be able to view any of nine basic floor plans on the Web page. The Web page should allow the customer to be able to pick a lot, pick a floor plan, and see a final cost. In addition, the developer wants a form to calculate and display the down payment needed from the customer to start construction (one-third the cost of the house). Use the concepts and techniques presented in this project to create the Web page.

## JavaScript

# P R O J E C T 3

# Enhancing the Use of Image and Form Objects

O B J E C T I V E S

You will have mastered the material in this project when you can:

- Define rolling banner
- Create an image object
- Write a rolling banner function
- Define array
- Describe how to create an array instance
- Call the rolling banner function
- Create a dynamic greeting
- Describe the Switch statement
- Write a user-defined function that calculates the number of days to a future date
- Discuss the getMonth() and getTime()methods
- Describe the onmouseover event handler
- Write a user-defined function that changes an image when the mouse pointer passes over a related link
- Write a user-defined function that displays a menu of items and the price for an item that is selected from the menu
- Describe the onchange event handler
- Write a user-defined function that calculates the total cost of an item selected from a menu
- Write a user-defined function to format the total cost as currency

1959

# What a Doll!

## Barbie® Doll Fans Are Tickled Pink About Custom Dolls

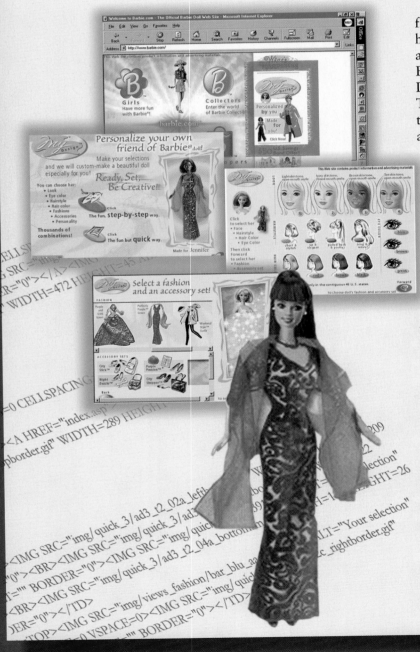

**W**alk down the doll aisle in any toy store, and you will find shelves brimming with hundreds of Barbie dolls and pink accessories. Happy Holidays Barbie. Dentist Barbie. Barbie Dream House. Barbie Motorhome. This merchandise is sold in more than 150 countries worldwide and accounts for more than 30 percent of Mattel's $4.8 billion annual revenues.

This ubiquitous doll has come a long way from her creation in 1959. At that time, Mattel cofounder Ruth Handler realized young girls wanted to play with teenage dolls, in addition to baby dolls. She bought a fashionable mature doll in Switzerland, made modifications, and named the creation after her daughter, Barbara. The original Barbie dolls sold for $3; they could be worth more than $5,000 today if they are in mint condition. Handler created the Barbie doll's boyfriend in 1961 and named him after her son, Ken.

More than one billion Barbie dolls and her family members have been sold since 1959 — enough to circle the Earth more than seven times if laid head to toe. The average American girl between the ages of three- to ten-years-old now owns ten Barbie dolls.

Now each of these children can add a personalized friend of Barbie to her collection. The Barbie.com Web site (www.barbie.com) contains a My Design™page that uses JavaScript and allows users to customize a doll and see the results. For starters, the child names the doll. Then she clicks a button to choose a light, ivory, brown, or tan skin tone and either an open or closed mouth. Next come selections for eye color, hair color and style, outfits, and accessories. The last set of choices specifies the doll's birthday, career, hobbies, and friends.

The user can print a photo of the unique doll. In addition, adult users can place an order for Mattel to produce an actual doll based on these specifications. Even though the various combinations of features can result in thousands of unique dolls, Mattel has the production facilities to manufacture the doll in six to eight weeks.

The Barbie.com Web site developers used JavaScript in the My Design page. The onmouseover and onmouseout event handlers add simple animation to the page and change button colors to draw users' attention to their choices.

JavaScript also is prevalent in the Fashion Avenue™Fun page. With a "Girls have more fun with Barbie" theme, the page uses JavaScript arrays to display an image of Barbie, Ken, or her little sisters, Skipper and Kelly. A user selects one of these dolls, clicks forward and back arrows to view outfits for the doll, and then clicks Try It to see the outfit appear on the doll. After the user makes each selection, the JavaScript code executes to read the arrays and display the requested images on the screen.

In this project, you will use arrays and the onmouseover event handler to create a Web page for Midwest Caterers that features picnics, dinner parties, and weddings. Both your page and the Barbie page demonstrate JavaScript's powerful functions. JavaScript applications provide you with interactivity and variety and are limited only by your creativity.

# JavaScript

# Enhancing the Use of Image and Form Objects

P R O J E C T

**3**

**CASE PERSPECTIVE**

Midwest Catering hired you as a part-time server when you started college last year. Your job is taking a new direction since you talked to the owner, Dennis Sullivan, and described the Web development course you just completed. Dennis knows that advertising on the Internet would expand his business. Most of the parties that Midwest caters center on holidays and three main specialties: picnics, dinner parties, and weddings. Dennis wants a Web page that highlights these catering services.

You have learned how to create a Web page that can display a greeting that counts down the number of days to any given holiday. If the holiday is more than a month away, you can design the Web page to display a generic greeting. Dennis likes these ideas. In addition, he wants the Web page to provide a way for clients to estimate prices before they place their orders. With these concepts in mind, Dennis tells you to start development of the Web page immediately.

# Introduction

In Project 2, you learned about different object properties, methods, built-in functions, and event handlers. You used the If statement and If…Else statement to validate form text box values. You learned how to pass values to user-defined functions that executed mathematical expressions and returned a result. You learned about the While loop and how to open a second window to display a message. This project continues to emphasize these topics and introduces new ones.

The new topics in this project include using the Date() object's getMonth() and getTime() methods and the Math ceil() method to calculate the number of days to a specific date. You will learn how to use image objects and arrays to create an animated title called a rolling banner or image rollover. You will learn how to use the Switch statement and arrays to display prices based on a selection from an HTML Select drop-down list box. In Project 2, you wrote the dollarFormat() function to format output of one text box as currency. In this project, you will learn how to make any value a string object instance so it can be used with the dollarFormat() function from any text box. Finally, you will learn the onmouseover event handler to call functions to change the current graphic image to another graphic image. You use the onchange event handler to call functions associated with a Select drop-down list box.

# Project Three — Creating the Midwest Catering Web Page

In your discussion with Dennis, you determined the following.

**Needs:** The Web page appears with the name of the company (Figure 3-1a).

**FIGURE 3-1a**

After three seconds, the title changes and rolls through three more images (Figures 3-1b, 3-1c, and 3-1d). Beneath the banner is the dynamic greeting, which displays a countdown to selected holidays (Figure 3-1a). As shown in Figure 3-1d on the next page, Picnics, Dinner Parties, and Weddings display as links between two photos of food. When you drag the mouse over a link, the graphic images change and display food items normally associated with that type of food service.

**FIGURE 3-1b**

**FIGURE 3-1c**

**FIGURE 3-1d**

**FIGURE 3-1e**

**Forms:** When you click a link, you jump to a section of the Web page that describes the type of food service available for that event. A select drop-down list provides a menu of meal choices (Figure 3-1e). When the you select an item, the price per person displays in a text box. You then can enter the number of guests in another text box, to view the total extended price.

**Calculations:** The calculation for determining the total price is the number of guests multiplied by the price.

## Starting Notepad and Opening the Cater.htm File

The first step is to start Notepad and open the HTML file, cater.htm, on the JavaScript Data Disk as shown in the following steps.

### TO START NOTEPAD AND OPEN THE HTML FILE

**1** Start Notepad.

**2** When the Notepad window displays, click the Maximize button.

**3** Open the file, cater.htm, on the JavaScript Data Disk in drive A.

*The cater.htm document opens in the Notepad window (Figure 3-2).*

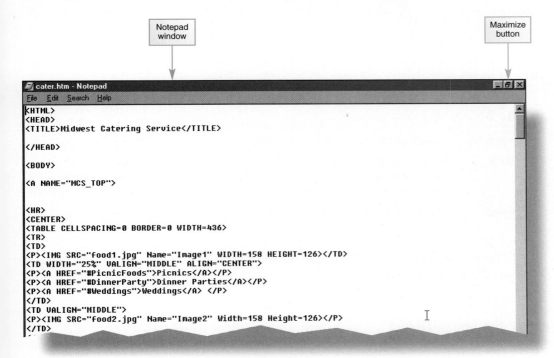

FIGURE 3-2

## Rolling Banners

The next step is to create the rolling banner. The page title, shown in Figure 3-1 (on pages J 3.5 and J 3.6), is similar to a rolling banner. A **rolling banner** is a set of images, all the same size, that display in the same location for a few seconds, one after the other. This banner includes the company name followed by the types of food service events Midwest Catering offers.

To create a rolling banner, perform the following three steps: (1) create an image object; (2) write the rolling banner function; and (3) add the event handler to call the function. The order in which you perform these steps is not critical, but all three steps must be completed before the banner will work.

### More About

### Rolling Banners

Rolling banners also are called image rollovers and dynamic images. For more information, visit www.scsite.com/js/p3.htm and then click Rolling Banners.

## Creating an Image Object

To create an image object, add the Name attribute to the HTML IMG SRC tag to allow the JavaScript code to reference the object. The Name attribute allows JavaScript to assign a new graphic image to the same location as the original image. Table 3-1 shows the general form of the IMG SRC tag with the name, width, and height attributes.

| Table 3-1 – Image Object | |
| --- | --- |
| **General form:** | \<IMG SRC = "Image_File_Name.Type" Name = "Object_Name" Width = pixels Height = pixels\> |
| **Comment:** | where an initial image displays at the location where the tag appears. The name identifies the object for JavaScript. The Width and Height attributes define the image size in pixels. |
| **Example:** | \<IMG SRC = "banner1.jpg" Name = "Banner" Width = 350 Height = 65\> |

Table 3-2 shows the general form of the statement to assign a new image to the defined location.

| Table 3-2 – Assign New Image | |
| --- | --- |
| **General form:** | document.objectname.src = "new image file name" |
| **Comment:** | where the new graphic image displays in the same location as the original by assigning a new file name to the image object source (SRC) property. The object name in the JavaScript code that must match the object name in the IMAGE tag. |
| **Example:** | document.Banner.src = "banner2.jpg" |

To create the location for the image object, which will display the rolling banner, perform the following steps.

**Steps** **To Create the Location for the Image Object**

**1** **Position the insertion point on line 10 (Figure 3-3).**

**FIGURE 3-3**

**Type** `<CENTER>`
`<IMG SRC=`
`"banner1.jpg"`
`Name="Banner"`
`Width=320`
`Height=65></CENTER>`
**as the code.**

*The image object is Banner
and has a set width and
height (Figure 3-4).*

```
cater.htm - Notepad
File   Edit   Search   Help
<HTML>
<HEAD>
<TITLE>Midwest Catering Service</TITLE>

</HEAD>

<BODY>

<A NAME="MCS_TOP">
<CENTER><IMG SRC="banner1.jpg" Name="Banner" Width=320 Height=65></CENTER>

<HR>
<CENTER>
<TABLE CELLSPACING=0 BORDER=0 WIDTH=436>
<TR>
<TD>
<P><IMG SRC="food1.jpg" Name="Image1" WIDTH=158 HEIGHT=126></TD>
<TD WIDTH="25%" VALIGN="MIDDLE" ALIGN="CENTER">
<P><A HREF="#PicnicFoods">Picnics</A></P>
<P><A HREF="#DinnerParty">Dinner Parties</A></P>
<P><A HREF="#Weddings">Weddings</A> </P>
</TD>
<TD VALIGN="MIDDLE">
<P><IMG SRC="food2.jpg" Name="Image2" Width=158 Height=126></P>
</TD>
</TR>
</TABLE>
</CENTER>
```

image object name

image width

image height

**FIGURE 3-4**

The width and height defined for the image source object is approximately the same size as a <H1> HTML tag to format text. The banner1.jpg image is the Midwest Catering logo. Because more than one image replaces the banner1.jpg image file, you must create a user-defined function, called bancycle(), to display the different images.

## Writing the Rolling Banner Function

To write the rolling banner function, perform the following six steps: (1) define an array of images; (2) establish a counter; (3) increment the counter by 1; (4) test the counter against the number of items in the array; (5) assign the array element of the counter to the image object; and (6) call the function again using the setTimeout() method. Using the setTimeout() method in the function employs the recursive method discussed in Project 2. This recursive call continuously changes the images until the user closes the browser. The first step in creating the rolling banner is to create an array and store the image file names in the array.

An **array** is a collection of data items, represented by one variable name. A subscript references individual data items in the array. A **subscript** is a number that designates an individual item or occurrence in the array as shown in example 2 of Table 3-3 on the next page. The first item of a JavaScript array is element zero. Subscripts are placed after the array name in square [ ] brackets as shown in the examples in Table 3-3. A subscript is any valid JavaScript variable or numeric value.

Arrays are built-in objects. To use data in an array, create an instance of the object in which to store the data. Recall from the Introduction that an object instance is an object created from a built-in object. Table 3-3 shows the general form of creating an array object instance from the Array object using the *new* keyword.

*More About*

**Arrays**

Array objects are useful for storing large quantities of items. For more information on using arrays, visit www.scsite.com/js/p3.htm and then click Arrays.

*More About*

**Subscripts**

In JavaScript, the default first element is zero. If you create a simulated array instead of using the Array object, however, the element zero is used to indicate the number of items in the array. To store a value in the element zero would destroy the array. For more information, visit www.scsite.com/js/p3.htm and then click Subscripts.

| Table 3-3 – Creating an Array | |
|---|---|
| **General form:** | var myarrayname = new Array() |
| **Comment:** | where Array is a built-in object and the new command creates a new object instance of the array. Assign data items to the array in one of two ways: (1) place data in the array object or (2) assign the items separately. |
| **Examples:** | `var banners = new Array("graphic1.jpg", "graphic2.jpg", "graphic3.jpg", "graphic4.jpg")`<br>or<br>`var banners = new Array()`<br>`banners[0] = "graphic1.jpg"`<br>`banners[1] = "graphic2.jpg"`<br>`banners[2] = "graphic3.jpg"`<br>`banners[3] = "graphic4.jpg"` |

Once the array assigns the data elements, retrieve or use the data by referencing the array name with the subscript. The data in an array is stored sequentially as shown in Figure 3-5. For example, to reference the first item (graphic.jpg) use banners[0]. To reference the third element in the array use the contents of banners[2].

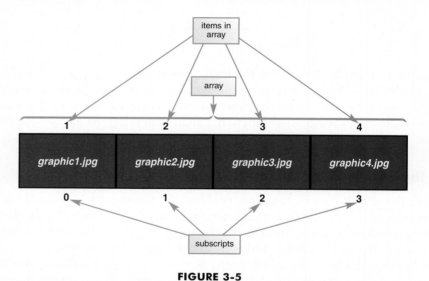

**FIGURE 3-5**

Table 3-4 shows the JavaScript code for the bancycle() function. Because this is the first function written in this project, it includes the code to create the JavaScript section in the HEAD section. Recall from previous projects that Web developers place user-defined functions in the HEAD section.

**Table 3-4**

| LINE | CODE |
|------|------|
| 4 | `<SCRIPT  LANGUAGE="JAVASCRIPT">` |
| 5 | `<!-- Hide from old browsers` |
| 6 | `    var banners = new Array("banner1.jpg","banner2.jpg","banner3.jpg","banner4.jpg")` |
| 7 | `    var bnrCntr = 0` |
| 8 | `    function bancycle() {` |
| 9 | `        bnrCntr = bnrCntr + 1` |
| 10 | `        if (bnrCntr == 4) {` |
| 11 | `        bnrCntr = 0` |
| 12 | `        }` |
| 13 | `        document.Banner.src = banners[bnrCntr]` |
| 14 | `        setTimeout("bancycle()",3000)` |
| 15 | `    }` |
| 16 | |
| 17 | |
| 18 | `//-->` |
| 19 | `</SCRIPT>` |

The bancycle() function begins in line 6 by creating an array of image file names. Line 7 initializes the counter variable named bnrCntr to zero, which serves as the subscript. Zero represents the first element in the array, which is the first banner image of the rolling banner displayed on the Web page. Line 8 defines the function name. Line 9 increments the bnrCntr by 1, and line 10 tests the counter against the number of items in the array, which is four. If bnrCntr is equal to four, line 11 assigns a zero (0) to bnrCntr. Line 13 assigns the contents of banners[bnrCntr] to the image object, so the new image displays. The function then calls itself with a three-second delay (line 14). The brace (line 15) completes the function. The blank lines at 16 and 17 reserve space for future user-defined functions, while lines 18 and 19 complete the JavaScript section.

To enter the bancycle() function to create a rolling banner, perform the following steps.

 **To Enter a Function to Create a Rolling Banner**

**1** **Position the insertion point on line 4.**

**2** **Enter the JavaScript code shown in Table 3-4.**

*The bancycle() function displays (Figure 3-6).*

```
cater.htm - Notepad
File   Edit   Search   Help
<HTML>
<HEAD>
<TITLE>Midwest Catering Service</TITLE>
<SCRIPT  LANGUAGE="JAVASCRIPT">
<!-- Hide from old browsers
    var banners = new Array("banner1.jpg","banner2.jpg","banner3.jpg","banner4.jpg")
    var bnrCntr = 0
    function bancycle() {
        bnrCntr = bnrCntr + 1
        if (bnrCntr == 4) {
            bnrCntr = 0
        }
        document.Banner.src = banners[bnrCntr]
        setTimeout("bancycle()",3000)
    }

//-->
</SCRIPT>
</HEAD>

<BODY>
```

line 4

array items

subscript

**FIGURE 3-6**

Once the bancycle() function is called, the setTimeout() method on line 14 will continue to call the function until the user displays a new Web page or quits the browser.

## Calling the Rolling Banner Function

The next step is to enter the event handler that calls the bancycle() function. In this project, place an onload event handler in the BODY tag using the setTimeout() method as you did in the bancycle() function. The setTimeout() method is used to delay changing the first image. A three-second delay is sufficient to allow the average user time to read the banner. To enter the onload event handler to call the bancycle() function, perform the following steps.

 **To Enter the onload Event Handler to Call a Function**

**1** Position the insertion point immediately to the left of the Y in BODY on line 22, inside the > symbol (Figure 3-7).

```
cater.htm - Notepad
File  Edit  Search  Help
<HTML>
<HEAD>
<TITLE>Midwest Catering Service</TITLE>
<SCRIPT  LANGUAGE="JAVASCRIPT">
<!--  Hide from old browsers
    var banners = new Array("banner1.jpg","banner2.jpg","banner3.jpg","banner4.jpg")
    var bnrCntr = 0
    function bancycle() {
            bnrCntr = bnrCntr + 1
            if (bnrCntr == 4) {
                bnrCntr = 0
            }
        document.Banner.src = banners[bnrCntr]
        setTimeout("bancycle()",3000)
    }

//-->
</SCRIPT>
</HEAD>

line 22 ──▶ <BODY>

<A NAME="MCS_TOP">
<CENTER><IMG SRC="banner1.jpg" Name="Banner" Width=320 Height=65></CENTER>

<HR>
```

**FIGURE 3-7**

**2** Type onload= "setTimeout ('bancycle()',3000)" and do not press the ENTER key (Figure 3-8).

```
//-->
</SCRIPT>
</HEAD>
                                        onload Event
                                        Handler
<BODY onload="setTimeout('bancycle()',3000)">

<A NAME="MCS_TOP">
<CENTER><IMG SRC="banner1.jpg" Name="Banner" Width=320 Height=65></CENTER>

<HR>
<CENTER>
<TABLE CELLSPACING=0 BORDER=0 WIDTH=436>
<TR>
<TD>
<P><IMG SRC="food1.jpg" Name="Image1" WIDTH=158 HEIGHT=126></TD>
<TD WIDTH="25%" VALIGN="MIDDLE" ALIGN="CENTER">
<P><A HREF="#PicnicFoods">Picnics</A></P>
<P><A HREF="#DinnerParty">Dinner Parties</A></P>
```
Start | 🜚 🜙 🜛 🜜 | cater.htm - Notepad | 🔊 🜝 8:52 AM

**FIGURE 3-8**

The three steps for creating a rolling banner are complete. Recall that the three steps are (1) create an image object; (2) write the rolling banner function; and (3) add the event handler. The next step is to write the code to create the dynamic greeting for the holiday countdown.

# Creating a Dynamic Greeting

The dynamic greeting in this project displays below the rolling banner on the Web page. The greeting notifies the user of the number of days until a given holiday. This project focuses on St. Patrick's Day, Independence Day, Halloween, and Christmas as the holidays.

The steps in writing a user-defined function to create a dynamic greeting include: (1) initialize a generic greeting; (2) create a Date() object instance; (3) determine the month number; (4) depending on month, set the holiday date; (5) subtract the number of days between the holiday and the current date; (6) test the current date, if before the holiday calculate the number of days until the holiday; and (7) assign a new message. Repeat steps 2 through 7 for each of the four holidays.

You need a variable to contain the new message assigned in step 7. Name this variable holidayCntMsg and use it to assign an initial generic greeting. The generic greeting does not reference any holidays. Use the holidayCntMsg variable to change the greeting in step 7 for the countdown to a specific holiday.

To test the current month and set the holiday date requires a set of multiple conditionals. The testing can be accomplished with nested If...Else statements. An easier way to test multiple conditions, however, is the Switch statement.

## The Switch Statement

Recall in Project 2 that you used nested If...Else statements to test multiple conditions. The **Switch statement** is another way of testing multiple conditions as shown by the flowchart in Figure 3-9. The comparison begins with the first case statement, and continues until all conditions are tested. Table 3-5 on the next page describes the general form of the Switch statement.

**More** *About*

**The Switch Statement**

For more information on the Switch statement, visit www.scsite.com/js/p3.htm and click Switch. Then click Chapter 12, Overview of JavaScript Statements and locate the Switch statement.

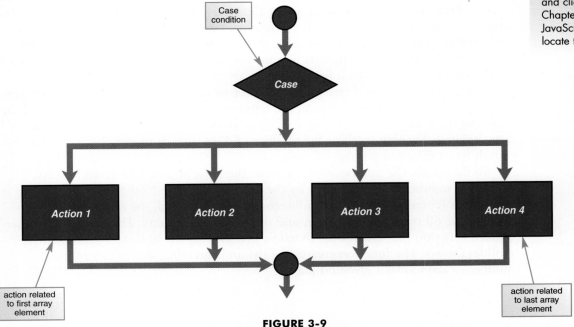

**FIGURE 3-9**

**Table 3-5 – Switch Statement**

| | |
|---|---|
| **General form:** | Switch (expression) {<br>       case value :<br>            JavaScript statements<br>            break<br>       case value :<br>            JavaScript statements<br>            break<br>      default :<br>            JavaScript statements<br>} |
| **Comment:** | where the expression is any valid JavaScript expression or variable and the case value is any valid JavaScript variable or constant. The condition compares the case value to the expression. If the condition is True, the JavaScript statements after the Case Condition statement execute. The Break statement passes control to the first statement after the closing brace for the Switch statement when a case condition is True. If the condition is False, the next case condition executes. The default statement is optional, and executes if none of the case conditions is True. |
| **Example:** | (the getDay() method returns the day of the week):<br>`var curDay = new Date()`<br>`var day = curDay.getDay()`<br>`switch (day) {`<br>`        case 0 :`<br>`                document.write("Today is Sunday")`<br>`                break`<br>`        case 6 :`<br>`                document.write("Today is Saturday")`<br>`                break`<br>`        default :`<br>`                document.write("Today is a weekday")`<br>`}` |

## More About

### The Date() Object

A specific date can be set as Date("month, day, year hours:minutes:seconds") or Date(year, month, day) or Date(year, month, day, hours, minutes, seconds).

## More About

### getTime()

You can divide by 86,400,000, but the expression 1000 * 60 * 60 * 24 is used to explain how the value is derived. For more information on the Date() object and the Date() method getTime(), visit www.scsite.com/js/p3.htm and then click getTime().

## The getMonth() and getTime() Methods

To create the dynamic greeting, use the getMonth() and getTime() methods of the Date() object. Recall from Project 1 that the Date() object returns the current system date to an object instance. Using the new object with the current system date, the getMonth() method returns the number of the current month. Because the system starts counting from zero, the first month, January, is zero. February is one and so on through December, which becomes 11.

The getTime() method returns the number of milliseconds that have elapsed since January 1, 1970 at 00:00:00. Using the number of milliseconds is easier to use than counting the number of days between dates. To count the number of days between dates requires keeping track of the number of days in each month, because each month has a different number of days.

To determine the number of days, from the current date to a given holiday, divide the number of milliseconds by the product of 1000 * 60 * 60 * 24. This expression represents the 1,000 milliseconds in one second, the 60 seconds in a minute, the 60 minutes in an hour, and the 24 hours in a day. The name of the user-defined function that creates the dynamic greeting for the holiday countdown is HolidayDays(). The function creates the dynamic greeting, which determines the number of days until a given holiday.

## Creating the HolidayDays() Function

The first holiday used in the function is St. Patrick's Day. The flowchart in Figure 3-10 shows the logic of the Switch statement used in the HolidayDays() function. Table 3-6 shows the JavaScript code for the function.

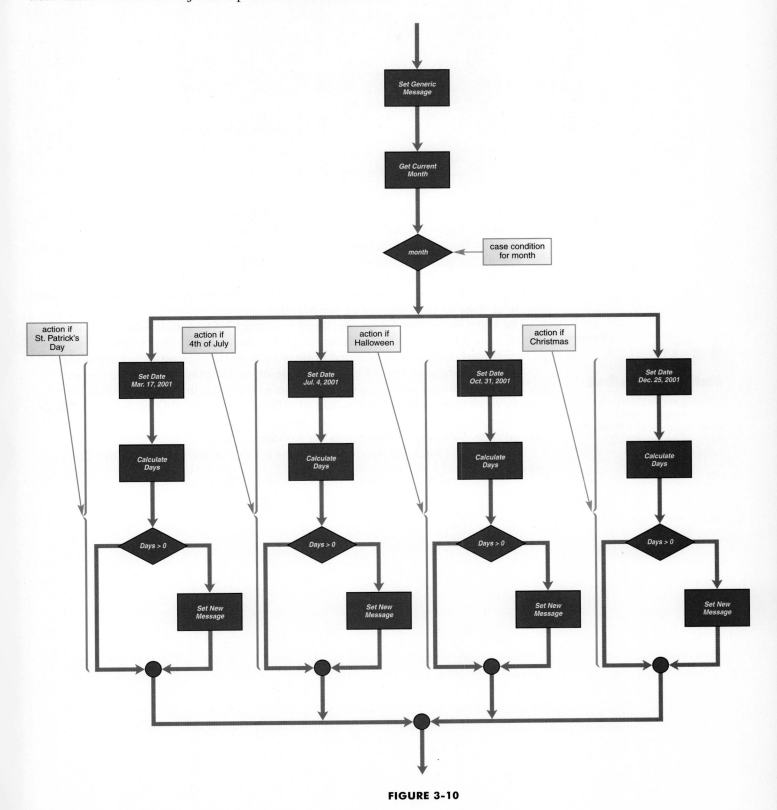

**FIGURE 3-10**

**Table 3-6**

| LINE | CODE |
|------|------|
| 17 | `var holidayCntMsg = "Leave the party to Midwest Catering"` |
| 18 | `var curDay = new Date()` |
| 19 | `var tMonth = curDay.getMonth()` |
| 20 | `function HolidayDays() {` |
| 21 | `switch (tMonth) {` |
| 22 | `    case 2:` |
| 23 | `        var tHoliday = new Date("March 17, 2001")` |
| 24 | `        var curHoliday = tHoliday.getTime()-curDay.getTime()` |
| 25 | `        if (curHoliday > 0) {` |
| 26 | `            curHoliday = Math.ceil(curHoliday / (1000 * 60 * 60 * 24))` |
| 27 | `            holidayCntMsg = "Only "+curHoliday+" days until St. Patrick s Day!"` |
| 28 | `        }` |
| 29 | `    break` |

Line 17 establishes the default greeting which displays if no holiday exists for a given month. Line 18 assigns curDay the current system date. Recall from project two that the Date() object returns the current system date, time, and time zone, and that specific information must be extracted from the string object. In line 19, the getMonth() method returns the number of the current month. Recall earlier that January returns a zero. Thus, the month of March returns a two. In line 22, the case statement (case 2) tests the month for March.

The Date() object sets a specific date (St. Patrick's Day) to an object instance in line 23. Line 24 subtracts the number of days of the current system date using the getTime() method from the assigned holiday date storing the result in curHoliday.

The If statement in line 24 tests the value of curHoliday. If the value is greater than zero that means current system date has not passed the holiday. Divide the number of milliseconds by the product of (1000 * 60 * 60 * 24) as shown in line 26. The entire expression is rounded to the nearest highest integer using the Math ceil() method (line 26). Line 27 constructs the holidayCntMsg.

To enter the HolidayDays()function steps for St Patrick's Day, perform the following steps.

**More About**

**Math ceil() Method**

The ceil() method returns the highest integer. Given the value -2.89, ceil(-2.89) returns 2. Given the value 3.02, ceil(3.02) returns 4.

**Steps** **To Enter the HolidayDays() User-Defined Function Steps for St. Patrick's Day**

**1** **Position the insertion point on line 17.**

**2** **Enter the JavaScript code shown in Table 3-6. For the date in line 23, enter the current year.**

*The JavaScript code for the St. Patrick's Day displays a holiday message (Figure 3-11).*

```
cater.htm - Notepad
File  Edit  Search  Help
<HTML>
<HEAD>
<TITLE>Midwest Catering Service</TITLE>
<SCRIPT  LANGUAGE="JAVASCRIPT">
<!--  Hide from old browsers
    var banners = new Array("banner1.jpg","banner2.jpg","banner3.jpg","banner4.jpg")
    var bnrCntr = 0
    function bancycle() {
          bnrCntr = bnrCntr + 1
          if (bnrCntr == 4) {
             bnrCntr = 0
          }
       document.Banner.src = banners[bnrCntr]
       setTimeout("bancycle()",3000)
    }

var holidayCntMsg = "Leave the party to Midwest Catering"
var curDay = new Date()
var tMonth = curDay.getMonth()
function HolidayDays() {
switch (tMonth) {
    case 2:
       var tHoliday = new Date("March 17, 2001")
       var curHoliday = tHoliday.getTime()-curDay.getTime()
       if (curHoliday > 0) {
          curHoliday = Math.ceil(curHoliday / (1000 * 60 * 60 * 24))
          holidayCntMsg = "Only "+curHoliday+" days until St. Patrick's Day!"
       }
       break

//-->
</SCRIPT>
</HEAD>
```

line 17

replace 2001 with current year

Start    cater.htm - Notepad    8:54 AM

**FIGURE 3-11**

The next section of the function completes the code for the Independence Day holiday and is shown in Table 3-7.

**Table 3-7**

| LINE | CODE |
|------|------|
| 30 | case 5 \|\| 6: |
| 31 | var tHoliday = new Date("July 4, 2001") |
| 32 | var curHoliday = tHoliday.getTime()-curDay.getTime() |
| 33 | if (curHoliday > 0) { |
| 34 | curHoliday = Math.ceil(curHoliday / (1000 * 60 * 60 * 24)) |
| 35 | holidayCntMsg = "Only "+curHoliday+" days until the 4<SUP>th</SUP> of July!" |
| 36 | } |
| 37 | break |

To wait until July to begin the count down until the holiday, only three days are left. Because this is a popular summer holiday, the count down for Independence Day begins in June. The Case statement (line 30) is a multiple condition using the OR conditional operator (||) to test for months 5 (June) or 6 (July). Recall from the Introduction section before Project 1, that in an OR condition if either condition is True, the entire condition is True. Line 31 sets the date for July 4. The <SUP> tag on line 35 is the SUPERSCRIPT tag.

To enter the statements to count down the days to the Independence Day holiday, perform the following steps.

 **Steps** ## To Enter the HolidayDays() User-Defined Function Steps for Independence Day

**1** **Position the insertion point on line 30.**

**2** **Enter the JavaScript code shown in Table 3-7 on the previous page. For the date in line 31, enter the current year.**

*The JavaScript code for the Independence Day holiday message displays (Figure 3-12).*

```
cater.htm - Notepad
File  Edit  Search  Help
        document.Banner.src = banners[bnrCntr]
        setTimeout("bancycle()",3000)
    }

var holidayCntMsg = "Leave the party to Midwest Catering"
var curDay = new Date()
var tMonth = curDay.getMonth()
function HolidayDays() {
switch (tMonth) {
    case 2:
        var tHoliday = new Date("March 17, 2001")
        var curHoliday = tHoliday.getTime()-curDay.getTime()
        if (curHoliday > 0) {
            curHoliday = Math.ceil(curHoliday / (1000 * 60 * 60 * 24))
            holidayCntMsg = "Only "+curHoliday+" days until St. Patrick's Day!"
        }
        break
    case 5 || 6:
        var tHoliday = new Date("July 4, 2001")
        var curHoliday = tHoliday.getTime()-curDay.getTime()
        if (curHoliday > 0) {
            curHoliday = Math.ceil(curHoliday / (1000 * 60 * 60 * 24))
            holidayCntMsg = "Only "+curHoliday+" days until the 4<SUP>th</SUP> of July!"
        }
        break

//-->
</SCRIPT>
</HEAD>

<BODY onload="setTimeout('bancycle()',3000)">

<A NAME="MCS_TOP">
<CENTER><IMG SRC="banner1.jpg" Name="Banner" Width=320 Height=65></CENTER>
```

replace 2001 with current year

line 30

**FIGURE 3-12**

The next section of the function code completes the count down for Halloween (Table 3-8).

**Table 3-8**

| LINE | CODE |
|---|---|
| 38 | case 9: |
| 39 | var tHoliday = new Date("October 31, 2001") |
| 40 | var curHoliday = tHoliday.getTime()-curDay.getTime() |
| 41 | if (curHoliday > 0) { |
| 42 | curHoliday = Math.ceil(curHoliday / (1000 * 60 * 60 * 24)) |
| 43 | holidayCntMsg = "Only "+curHoliday+" days until Halloween!" |
| 44 | } |
| 45 | break |

The count down begins in October, which the getMonth() method will determine as nine, as shown in line 38. The date for Halloween, is set in line 39.

To enter the function statements for Halloween, perform the following steps.

 **To Enter the HolidayDays() User-Defined Function Steps for Halloween**

**1** Position the insertion point on line 38.

**2** Enter the JavaScript code shown in Table 3-8. For the date in line 39, enter the current year.

*The JavaScript code for the Halloween holiday message displays (Figure 3-13).*

```
cater.htm - Notepad
File  Edit  Search  Help
     switch (tMonth) {
        case 2:
           var tHoliday = new Date("March 17, 2001")
           var curHoliday = tHoliday.getTime()-curDay.getTime()
           if (curHoliday > 0) {
              curHoliday = Math.ceil(curHoliday / (1000 * 60 * 60 * 24))
              holidayCntMsg = "Only "+curHoliday+" days until St. Patrick's Day!"
           }
           break
        case 5 || 6:
           var tHoliday = new Date("July 4, 2001")
           var curHoliday = tHoliday.getTime()-curDay.getTime()
           if (curHoliday > 0) {
              curHoliday = Math.ceil(curHoliday / (1000 * 60 * 60 * 24))
              holidayCntMsg = "Only "+curHoliday+" days until the 4<SUP>th</SUP> of July!"
           }
           break
        case 9:
           var tHoliday = new Date("October 31, 2001")
           var curHoliday = tHoliday.getTime()-curDay.getTime()
           if (curHoliday > 0) {
              curHoliday = Math.ceil(curHoliday / (1000 * 60 * 60 * 24))
              holidayCntMsg = "Only "+curHoliday+" days until Halloween!"
           }
           break

//-->
</SCRIPT>
</HEAD>

<BODY onload="setTimeout('bancycle()',3000)">

<A NAME="MCS_TOP">
<CENTER><IMG SRC="banner1.jpg" Name="Banner" Width=320 Height=65></CENTER>

Start          cater.htm - Notepad                    8:56 AM
```

line 38

replace 2001 with current year

**FIGURE 3-13**

The code to finish the function for the Christmas holiday message is shown in Table 3-9. This case section follows the same logic as the code discussed in Table 3-8.

**Table 3-9**

| LINE | CODE |
|------|------|
| 46 | `        case 11:` |
| 47 | `           var tHoliday = new Date("December 25, 2001")` |
| 48 | `           var curHoliday = tHoliday.getTime()-curDay.getTime()` |
| 49 | `           if (curHoliday > 0) {` |
| 50 | `              curHoliday = Math.ceil(curHoliday / (1000 * 60 * 60 * 24))` |
| 51 | `              holidayCntMsg = "Only "+curHoliday+" days until Christmas!"` |
| 52 | `           }` |
| 53 | `           break` |
| 54 | `        }` |
| 55 | `     return holidayCntMsg` |
| 56 | `  }` |

The case condition for December tests for an 11 in line 46. The return command in line 55 sends the contents of the holidayCntMsg variable back to the calling function. If the current system month does not match any of the holiday months, the function returns the generic greeting originally set in line 17.

To enter the JavaScript code for the Christmas holiday, perform the following steps.

 **To Enter the HolidayDays() User-Defined Function Steps for Christmas**

**1** **Position the insertion point on line 46.**

**2** **Enter the JavaScript code shown in Table 3-9 on the previous page. For the date in line 47, enter the current year.**

*The final section of the function displays (Figure 3-14).*

```
cater.htm - Notepad
File  Edit  Search  Help
        case 5 || 6:
            var tHoliday = new Date("July 4, 2001")
            var curHoliday = tHoliday.getTime()-curDay.getTime()
            if (curHoliday > 0) {
                curHoliday = Math.ceil(curHoliday / (1000 * 60 * 60 * 24))
                holidayCntMsg = "Only "+curHoliday+" days until the 4<SUP>th</SUP> of July!"
            }
            break
        case 9:
            var tHoliday = new Date("October 31, 2001")
            var curHoliday = tHoliday.getTime()-curDay.getTime()
            if (curHoliday > 0) {
                curHoliday = Math.ceil(curHoliday / (1000 * 60 * 60 * 24))
                holidayCntMsg = "Only "+curHoliday+" days until Halloween!"
            }
            break
        case 11:
            var tHoliday = new Date("December 25, 2001")
            var curHoliday = tHoliday.getTime()-curDay.getTime()
            if (curHoliday > 0) {
                curHoliday = Math.ceil(curHoliday / (1000 * 60 * 60 * 24))
                holidayCntMsg = "Only "+curHoliday+" days until Christmas!"
            }
            break
        }
        return holidayCntMsg
    }

//-->
</SCRIPT>
</HEAD>

<BODY onload="setTimeout('...cle()',3000...
```

replace 2001 with current year

line 46

return message string

end of function

**FIGURE 3-14**

## Calling the HolidayDays() Function

The next step inserts the JavaScript code in the BODY section that calls the HolidayDays() function and displays the appropriate greeting (Figures 3-1a through 3-1e on page J 3.5 and J 3.6). The dynamic greeting displays at the top of the page below the rolling banner images. Table 3-10 provides the code for the HolidayDays() function call and the write() method that displays the message.

| Table 3-10 | |
|---|---|
| LINE | CODE |
| 67 | `<SCRIPT LANGUAGE="JAVASCRIPT">` |
| 68 | `<-- Hide from old browsers` |
| 69 | `    var holidayMsg = HolidayDays()` |
| 70 | `    document.write("<H2><CENTER>"+holidayMsg+"</CENTER></H2>")` |
| 71 | |
| 72 | `//-->` |
| 73 | `</SCRIPT>` |

Recall from previous projects that JavaScript code entered in the BODY section must be in a SCRIPT section. To enter the function call that displays the dynamic message on the Web page, perform the following steps.

 **Steps** **To Enter a Function Call and Display a Message**

**1** **Position the insertion point on line 67.**

**2** **Enter the JavaScript code shown in Table 3-10.**

*The embedded HTML tags display the message center-aligned with the Heading 2 style.*

line 67

```
🖉 cater.htm - Notepad                                                    _ 🗗 ✕
File   Edit   Search   Help
          case 11:
              var tHoliday = new Date("December 25, 2001")
              var curHoliday = tHoliday.getTime()-curDay.getTime()
              if (curHoliday > 0) {
                  curHoliday = Math.ceil(curHoliday / (1000 * 60 * 60 * 24))
                  holidayCntMsg = "Only "+curHoliday+" days until Christmas!"
              }
              break
          }
      return holidayCntMsg
      }

//-->
</SCRIPT>
</HEAD>

<BODY onload="setTimeout('bancycle()',3000)">

<A NAME="MCS_TOP">
<CENTER><IMG SRC="banner1.jpg" Name="Banner" Width=320 Height=65></CENTER>
<SCRIPT LANGUAGE="JAVASCRIPT">
<!-- Hide from old browsers
     var holidayMsg = HolidayDays()
     document.write("<H2><CENTER>"+holidayMsg+"</CENTER></H2>")

//-->
</SCRIPT>
<HR>
<CENTER>
<TABLE CELLSPACING=0 BORDER=0 WIDTH=436>
<TR>
<TD>
<P><IMG SRC="food1.jpg" Name="Image1" WIDTH=158 HEIGHT=126></TD>
<TD WIDTH="25%" VALIGN="MIDDLE" ALIGN="CENTER">
🏁 Start    🌐 🖼 🎮 🗐            🖉 cater.htm - Notepad                    🔊🕙 8:58 AM
```

Heading 2 style font tag

center-align tag

**FIGURE 3-15**

The JavaScript code to display the rolling banner and the greeting is complete. This is a good time to test the JavaScript code entered thus far.

## Saving the HTML File and Viewing the Web Page

Save the HTML file with the JavaScript code using the name, mwcatering.htm, on the JavaScript Data Disk in drive A. Recall that you must add the .htm extension to the file name, because Notepad automatically saves all files with a .txt extension. To save and test the Web page, perform the steps on the next page.

**TO SAVE THE HTML FILE AND TEST THE WEB PAGE**

**1** With the JavaScript Data Disk in drive A, click File on the menu bar and then Save As.

**2** Type a:\mwcatering.htm in the File name text box and then click the Save button in the Save As dialog box.

**3** Start your browser and open mwcatering.htm.

*Figure 3-16 displays the first image of the rolling banner and the count down to Halloween message. The dynamic message that displays depends on the current system date.*

**FIGURE 3-16**

If the browser does not display the Web page correctly, close any error message dialog boxes and then click the Notepad button on the taskbar. Check the JavaScript code according to Figures 3-3 through 3-15 on pages J 3.8 through J 3.21. Correct any errors, save the file, activate the browser, and then click the Refresh button.

# The onmouseover Event Handler

Recall from the requirements that the two images in Figure 3-1d (page J 3.6) change when the user places the mouse over one of the food service category links. To make these images change, assign a new image name to the image object. Each food service category link contains an onmouseover event handler that calls a function. The function assigns a new image to the image objects.

Web designers must be careful when writing onmouseover event handlers. While waiting for a Web page to load, a user might drag the mouse over an object associated with an event handler and trigger an action they were not expecting. Depending on the action, an error message may display, or the user may become lost or confused. If you get an error message associated with an onmouseover event handler, refresh the Web page, and make sure the page is completely loaded before moving the mouse.

In this project, the mouse event handler is associated with anchor links. A mouse event handler can be associated, however, with other objects such as buttons or graphics. Table 3-11 describes other mouse related event handlers.

**Table 3-11**

| EVENT HANDLER | COMMENT |
| --- | --- |
| onmouseout | Triggers JavaScript code when the mouse pointer is dragged off an object |
| onmousedown | Triggers JavaScript code when the mouse button is pressed |
| onmouseup | Triggers JavaScript code when the mouse button is released |
| onmousemove | Triggers JavaScript code when a user moves the mouse pointer |

**More About**

**Mouse Event Handlers**

For more information, visit www.scsite.com/js/p3.htm, click Event Handlers, and then click Chapter 2, Handling Events.

### Entering the onmouseover Event Handler

The user-defined functions for each of the food service categories are onPicnic(), onDinnerParty(), and onWedding(). For example, the link for Picnics in line 81 in Figure 3-17 reads <A HREF="#PicnicFood">. With the addition of the onmouseover event it will read <A HREF="#PicnicFood" onmouseover="onPicnic()">. To call the functions using the onmouseover event handlers, perform the following steps.

 **To Call the Functions Using the onmouseover Event Handler**

**1** **Position the insertion point immediately after the "and before the > on line 81.**

**2** **Press the SPACEBAR once. Type** onmouseover="onPicnic ()" **and do not press the ENTER key.**

*The onmouseover event handler to call the onPicnic() function displays (Figure 3-17).*

```
mwcatering.htm - Notepad
File  Edit  Search  Help
<BODY onload="setTimeout('bancycle()',3000)">

<A NAME="MCS_TOP">
<CENTER><IMG SRC="banner1.jpg" Name="Banner" Width=320 Height=65></CENTER>
<SCRIPT LANGUAGE="JAVASCRIPT">
<!-- Hide from old browsers
     var holidayMsg = HolidayDays()
     document.write("<H2><CENTER>"+holidayMsg+"</CENTER></H2>")

//-->
</SCRIPT>
<HR>
<CENTER>
<TABLE CELLSPACING=0 BORDER=0 WIDTH=436>
<TR>
<TD>
<P><IMG SRC="food1.jpg" Name="Image1" WIDTH=158 HEIGHT=126></TD>
<TD WIDTH="25%" VALIGN="MIDDLE" ALIGN="CENTER">
<P><A HREF="#PicnicFoods" onmouseover="onPicnic()">Picnics</A></P>
<P><A HREF="#DinnerParty">Dinner Parties</A></P>
<P><A HREF="#Weddings">Weddings</A> </P>
</TD>
<TD VALIGN="MIDDLE">
<P><IMG SRC="food2.jpg" Name="Image2" Wi         t=126></P>
</TD>
</TR>
</TABLE>
</CENTER>
```

line 81

mouse event handler

**FIGURE 3-17**

**3** **Position the insertion point immediately after the " and before the > on line 82.**

**4** **Press the SPACEBAR once. Type** onmouseover="onDinner Party()" **and do not press the ENTER key.**

*The onmouseover event handler to call the onDinnerParty() function displays (Figure 3-18).*

**FIGURE 3-18**

**5** **Position the insertion point immediately after the " and before the > on line 83.**

**6** **Press the SPACEBAR once. Type** onmouseover= "onWedding()" **and do not press the ENTER key.**

*The onmouseover event handler to call the onWedding() function displays (Figure 3-19).*

**FIGURE 3-19**

## Entering the Functions

The next step is to enter the functions that the onmouseover event handlers trigger to change the images. Lines 79 and 86 contain the initial images, which display on the left and right sides of the links before the user drags the mouse over one of the links. The initial images display as shown in Figure 3-20.

**FIGURE 3-20a**

**FIGURE 3-20b**

**Table 3-12**

| LINE | CODE |
|------|------|
| 58 | `function onPicnic() {` |
| 59 | `    document.Image1.src = "catering2.jpg"` |
| 60 | `    document.Image2.src = "catering3.jpg"` |
| 61 | `    }` |

Table 3-12 shows the statements that assign the new images to the image object for the onPicnic() function.

In line 58, document.Image1.src contains the image on the left and in line 59, document.Image2.src contains the image on the right. To enter the onPicnic() function, which changes the images when the user drags the mouse over the Picnics Link, move to the HEAD section and then perform the following steps.

 **To Enter the onPicnic() Function**

**1** **Position the insertion point on line 58.**

**2** **Enter the JavaScript code shown in Table 3-12.**

*The onPicnic() function displays (Figure 3-21).*

```
        case 9:
            var tHoliday = new Date("October 31, 2001")
            var curHoliday = tHoliday.getTime()-curDay.getTime()
            if (curHoliday > 0) {
                curHoliday = Math.ceil(curHoliday / (1000 * 60 * 60 * 24))
                holidayCntMsg = "Only "+curHoliday+" days until Halloween!"
            }
             break
        case 11:
            var tHoliday = new Date("December 25, 2001")
            var curHoliday = tHoliday.getTime()-curDay.getTime()
            if (curHoliday > 0) {
                curHoliday = Math.ceil(curHoliday / (1000 * 60 * 60 * 24))
                holidayCntMsg = "Only "+curHoliday+" days until Christmas!"
            }
            break
        }
    return holidayCntMsg
    }

    function onPicnic() {
        document.Image1.src = "catering2.jpg"
        document.Image2.src = "catering3.jpg"
        }


//-->
</SCRIPT>
</HEAD>

<BODY onload="setTimeout('bancycle()',3000)">

<A NAME="MCS_TOP">
<CENTER><IMG SRC="banner1.jpg" Name="Banner" Width=320 Height=65></CENTER>
<SCRIPT LANGUAGE="JAVASCRIPT">
```

Image1 object location reference

Image2 object location reference

line 58

**FIGURE 3-21**

Table 3-13 provides the code for the onDinnerParty() function.

**Table 3-13**

| LINE | CODE |
|------|------|
| 63 | `function onDinnerParty() {` |
| 64 | `    document.Image1.src = "catering4.jpg"` |
| 65 | `    document.Image2.src = "catering5.jpg"` |
| 66 | `    }` |

Lines 64 and 65 assign the image file names to the image objects. To enter the onDinnerParty() function, perform the following steps.

## *Steps* To Enter the onDinnerParty() Function

**1** Position the insertion point on line 63.

**2** Enter the JavaScript code shown in Table 3-13.

*The onDinnerParty() function displays (Figure 3-22).*

(line 63)

```
        case 11:
            var tHoliday = new Date("December 25, 2001")
            var curHoliday = tHoliday.getTime()-curDay.getTime()
            if (curHoliday > 0) {
                curHoliday = Math.ceil(curHoliday / (1000 * 60 * 60 * 24))
                holidayCntMsg = "Only "+curHoliday+" days until Christmas!"
            }
            break
    }
    return holidayCntMsg
}

function onPicnic() {
    document.Image1.src = "catering2.jpg"
    document.Image2.src = "catering3.jpg"
}

function onDinnerParty() {
    document.Image1.src = "catering4.jpg"
    document.Image2.src = "catering5.jpg"
}

//-->
</SCRIPT>
</HEAD>
```

Start | mwcatering.htm - Not... | Midwest Catering Service - | 9:07 AM

**FIGURE 3-22**

Table 3-14 provides the code for the onWedding() function.

Lines 69 and 70 change the images. To enter the onWedding() function, perform the following steps.

| Table 3-14 | |
|------|------|
| *LINE* | *CODE* |
| 68 | function onWedding() { |
| 69 | document.Image1.src = "catering6.jpg" |
| 70 | document.Image2.src = "catering7.jpg" |
| 71 | } |

## *Steps* To Enter the onWedding() Function

**1** Position the insertion point on line 68.

**2** Enter the JavaScript code shown in Table 3-14.

*The onWedding() function displays (Figure 3-23).*

(line 68)

```
        case 11:
            var tHoliday = new Date("December 25, 2001")
            var curHoliday = tHoliday.getTime()-curDay.getTime()
            if (curHoliday > 0) {
                curHoliday = Math.ceil(curHoliday / (1000 * 60 * 60 * 24))
                holidayCntMsg = "Only "+curHoliday+" days until Christmas!"
            }
            break
    }
    return holidayCntMsg
}

function onPicnic() {
    document.Image1.src = "catering2.jpg"
    document.Image2.src = "catering3.jpg"
}

function onDinnerParty() {
    document.Image1.src = "catering4.jpg"
    document.Image2.src = "catering5.jpg"
}

function onWedding() {
    document.Image1.src = "catering6.jpg"
    document.Image2.src = "catering7.jpg"
}
```

Start | mwcatering.htm - Not... | Midwest Catering Service - | 9:08 AM

**FIGURE 3-23**

Now is a good point to save the Web page and test the JavaScript code in the browser.

### TO SAVE AND TEST THE WEB PAGE

**1** With the JavaScript Data Disk in drive A, click File on the menu bar and then click Save.

**2** Click the browser button on the taskbar and then click the Refresh button on the toolbar.

**3** Point to the Weddings link and wait a few seconds.

**4** Point to the Picnics link and wait a few seconds.

*The images on both sides of the link change as you point to a link. Figure 3-24 displays the new images for the Picnics link.*

**FIGURE 3-24**

If the browser does not display the Web page correctly, close any error message dialog boxes and then click the Notepad button on the taskbar. Check the JavaScript code according to Figures 3-17 through 3-23 on pages J 3.23 through J 3.27. Correct any errors, save the file, activate the browser, and then click the Refresh button. The next step in the project is to display the per-person menu prices in a text box.

# Using Selection Lists to Display Menu Items

Each of the three food service categories has a selection list that offers menu choices. Figure 3-25 shows the Picnics selection list. To display a price, the user clicks the down arrow associated with the upper-left list box (Figure 3-25). To select an item from the list, the user clicks the desired item. Each item in the list has a per-person price. An array object contains the corresponding per-person price to match the list.

**FIGURE 3-25**

When the user selects an item, the price would display in the price text box shown in Figure 3-25. To obtain the correct price from the array, use the selectedIndex property. The **selectedIndex property** provides the position of the item selected in the list, which corresponds to the position of the price in the array. Figure 3-26 on the next page shows the function call from the PicnicMenu form and the relationship of the selectedIndex property to the array in the setPicnicPrice() function.

## More About

### Select Lists

For more information, visit www.scsite.com/js/p3.htm, click Select, click Chapter 7, Forms, and then click Select.

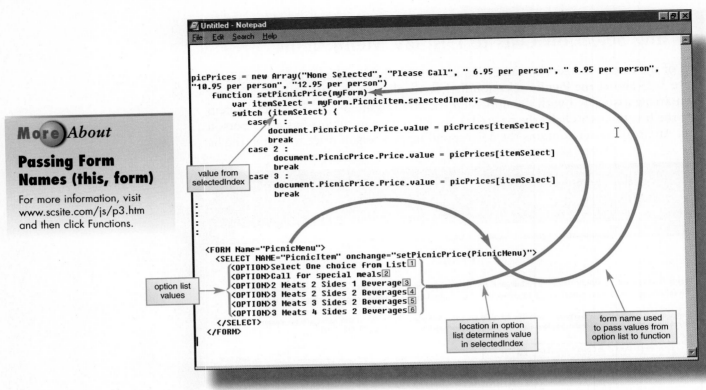

**FIGURE 3-26**

## More About

### Passing Form Names (this, form)

For more information, visit www.scsite.com/js/p3.htm and then click Functions.

## The onchange Event Handler

To display the price in the text box associated with the item, use the onchange event handler. The **onchange event handler** triggers an event whenever the object it is associated with changes. In this project, when a user selects an item, the list changes and triggers the onchange event handler.

For each of the price lists, the functions are setPicnicPrice(), setDinnerPrice(), and setWeddingPrice(). Associate each function with an onchange event handler in the SELECT tag. To call the setPicnicPrice(), setDinnerPrice(), and setWeddingPrice() functions for each option list form using the onchange event handler, move down into the BODY section and perform the following steps.

## Steps To Call the Functions Using the onchange Event Handler

**1** Position the insertion point immediately after the right " and before the > on line 116.

**2** Press the SPACEBAR once. Type
onchange=
"setPicnic
Price(PicnicMenu)" **and do not press the** ENTER **key.**

*The onchange event handler that calls the setPicnicPrice() function displays (Figure 3-27).*

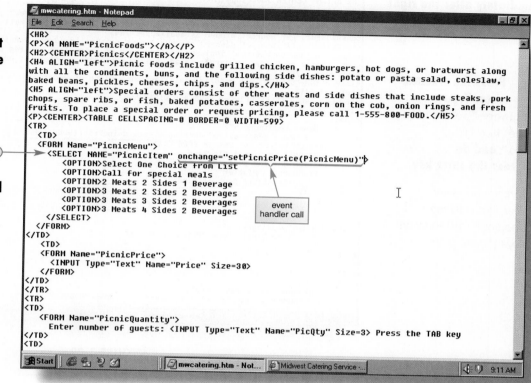

**FIGURE 3-27**

**3** Position the insertion point immediately after the right " and before the > on line 162.

**4** Press the SPACEBAR once. Type
onchange=
"setDinnerPrice
(DinnerMenu)" **and do not press the** ENTER **key.**

*The onchange event handler that calls the setDinnerPrice() function displays (Figure 3-28).*

**FIGURE 3-28**

**5** Position the insertion point immediately after the right " and before the > on line 216.

**6** Press the SPACEBAR once. Type onchange="setWedding Price(Wedding Menu)" **and do not press the ENTER key.**

*The onchange event handler that calls the setWeddingPrice() function displays (Figure 3-29).*

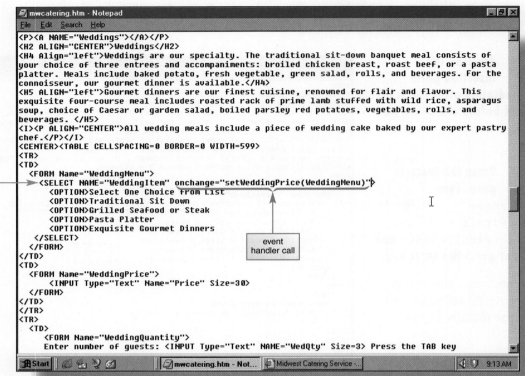

**FIGURE 3-29**

The next step is to write the user-defined functions to determine the item selected from the option list and display the price in the text box.

## Entering the User-Defined Functions for the onchange Event Handler

The user-defined functions called by the onchange event handlers, display the price for the item selected in the option list. Each function performs the following steps: (1) defines an array for the prices; (2) clears the text boxes; (3) uses the selectedIndex property to set the subscript variable; and (4) sets the price to the price text box. Table 3-15 provides the code for the setPicnicPrice() function.

**Table 3-15**

| LINE | CODE |
|------|------|
| 73 | `picPrices = new Array("None Selected", "Please Call", "$10.95 per person", "$10.95 per person", "$11.95 per person", "$13.95 per person")` |
| 74 | `function setPicnicPrice(myForm) {` |
| 75 | `document.PicnicPrice.Price.value = ""` |
| 76 | `document.PicnicQuantity.PicExtPrice.value = ""` |
| 77 | `document.PicnicQuantity.PicQty.value = ""` |
| 78 | `var itemSelect = myForm.PicnicItem.selectedIndex;` |
| 79 | `switch (itemSelect) {` |
| 80 | `case 1 :` |
| 81 | `document.PicnicPrice.Price.value = picPrices[itemSelect]` |
| 82 | `break` |
| 83 | `case 2 :` |
| 84 | `document.PicnicPrice.Price.value = picPrices[itemSelect]` |
| 85 | `break;` |
| 86 | `case 3 :` |
| 87 | `document.PicnicPrice.Price.value = picPrices[itemSelect]` |
| 88 | `break;` |
| 89 | `case 4 :` |
| 90 | `document.PicnicPrice.Price.value = picPrices[itemSelect]` |
| 91 | `break` |
| 92 | `case 5 :` |
| 93 | `document.PicnicPrice.Price.value = picPrices[itemSelect]` |
| 94 | `}` |
| 95 | `document.PicnicQuantity.PicQty.focus()` |
| 96 | `}` |

Line 73 defines the price array. The first item, None Selected, fills the zero element location, which is never used. Lines 75 through 77 clear out the text boxes each time the user selects a new item in the drop-down list. Lines 79 through 91 contain the JavaScript Switch statement. Line 78 shows the assignment of the index value from the selectedIndex property to the variable itemSelect. The index starts numbering the items in the list at zero. In the setPicnicPrice function, if the user selects the 2 Meats 2 Sides 1 Beverage choice, then the itemSelect value is 2 (Case Condition statement on line 83). The index value assigned to itemSelect becomes the subscript in lines 81, 84, 87, 90, and 93. These statements assign the corresponding price to the text box. Line 95 sets the focus to the number of guests text box to allow the user to enter the number of guests. To enter the function that assigns the picnic prices from the picnic menu to the text box, perform the steps on the next page.

## To Enter the Function to Assign the Prices for Picnics

**1** **Position the insertion point on line 73.**

**2** **Enter the JavaScript code shown in Table 3-15.**

*The setPicnicPrice() function displays (Figure 3-30).*

```
                 mwcatering.htm - Notepad
File   Edit   Search   Help
          Function onWedding() {
              document.Image1.src = "catering6.jpg"
              document.Image2.src = "catering7.jpg"
          }

line 73  → picPrices = new Array("None Selected", "Please Call", "$10.95 per person", "$10.95 per
         person", "$11.95 per person", "$13.95 per person")
          function setPicnicPrice(myForm) {
              document.PicnicPrice.Price.value = ""                    ← clear text
              document.PicnicQuantity.PicExtPrice.value = ""             boxes
              document.PicnicQuantity.PicQty.value = ""
              var itemSelect = myForm.PicnicItem.selectedIndex;
              switch (itemSelect) {
                  case 1 :
                      document.PicnicPrice.Price.value = picPrices[itemSelect]
                      break
                  case 2 :
                      document.PicnicPrice.Price.value = picPrices[itemSelect]
                      break;
                  case 3 :                                              ← assign price
                      document.PicnicPrice.Price.value = picPrices[itemSelect]   to text box
                      break;
                  case 4 :
                      document.PicnicPrice.Price.value = picPrices[itemSelect]
                      break
                  case 5 :
                      document.PicnicPrice.Price.value = picPrices[itemSelect]
              }
              document.PicnicQuantity.PicQty.focus()                   ← set focus to Enter
          }                                                              number of guests
                                                                         text box
//-->
</SCRIPT>
</HEAD>
```

line wraps as code is entered

**FIGURE 3-30**

The user-defined function for dinner party prices is similar to the picnic function as shown in Table 3-16. The Switch statement tests the selected item and assigns the price to the price text box (document.DinnerPrice.Price.value) and the focus is set to the Enter number of guests text box.

**Table 3-16**

| LINE | CODE |
|------|------|
| 99 | dinnerPrices = new Array("None Selected", "$13.95 per person", "$16.95 per person", "$18.95 per person", "$12.95 per person", "$12.95 per person") |
| 100 | function setDinnerPrice(myForm) { |
| 101 |     document.DinnerPrice.Price.value = "" |
| 102 |     document.DinnerQuantity.DinExtPrice.value = "" |
| 103 |     document.DinnerQuantity.DinQty.value = "" |
| 104 |     var itemSelect = myForm.DinnerItem.selectedIndex; |
| 105 |     switch (itemSelect) { |
| 106 |         case 1 : |
| 107 |             document.DinnerPrice.Price.value = dinnerPrices[itemSelect] |
| 108 |             break |
| 109 |         case 2 : |
| 110 |             document.DinnerPrice.Price.value = dinnerPrices[itemSelect] |
| 111 |             break |
| 112 |         case 3 : |
| 113 |             document.DinnerPrice.Price.value = dinnerPrices[itemSelect] |
| 114 |             break |
| 115 |         case 4 : |
| 116 |             document.DinnerPrice.Price.value = dinnerPrices[itemSelect] |
| 117 |             break |
| 118 |         case 5 : |
| 119 |             document.DinnerPrice.Price.value = dinnerPrices[itemSelect] |
| 120 |             break |
| 121 |     } |
| 122 |     document.DinnerQuantity.DinQty.focus() |
| 123 | } |

Line 99 defines and fills the dinnerPrices array. The None Selected value fills the zero element in the array. Lines 101 through 103 clear the text boxes each time the function is called. The selectedIndex property (line 104) determines the item selected. Lines 105 through 120 set the corresponding price from the array to the text box. Line 122 sets the focus to the Enter number of guests text box to allow the user to enter the number of guests. To enter the function that assigns the prices for the dinner parties menu to the price text box, perform the steps on the next page.

**Steps** **To Enter the Function to Assign the Prices for Dinner Parties**

**1** **Position the insertion point on line 99.**

**2** **Enter the JavaScript code shown in Table 3-16.**

*The setDinnerPrice() function displays (Figure 3-31).*

line 99

```
                  case 5 :
                        document.PicnicPrice.Price.value = picPrices[itemSelect]
            }
            document.PicnicQuantity.PicQty.focus()
      }

dinnerPrices = new Array("None Selected", "$13.95 per person", "$16.95 per person", "$18.95
per person", "$12.95 per person", "$12.95 per person")
      function setDinnerPrice(myForm) {
            document.DinnerPrice.Price.value = ""
            document.DinnerQuantity.DinExtPrice.value = ""
            document.DinnerQuantity.DinQty.value = ""
            var itemSelect = myForm.DinnerItem.selectedIndex;
            switch (itemSelect) {
                  case 1 :
                        document.DinnerPrice.Price.value = dinnerPrices[itemSelect]
                        break
                  case 2 :
                        document.DinnerPrice.Price.value = dinnerPrices[itemSelect]
                        break
                  case 3 :
                        document.DinnerPrice.Price.value = dinnerPrices[itemSelect]
                        break
                  case 4 :
                        document.DinnerPrice.Price.value = dinnerPrices[itemSelect]
                        break
                  case 5 :
                        document.DinnerPrice.Price.value = dinnerPrices[itemSelect]
                        break
            }
            document.DinnerQuantity.DinQty.focus()
      }

//-->
```

*line wraps as code is entered*

*clear text boxes*

*assign price to text box*

*set focus to Enter number of guests text box*

mwcatering.htm - Notepad | File Edit Search Help

Start | mwcatering.htm - Not... | Midwest Catering Service -... | 9:16 AM

**FIGURE 3-31**

The third function required is for the wedding prices (Table 3-17). The process for setting wedding prices is identical to the process for setting picnic and dinner party functions.

**Table 3-17**

| LINE | CODE |
|------|------|
| 125 | weddingPrices = new Array("None Selected", "$13.95 per person", $16.95 per person , $18.95 per person", "$28.95 per person") |
| 126 | function setWeddingPrice(myForm) { |
| 127 | document.WeddingPrice.Price.value = "" |
| 128 | document.WeddingQuantity.WedExtPrice.value = "" |
| 129 | document.WeddingQuantity.WedQty.value = "" |
| 130 | var itemSelect = myForm.WeddingItem.selectedIndex; |
| 131 | switch (itemSelect) { |
| 132 | case 1 : |
| 133 | document.WeddingPrice.Price.value = weddingPrices[itemSelect] |
| 134 | break |
| 135 | case 2 : |
| 136 | document.WeddingPrice.Price.value = weddingPrices[itemSelect] |
| 137 | break |
| 138 | case 3 : |
| 139 | document.WeddingPrice.Price.value = weddingPrices[itemSelect] |
| 140 | break |
| 141 | case 4 : |
| 142 | document.WeddingPrice.Price.value = weddingPrices[itemSelect] |
| 143 | break |
| 144 | } |
| 145 | document.WeddingQuantity.WedQty.focus() |
| 146 | } |

To enter the function to assign the prices for wedding receptions, perform the following steps.

## To Enter the Function to Assign the Prices for Weddings

**1** **Position the insertion point on line 125.**

**2** **Enter the JavaScript code shown in Table 3-17.**

*The setWeddingPrice() function displays (Figure 3-32).*

```
                    }
        document.DinnerQuantity.DinQty.focus()
    }

weddingPrices = new Array("None Selected", "$13.95 per person", "$16.95 per person", "$18.95
per person", "$28.95 per person")
    function setWeddingPrice(myForm) {
        document.WeddingPrice.Price.value = ""
        document.WeddingQuantity.WedExtPrice.value = ""
        document.WeddingQuantity.WedQty.value = ""
        var itemSelect = myForm.WeddingItem.selectedIndex;
        switch (itemSelect) {
            case 1 :
                document.WeddingPrice.Price.value = weddingPrices[itemSelect]
                break
            case 2 :
                document.WeddingPrice.Price.value = weddingPrices[itemSelect]
                break
            case 3 :
                document.WeddingPrice.Price.value = weddingPrices[itemSelect]
                break
            case 4 :
                document.WeddingPrice.Price.value = weddingPrices[itemSelect]
                break
        }
        document.WeddingQuantity.WedQty.focus()
    }
```

*mwcatering.htm - Notepad*
File   Edit   Search   Help

line 125

clear text boxes

line wraps as code is entered

assign price to text box

set focus to Enter number of guests text box

**FIGURE 3-32**

The function for each category displays the price per person and positions the insertion point in the Enter number of guests text box. The next section calculates the extended price based on the number of guests entered.

# Calculating the Extended Price Function

The instructions on the Web page, as shown in Figure 3-33 for the Picnic category, instruct the user to enter a number in the Enter number of guests text box and then press the TAB key.

**FIGURE 3-33**

When the user enters a number and presses the TAB key, the value of the Enter number of guests text box changes. This action triggers the onchange event handler and calls the appropriate function to calculate the extended price. Because each food service category has its own form and menu of prices, you cannot write a general-purpose function to calculate the prices.

The names of the three functions that calculate the extended price are picPrice(), dinPrice(), and wedPrice(). To call the functions that calculate the extended prices using the onchange event handler, perform the following steps.

**Steps** ## To Call the Functions that Calculate the Extended Prices Using the onchange Event Handler

**1** **Position the insertion point on line 221, immediately before the >.**

**2** **Press the SPACEBAR once. Type**
onchange="picPrice (PicnicQuantity)" **and do not press the ENTER key.**

*Figure 3-34 displays the placement of the onchange event handler to call the picPrice function.*

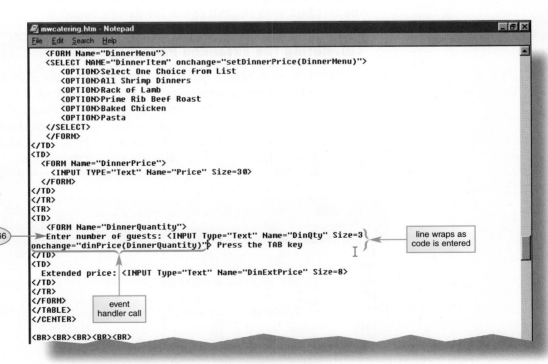

```
<TR>
  <TD>
  <FORM Name="PicnicMenu">
    <SELECT NAME="PicnicItem" onchange="setPicnicPrice(PicnicMenu)">
      <OPTION>Select One Choice from List
      <OPTION>Call for special meals
      <OPTION>2 Meats 2 Sides 1 Beverage
      <OPTION>3 Meats 2 Sides 2 Beverages
      <OPTION>3 Meats 3 Sides 2 Beverages
      <OPTION>3 Meats 4 Sides 2 Beverages
    </SELECT>
  </FORM>
</TD>
  <TD>
  <FORM Name="PicnicPrice">
    <INPUT Type="Text" Name="Price" Size=30>
  </FORM>
</TD>
</TR>
<TR>
  <TD>
  <FORM Name="PicnicQuantity">
    Enter number of guests: <INPUT Type="Text" Name="PicQty" Size=3
onchange="picPrice(PicnicQuantity)"> Press the TAB key
</TD>
<TD>
Extended price: <INPUT Type="Text" Name="PicExtPrice" Size=8>
</TD>
</TR>
</FORM>
</TABLE>
</CENTER>
</P>
<BR><BR>
<P ALIGN="CENTER"><BR>
```

line 221 → (pointing to the FORM Name="PicnicQuantity" area)

line wraps as code is entered

event handler call

**FIGURE 3-34**

**3** **Position the insertion point on line 266, immediately before the >.**

**4** **Press the SPACEBAR once. Type**
onchange="dinPrice (DinnerQuantity)" **and do not press the ENTER key.**

*Figure 3-35 displays the placement of the onchange event handler to call the dinPrice function.*

```
  <FORM Name="DinnerMenu">
  <SELECT NAME="DinnerItem" onchange="setDinnerPrice(DinnerMenu)">
    <OPTION>Select One Choice from List
    <OPTION>All Shrimp Dinners
    <OPTION>Rack of Lamb
    <OPTION>Prime Rib Beef Roast
    <OPTION>Baked Chicken
    <OPTION>Pasta
  </SELECT>
  </FORM>
</TD>
<TD>
  <FORM Name="DinnerPrice">
    <INPUT TYPE="Text" Name="Price" Size=30>
  </FORM>
</TD>
</TR>
<TR>
  <TD>
  <FORM Name="DinnerQuantity">
    Enter number of guests: <INPUT Type="Text" Name="DinQty" Size=3
onchange="dinPrice(DinnerQuantity)"> Press the TAB key
</TD>
<TD>
  Extended price: <INPUT Type="Text" Name="DinExtPrice" Size=8>
</TD>
</TR>
</FORM>
</TABLE>
</CENTER>

<BR><BR><BR><BR><BR>
```

line 266 → (pointing to the FORM Name="DinnerQuantity" area)

line wraps as code is entered

event handler call

**FIGURE 3-35**

**5** Position the insertion point on line 314, immediately before the >.

**6** Press the SPACEBAR once. Type onchange="wedPrice (WeddingQuantity)" and do not press the ENTER key.

*Figure 3-36 displays the placement of the onchange event handler to call the wedPrice function.*

```
<FORM Name="WeddingMenu">
  <SELECT NAME="WeddingItem" onchange="setWeddingPrice(WeddingMenu)">
     <OPTION>Select One Choice from List
     <OPTION>Traditional Sit Down
     <OPTION>Grilled Seafood or Steak
     <OPTION>Pasta Platter
     <OPTION>Exquisite Gourmet Dinners
  </SELECT>
  </FORM>
</TD>
<TD>
  <FORM Name="WeddingPrice">
     <INPUT Type="Text" Name="Price" Size=30>
  </FORM>
</TD>
</TR>
<TR>
  <TD>
     <FORM Name="WeddingQuantity">
     Enter number of guests: <INPUT Type="Text" NAME="WedQty" Size=3
onchange="wedPrice(WeddingQuantity)"> Press the TAB key
     </TD>
<TD>
     Extended price: <INPUT Type="Text" Name="WedExtPrice" Size=8>
</TD>
</TR>
</FORM>
</TABLE>
</CENTER>

<BR>
<P ALIGN="CENTER">
<A HREF="#TOP">Top of Page</A></p>
<P><HR>
<H6 ALIGN="CENTER">For more information, please call us at 1-555-800-FOOD or e-mail us at
```

line 314

line wraps as code is entered

event handler call

**FIGURE 3-36**

The next section describes the JavaScript code for each of the user-defined functions that will calculate the extended price and set the formatted extended price in the text box with the call to the formatting function.

### Calculating the Extended Price

After the user selects an item from the menu, the insertion point automatically is placed in the Enter number of guests text box. For each service category, a function calculates the extended price and displays in a text box. The onchange event handlers just entered call the appropriate functions. When the user presses the TAB key to move out of the Enter number of guests text box, the onchange event handler triggers and calls the function to calculate the extended price.

Table 3-18 provides the code for the picPrice() user-defined function.

**Table 3-18**

| LINE | CODE |
| --- | --- |
| 148 | function picPrice(myForm) { |
| 149 | var picnicQty = myForm.PicQty.value |
| 150 | var EstPrice = picnicQty * document.PicnicPrice.Price.value.substring(1,6) |
| 151 | var EstPrice = new String(EstPrice) |
| 152 | document.PicnicQuantity.PicExtPrice.value = dollarFormat(EstPrice) |
| 153 | } |

Line 150 multiplies the picnicQty, which represents the number of guests, by the per-person price. The substring method extracts the numeric value from the per-person price. On line 151, the result is stored in EstPrice and converted to a string object. This procedure allows the dollarFormat() function to accept the EstPrice value as a string. Line 152 calls the dollarFormat() function. The dollarFormat() function returns the extended price to the text box formatted as currency. To enter the picPrice() function perform the following steps.

 ## To Enter the picPrice() Function

**1** **Position the insertion point on line 148.**

**2** **Enter the JavaScript code shown in Table 3-18.**

*The picPrice() function displays (Figure 3-37).*

```
function setWeddingPrice(myForm) {
    document.WeddingPrice.Price.value = ""
    document.WeddingQuantity.WedExtPrice.value = ""
    document.WeddingQuantity.WedQty.value = ""
    var itemSelect = myForm.WeddingItem.selectedIndex;
    switch (itemSelect) {
        case 1 :
            document.WeddingPrice.Price.value = weddingPrices[itemSelect]
            break
        case 2 :
            document.WeddingPrice.Price.value = weddingPrices[itemSelect]
            break
        case 3 :
            document.WeddingPrice.Price.value = weddingPrices[itemSelect]
            break
        case 4 :
            document.WeddingPrice.Price.value = weddingPrices[itemSelect]
            break
    }
    document.WeddingQuantity.WedQty.focus()
}

function picPrice(myForm) {
    var picnicQty = myForm.PicQty.value
    var EstPrice = picnicQty * document.PicnicPrice.Price.value.substring(1,6)
    var EstPrice = new String(EstPrice)
    document.PicnicQuantity.PicExtPrice.value = dollarFormat(EstPrice)
}

//-->
</SCRIPT>
</HEAD>

<BODY onload="setTimeout('bancycle()',3000)">
```

line 148 →

converts EstPrice to string object

**FIGURE 3-37**

The next step is to write the dinPrice() function shown in Table 3-19. This function uses the same logic and procedures as the picPrice() function.

| Table 3-19 | |
|---|---|
| LINE | CODE |
| 155 | `function dinPrice(myForm) {` |
| 156 | `    var dinnerQty = myForm.DinQty.value` |
| 157 | `    var EstPrice = dinnerQty * document.DinnerPrice.Price.value.substring(1,6)` |
| 158 | `    var EstPrice = new String(EstPrice)` |
| 159 | `    document.DinnerQuantity.DinExtPrice.value = dollarFormat(EstPrice)` |
| 160 | `}` |

To enter the dinPrice() function, perform the following steps.

 **To Enter the dinPrice() Function**

**1** **Position the insertion point on line 155.**

**2** **Enter the JavaScript code shown in Table 3-19.**

*The dinPrice() function displays (Figure 3-38).*

```
mwcatering.htm - Notepad
File  Edit  Search  Help
        switch (itemSelect) {
            case 1 :
                document.WeddingPrice.Price.value = weddingPrices[itemSelect]
                break
            case 2 :
                document.WeddingPrice.Price.value = weddingPrices[itemSelect]
                break
            case 3 :
                document.WeddingPrice.Price.value = weddingPrices[itemSelect]
                break
            case 4 :
                document.WeddingPrice.Price.value = weddingPrices[itemSelect]
                break
        }
        document.WeddingQuantity.WedQty.focus()
    }

    function picPrice(myForm) {
        var picnicQty =  myForm.PicQty.value
        var EstPrice = picnicQty * document.PicnicPrice.Price.value.substring(1,6)
        var EstPrice = new String(EstPrice)
        document.PicnicQuantity.PicExtPrice.value = dollarFormat(EstPrice)
    }

    function dinPrice(myForm) {
        var dinnerQty = myForm.DinQty.value
        var EstPrice = dinnerQty * document.DinnerPrice.Price.value.substring(1,6)
        var EstPrice = new String(EstPrice)
        document.DinnerQuantity.DinExtPrice.value = dollarFormat(EstPrice)
    }

//-->
</SCRIPT>
</HEAD>
Start        mwcatering.htm - Not...    Midwest Catering Service -        9:23 AM
```

line 155

**FIGURE 3-38**

The next step is to write the wedPrice() function. Table 3-20 shows the wedPrice() function, and it uses the same logic and procedures as the previous functions.

| Table 3-20 | |
| --- | --- |
| *LINE* | *CODE* |
| 162 | `function wedPrice(myForm) {` |
| 163 | `    var weddingQty =  myForm.WedQty.value` |
| 164 | `    var EstPrice = weddingQty * document.WeddingPrice.Price.value.substring(1,6)` |
| 165 | `    var EstPrice = new String(EstPrice)` |
| 166 | `    document.WeddingQuantity.WedExtPrice.value = dollarFormat(EstPrice)` |
| 167 | `}` |

To enter the wedPrice() function, perform the following steps.

 **To Enter the wedPrice() Function**

**1** **Position the insertion point on line 162.**

**2** **Enter the JavaScript code shown in Table 3-20.**

*The wedPrice() function displays (Figure 3-39).*

```
case 4 :
        document.WeddingPrice.Price.value = weddingPrices[itemSelect]
        break
    }
    document.WeddingQuantity.WedQty.focus()
}

function picPrice(myForm) {
    var picnicQty =  myForm.PicQty.value
    var EstPrice = picnicQty * document.PicnicPrice.Price.value.substring(1,6)
    var EstPrice = new String(EstPrice)
    document.PicnicQuantity.PicExtPrice.value = dollarFormat(EstPrice)
}

function dinPrice(myForm) {
    var dinnerQty = myForm.DinQty.value
    var EstPrice = dinnerQty * document.DinnerPrice.Price.value.substring(1,6)
    var EstPrice = new String(EstPrice)
    document.DinnerQuantity.DinExtPrice.value = dollarFormat(EstPrice)
}

function wedPrice(myForm) {                    ← line 162
    var weddingQty =  myForm.WedQty.value
    var EstPrice = weddingQty * document.WeddingPrice.Price.value.substring(1,6)
    var EstPrice = new String(EstPrice)
    document.WeddingQuantity.WedExtPrice.value = dollarFormat(EstPrice)
}

//-->
</SCRIPT>
</HEAD>

<BODY onload="setTimeout('bancycle()',3000)">

<A NAME="MCS_TOP">
```

**FIGURE 3-39**

The wedPrice() function completes the three functions that display the extended cost. Each function makes a call to the dollarFormat() function.

# The dollarFormat Function

Recall from Project 2 that the dollarFormat() function performs seven basic steps: (1) takes the string value passed to it and separates the dollars from the cents based on the position of the decimal point; (2) using the indexOf() method, determines the location of the decimal point; (3) establishes the value to the left of the decimal point as the dollar amount and the value to the right of the decimal point as the cents; (4) inserts commas in dollar amounts exceeding 999; (5) truncates cents to two decimal positions and not rounded; (6) reconstructs the string value with the commas and decimal values and inserts a dollar sign at the beginning; and (7) returns the completed formatted value. Table 3-21 on the next page provides the code for the dollarFormat() function.

**Table 3-21**

| LINE | CODE |
|------|------|

```
169      function dollarFormat(valuein) {
170          var formatStr = ""
171          var decipos = valuein.indexOf(".")
172          if (decipos = = -1)
173              decipos = valuein.length
174          var dollars = valuein.substring(0,decipos)
175          var Outdollars = ""
176          var dollen = dollars.length
177          if (dollen > 3) {
178              while (dollen > 0) {
179                  tDollars = dollars.substring(dollen-3, dollen)
180                      if (tDollars.length = = 3) {
181                              Outdollars = ","+tDollars+Outdollars
182                              dollen = dollen-3;
183                      } else {
184                              Outdollars = tDollars+Outdollars
185                              dollen = 0
186                      }
187              }
188              if (Outdollars.substring(0, 1) = = ",")
189                      dollars = Outdollars.substring(1, Outdollars.length)
190              else
191                      dollars = Outdollars
192          }
193          var cents = valuein.substring(decipos+1, decipos+3)
194          if (cents = = "")
195              cents = "00"
196          if (cents.length = = 1)
197              cents = cents+"0"
198          var formatStr = "$"+dollars+"."+cents
199          return formatStr
200      }
```

To enter the dollarFormat() function, perform the following steps.

**Steps** To Enter the dollarFormat() Function

**1** **Position the insertion point on line 169.**

line 169

**2** **Enter the JavaScript code shown in Table 3-21.**

The dollarFormat() function displays (Figure 3-40).

```
mwcatering.htm - Notepad
File  Edit  Search  Help
Function dollarFormat(valuein) {
        var formatStr = ""
        var decipos = valuein.indexOf(".")
        if (decipos == -1)
                decipos = valuein.length
        var dollars = valuein.substring(0,decipos)
        var Outdollars = ""
        var dollen = dollars.length
        if (dollen > 3) {
            while (dollen > 0) {
                    tDollars = dollars.substring(dollen-3, dollen)
                            if (tDollars.length == 3) {
                                    Outdollars = ","+tDollars+Outdollars
                                    dollen = dollen-3;
                            } else {
                                    Outdollars = tDollars+Outdollars
                                    dollen=0
                            }
            }
                    if (Outdollars.substring(0, 1) == ",")
                            dollars = Outdollars.substring(1, Outdollars.length)
                    else
                            dollars = Outdollars
        }
        var cents = valuein.substring(decipos+1, decipos+3)
        if (cents == "")
            cents = "00"
        if (cents.length == 1)
            cents = cents+"0"
        var formatStr = "$"+dollars+"."+cents
        return formatStr
    }

//-->
</SCRIPT>
```

Start | mwcatering.htm - Not... | Midwest Catering Service -... | 9:25 AM

**FIGURE 3-40**

The Web page now is complete. The next step is to save the Web page and test the JavaScript code in the browser. The data you must enter to test the Web page is provided in Table 3-22.

| Table 3-22 | | | | |
| --- | --- | --- | --- | --- |
| CATEGORY | SELECTION | PRICE | GUESTS | EXTENDED PRICE |
| Dinner Parties | Rack of Lamb | 16.95 | 15 | 254.25 |
| Weddings | Traditional Sit Down | 13.95 | 250 | 3,487.50 |
| Dinner Parties | Pasta | 12.95 | 10 | 129.50 |
| Picnics | 3 Meats 3 Sides 2 Beverages | 11.95 | 30 | 358.50 |

Perform the steps on the next page to save and test the Web page.

## TO SAVE AND TEST THE WEB PAGE

**(1)** With the JavaScript Data Disk in drive A, click File on the menu bar and then Save.

**(2)** Click the browser button on the taskbar and then click the Refresh button on the toolbar.

**(3)** Enter the data shown in Table 3-22 on the previous page by clicking the link name under the category column. Select the meal type in the Selection column. Enter the number of guests in the Guests column. Click the Top of Page link to try the next category.

*Figure 3-41 shows the test data results for the Picnics category. (Due to floating point math differences in some CPUs and browsers, your extended price may vary by one cent.)*

**FIGURE 3-41**

If the browser does not display the Web page correctly, close any error message dialog boxes, and click the Notepad button on the taskbar. Check the JavaScript code according to Figures 3-27 through 3-40 on pages J 3.31 through J 3.45. Correct any errors, save the file, activate the browser, and then click the Refresh button. The next step is to print the HTML file.

### Printing the HTML Notepad File

After you have completed and tested the Web page, you may want to print it. Print the HTML file with Notepad. To print the mwcatering.htm Notepad file, perform the following step.

## TO PRINT THE NOTEPAD FILE

 Make sure the Notepad window is active. Click File on the menu bar and then click Print.

*A Notepad Print dialog box displays briefly with a message that indicates the file is being printed and informs you that to cancel printing, click the Cancel button. The dialog box closes after the file has been sent to the printer.*

# Project Summary

The Web page you created in this project is the home page for Midwest Catering. The Web page presents a rolling banner that acts as an additional advertisement. A greeting either displays a generic message, or indicates the number of days to one of four specific holidays: St. Patrick's Day, Independence Day, Halloween, and Christmas.

The main body has a link to each of the food service categories. When the user drags the mouse over a category link, the images on both sides of the category link change to reflect the type of entrée offered. Each food service category has a detailed explanation about the category. Each category has a form that allows users to obtain a cost estimate. To receive an estimate, the user selects a choice from a select drop-down list and enters the number of guests.

In creating this project, you learned how to create a rolling banner using the Array object. You learned more about the Date() object and the getTime() and getMonth() methods to construct a message that displays the number of days until a specific holiday. You learned the math ceil() method to round a number to the highest integer when calculating the number of days to a given date.

You learned how to use the onmouseover event handler to change images. You learned how to use the selectedIndex property to determine which item in an option list was selected. You used an array to store price data and associated that data with items in the option list. Finally, you learned how to pass form values to calculate and display an extended price formatted as currency.

# What You Should Know

Having completed this project, you now should be able to perform the following tasks.

▶ Call the Functions Using the onchange Event Handler *(J 3.23, J 3.31)*

▶ Call the Functions that Calculate the Extended Prices Using the onchange Event Handler *(J 3.39)*

▶ Call the Functions Using the onmouseover Event Handler *(J 3.23)*

▶ Create the Location for the Image Object *(J 3.8)*

▶ Enter a Function to Create a Rolling Banner *(J 3.11)*

▶ Enter the Function to Assign the Prices for Picnics *(J 3.34)*

▶ Enter the Function to Assign the Prices for Dinner Parties *(J 3.36)*

▶ Enter the Function to Assign the Prices for Weddings *(J 3.37)*

▶ Enter the onload Event Handler to Call a Function *(J 3.12)*

▶ Enter the HolidayDays() User-Defined Function Steps for St. Patrick's Day *(J 3.17)*

▶ Enter the HolidayDays() User-Defined Function Steps for Independence Day *(J 3.18)*

▶ Enter the HolidayDays() User-Defined Function Steps for Halloween *(J 3.19)*

▶ Enter the HolidayDays() User-Defined Function Steps for Christmas *(J 3.20)*

▶ Enter a Function Call and Display a Message *(J 3.21)*

▶ Enter the onPicnic() Function *(J 3.26)*

▶ Enter the onDinnerParty() Function *(J 3.27)*

▶ Enter the onWedding() Function *(J 3.27)*

▶ Enter the picPrice() Function *(J 3.41)*

▶ Enter the dinPrice() Function *(J 3.42)*

▶ Enter the wedPrice() Function *(J 3.43)*

▶ Enter the dollarFormat() Function *(J 3.45)*

▶ Print the Notepad File *(J 3.47)*

▶ Save and Test the Web Page *(J 3.28, J 3.46)*

▶ Save the HTML File and Test the Web Page *(J 3.22)*

▶ Start Notepad and Open the HTML File *(J 3.7)*

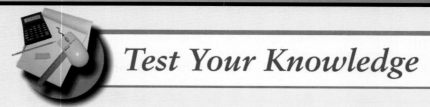

# *Test Your Knowledge*

## 1 True/False

**Instructions:** Circle T if the statement is true or F if the statement is false.

T  F    1. A rolling banner is a single graphic image created from several individual graphic image files.
T  F    2. An array is a collection of data items represented by one variable name.
T  F    3. A subscript is a number that designates an individual item or occurrence in an array.
T  F    4. The getMonth() method returns the name of the month from the current system date.
T  F    5. It is not possible to set a new date with the Date() object.
T  F    6. The getTime() method returns the current time from the current system date.
T  F    7. The Switch statement is another way of performing nested If...Else statements.
T  F    8. The onmouseover event handler triggers the JavaScript code assigned to it when the user drags the mouse over the object associated with the event handler.
T  F    9. The only disadvantage of the onmouseover event handler is that you must press the right mouse button for it to work.
T  F   10. The selectedIndex is a string method that returns the actual data in a select list object.

## 2 Multiple Choice

**Instructions:** Circle the correct response.

1. To create an image object, you use the _____ attribute in the IMG SRC tag.
   a. Object
   b. Location
   c. Name
   d. Width

2. A(n) _____ is a collection of data items referenced by one variable name.
   a. subscript
   b. banner
   c. array
   d. object

3. The value that indicates which element in an array you are referencing is called a(n) _____.
   a. superscript
   b. subscript
   c. array
   d. object

4. The _____ object can return either the current system date or be used to set a different date.
   a. Time
   b. System
   c. Date
   d. Array

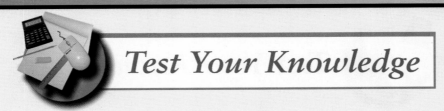

## Test Your Knowledge

5. The getMonth() method returns the _____ the current month.
   a. name of
   b. number of days left in
   c. number of days in
   d. numerical equivalent of
6. The getTime() method returns the _____ since January 1, 1970.
   a. milliseconds
   b. microseconds
   c. number of days
   d. number of hours
7. In the JavaScript Switch statement, the Case statement is used to _____.
   a. execute the first statement outside of the Switch statement
   b. compare the value given to the expression stated in the Switch statement
   c. indicate the default statements to be executed
   d. terminate the Switch statement
8. Which of the following mouse event handlers triggers the JavaScript code when the user presses the mouse button?
   a. onmouseover
   b. onmouseup
   c. onmousemove
   d. onmousedown
9. Which of the following event handlers triggers the JavaScript code when the value in a text box or select list is altered?
   a. onload
   b. onfocus
   c. onclick
   d. onchange
10. Which JavaScript property of the form object is used to identify the item that is selected in a select list?
    a. value
    b. selectedIndex
    c. <Option>
    d. <Select>

## 3 Understanding JavaScript Code Statements

**Instructions:** Carefully read each of the following descriptions of writing code statements to accomplish specific tasks. Record your answers on a separate sheet of paper. Number your answers to correspond to the code descriptions.

1. Write a JavaScript statement that assigns the values "Freshman", "Sophomore", "Junior", "Senior" to an Array object instance called ClassStanding.

*(continued)*

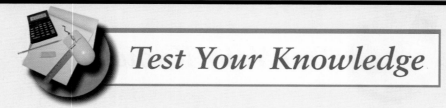

# Test Your Knowledge

### Understanding JavaScript Code Statements *(continued)*

2. Write a JavaScript statement that assigns the fifth element of an array called Course to an object named document.Schedule.Class.value.

3. Write a JavaScript statement that sets the date June 19, 2001 to an object instance named Anniversary.

4. Write a JavaScript statement that subtracts the current date from Anniversary and stores the result in AnnivReminder.

5. Using the variable AnnivReminder, write the JavaScript statements that test AnnivReminder for a result greater than zero. If the result is greater than zero, convert the milliseconds into the number of days.

6. Write a JavaScript statement that assigns the index value of an item selected from a list to a variable named itemNum. The form name is CategoryList and the select list name is Category.

## *4* Using onmouseover, onmouseout, onmousedown, and onmouseup to Simulate Animation

**Instructions:** Start your browser. Start Notepad. Maximize the Notepad window. Open the HTML file, mouse.htm, on the JavaScript Data Disk. The page has two images placed to the left and right of three lines of instructions (Figure 3-42). These images change through use of the mouse event handlers as explained in the instructions on the Web page. Enter the JavaScript code to change the images by performing the following tasks.

**FIGURE 3-42**

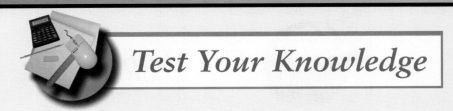

## Test Your Knowledge

1. Enter the mouse event handlers to call the functions. Position the insertion point between the Name= "Location1" and Width="75" attributes in the IMAGE tag on line 21.
2. Type `onmouseover="chngColor1()" onmouseout="chngColor2()"` and do not press the ENTER key.
3. Move to the next IMAGE tag. Position the insertion point between the Name="Location2" and Width="75" attributes.
4. Type `onmousedown="pressDown()" onmouseup="Release()"` and do not press the ENTER key.
5. Position the insertion point in the SCRIPT section on the blank line (line 7). Enter the following code to create the functions called in steps 2 and 4.

```
function chngColor1() {
        document.Location1.src = "redbox.jpg"
}


function chngColor2() {
        document.Location1.src = "bluebox.jpg"
}


function pressDown() {
        document.Location2.src = "redbutton2.jpg"
}


function Release() {
        document.Location2.src = "redbutton1.jpg"
}
```

6. Save the file using the file name, mousesolution.htm, on the JavaScript Data Disk in drive A.
7. Start your browser. Open the file, a:\mousesolution.htm, in the browser. Follow the instructions on the Web page. If you have any errors, activate Notepad and check steps 2 through 7.
8. Save the Notepad file, activate your browser, and then click the Refresh button on the toolbar.
9. If no errors, print the Web page and return to Notepad to print the HTML file. Hand in the printouts to your instructor.

*Use Help*

# 1 Exploring Online Documentation

**Instructions:** Start your browser and then type www.scsite.com/js/p3.htm in the Location text box. Click the link, Project 3 Use Help 1. Click Chapter 11, Predefined Core Objects and Functions. Complete the following tasks.

Read the Web page to find the answers to the following questions.

1. What are the predefined core objects?
2. What is an array?
3. What is the difference between defining an array in Navigator 2.0 and Navigator 3.0?
4. Describe the following Array object properties.
   a. concat
   b. pop
   c. push
   d. reverse
   e. sort
5. Describe how to refer to an array's elements and provide two examples. Scroll down to locate the Date object. Answer the following questions.
   a. Name the Date object properties.
   b. What is the limitation placed on prior dates?
   c. Describe the purpose of using parameters in the Date object and provide two examples.
   d. What are the general categories of the Date object's methods and what is their purpose?
6. Hand in the answers to your instructor.

# 2 Exploring Links to Other JavaScript Sites

**Instructions:** Start your browser and then type www.scsite.com/js/p3.htm in the Location text box. Click the link, Project 3 Use Help 2. Complete the following tasks.

1. Click Web Development. Read about Web development. Print the Web page.
2. Click the image link. Read about Image flipping or banners. Print the Web page.
3. Click the image rollovers link. Read the tutorial about image rollovers. Print the first page.
4. Click the date and time link. Read the about Time & Date. Print the first page.
5. Click the arrays and loops link. Read about arrays and loops. Print the first page.
6. Click the image changing link. Read how to accomplish image changing and cause a button to look repressed with onmousedown and up. Print the Web page.
7. Click the format link. Read how to add extra zeroes at the end of 2.2 to get 2.20 for an answer. Print the Web page.
8. Hand in the printouts to your instructor.

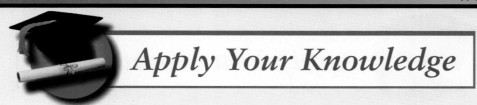

# *Apply Your Knowledge*

## *1* Using the onmouseover Event Handlers to Change Images

**Instructions:** Start Notepad. Open the Web page, travel.htm, on the JavaScript Data Disk. The High Flyers Travel agency Web page displays an image of a ship to the left of three vacation links, and a jet airliner to the right of the vacation links (Figure 3-43). Write three functions, called by onmouseover event handlers, that change the two images when the user moves the mouse pointer over each of the links. The names of the image objects are Image1 and Image2. To change the images, complete the following tasks.

**FIGURE 3-43**

1. Enter the onmouseover event handler to change the images for the Weekend Deals link.
   a. Locate the <A HREF="#Weekend"> link in the travel.htm file.
   b. Position the insertion point between the last " and >.
   c. Enter `onmouseover="Weekend()"` as the code.
2. Enter the onmouseover event handler to change the images for the Summer Vacations link.
   a. Locate the <A HREF="#Summer"> link in the travel.htm file.
   b. Position the insertion point between the last " and >.
   c. Enter `onmouseover="Summer()"` as the code.

*(continued)*

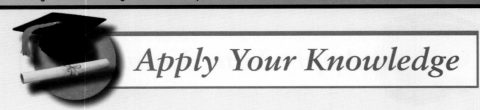

## Apply Your Knowledge

### Using the onmouseover Event Handlers to Change Images *(continued)*

3. Enter the onmouseover event handler to change the images for the Winter Vacations link.
   a. Locate the <A HREF="#Winter"> link in the travel.htm file.
   b. Position the insertion point between the last " and >.
   c. Enter onmouseover="Winter()" as the code.
4. Move to the HEAD section to insert a SCRIPT section. (*Hint:* do not forget the SCRIPT tags.)
5. Position the insertion point on line 4 and then enter the following code for the Weekend() function:

```
function Weekend() {
        document.Image1.src = "Sanfran.jpg"
        document.Image2.src = "Vegas.jpg"
}
```

6. Using the function in step 5 as a model, write the Summer() function. Assign summer1.jpg to Image1.src, and summer2.jpg to Image2.src.
7. Using the function in step 5 as a model, write the Winter() function. Assign winter1.jpg to Image1.src and winter2.jpg to Image2.src.
8. Save the HTML file using the file name, travelsolution.htm, on the JavaScript Data Disk in drive A.
9. Start your browser. Open the file a:\travelsolution.htm to test the JavaScript code. Move the mouse pointer over the Weekend Deals link and stop. If no errors occur, move the mouse pointer over the Summer Vacations link and stop. If no errors occur, move the mouse pointer over the Winter Vacations link. If any errors occur, double-check steps 1 through 7 and then save and test again.
10. Print the Web page and the HTML file. Hand in the printouts to your instructor.

# In the Lab

## 1 Using the Arrays Selection List Prices to Calculate a Total Price

**Problem:** As a Computer Science major, you are employed part-time at Campus Computers. While talking with the owner, Jermaine Wilson, you discuss your skills at developing Web pages. Jermaine would like a Web page that advertises his semester specials (Figure 3-44). He wants to display the basic computer specifications, then offer a few select upgrade options. Jermaine wants the user options to display in selection lists. The user clicks a Price button to display the total cost of the new computer.

**FIGURE 3-44**

**Instructions:** Start your browser and Notepad. Using Notepad, open the computer.htm file on the JavaScript Data Disk. Perform the following tasks.

1. Enter the beginning SCRIPT section in the HEAD section by entering the following code on line 4:

```
<SCRIPT LANGUAGE="JAVASCRIPT">
<!-- Hide from old browsers
```

*(continued)*

*In the Lab*

### Using the Arrays Selection List Prices to Calculate a Total Price *(continued)*

2. Create the arrays to store the prices for the RAM, hard disk, and communication device options. Position the insertion point on line 6 and enter the following lines of code:

```
var Ram = new Array(0, 49, 98, 159)
var Disk = new Array(0, 109, 179, 219, 299)
var Comm = new Array(0, 109, 79, 279)
```

3. Write the function to determine the option prices, using the selectedIndex property for each drop-down list item by entering the following code on line 9:

```
function Calc(myForm) {
   var ramItem = myForm.RAM.selectedIndex
   var diskItem = myForm.HardDrive.selectedIndex
   var commItem = myForm.CommCard.selectedIndex
   var totalPrice = 799+Ram[ramItem]+Disk[diskItem]+Comm[commItem]
   document.XOptions.PiecePrice.value = format(totalPrice)
}
```

4. Be sure to complete the SCRIPT section and the ending SCRIPT tags.
5. To call the Calc() function when the user clicks the Price button, enter `onclick="Calc(Xoptions)"` in the INPUT tag where the Price button appears on line 87.
6. Save the HTML file using the file name, computersolution.htm, on the JavaScript Data Disk in drive A.
7. Activate the browser. Open the file, a:\computersolution.htm, to test the JavaScript code. If any errors occur, double-check steps 1 through 5 and test again. If no errors occur, print the Web page, and return to Notepad to print the HTML file. Hand in the printouts to your instructor.

## 2 Using Arrays to Create a Rolling Banner and Display Prices for a Selection List

**Problem:** You work part-time for your Aunt Jennifer at her floral and garden shop. She recently has signed up with an Internet service provider so she can advertise with a Web page. Because you recently completed a Web design course, she asks you to develop her Web site. She wants customers to see a selection list of different arrangements, and when the user selects an item from the list, the price displays. She also wants a simple rolling banner that continuously displays her floral shop offerings (Figure 3-45). This banner displays in the table cell under the store title.

**FIGURE 3-45**

**Instructions:** Start your browser and Notepad. Using Notepad, open the florist.htm file on the JavaScript Data Disk and perform the following tasks.

1. Place the onload event handler in the BODY tag before the > on line 6, which calls a function named roller() to start the rolling banner, by entering `onload="roller()"` as the code.

2. Position the insertion pointer on line 4 and enter the SCRIPT section in the HEAD section by entering:
```
<SCRIPT LANGUAGE="JAVASCRIPT">
<!-- Hide from old browsers
```

3. Create an array, called banner, to hold the banner file images, and initialize a variable for a subscript by entering the following code starting at line 6:
```
var banner = new Array("florist1.jpg", "florist2.jpg", "florist3.jpg")
var banctr = 0
```

4. Enter the function, called roller(), to roll the three images by entering the following on line 8 indenting where appropriate:
```
function roller() {
    if (banctr == 3) {
        banctr=0
    }
    document.Bannerspot.src=banner[banctr]
    banctr = banctr + 1
    setTimeout("roller()",3000)
}
```

*(continued)*

## In the Lab

**Using Arrays to Create a Rolling Banner and Display Prices for a Selection List** *(continued)*

5. Place an onchange event handler to call the floralPrice() function in the SELECT tag on line 35 by entering onchange="floralPrice(FloralMenu)" between the double quote and the >.
6. On line 44, create an array, called floral, by entering var floral = new Array ("Select a floral piece","Please call for special prices","18.95 a dozen", "7.95 a dozen", "25.95 a set") as the code.
7. Complete the floralPrice function by entering the following JavaScript code:

```
function floralPrice(myform) {
        var itemSelect = myForm.FloralList.selectedIndex
        myForm.PiecePrice.value = floral[itemSelect]
}
```

8. Be sure to complete the SCRIPT section with a closing SCRIPT tag.
9. Save the HTML file using the file name, floristsolution.htm, on the JavaScript Data Disk in drive A.
10. Activate your browser. Open the floristsolution.htm file to test the JavaScript code. If any errors occur, double-check steps 1 through 8 and then save and test again. If no errors occur, print the Web page, return to Notepad, and then print the HTML file. Hand in the printouts to your instructor.

# 3 Creating Rolling Banners, Selection Lists, and Displaying Messages

**Problem:** While interviewing for a summer job with the owner of Three Rivers' Fencing, Yolanda Riveria, the discussion turns to your skills in Web page design. Being summer, Yolanda wants a Web site that focuses on deck prices. You suggest a selection list that displays the different deck offerings (Figure 3-46). The user selects an item from the list and then clicks a button to see a price. Yolanda wants a seasonal message that displays, mentioning different specials. Finally, because the company does more than fencing, she wants a rolling banner to remind people that Three Rivers' Fencing offers many services.

**Instructions:** Start your browser and Notepad. Using Notepad, open the fence.htm file on your JavaScript Data Disk and perform the following tasks. The Fence.htm file contains the HTML code for the drop-down list.

1. In the HEAD section, enter the SCRIPT tags for the functions.
2. Write the code for the rolling banner function. Name the function rollbanner(). The image files are "fence1.jpg", "fence2.jpg", and "fence3.jpg." The image object name is Banner.
3. Call this function with an onload event handler in the BODY tag.
4. Write the code for the drop-down list of deck prices function. Name the function displayPrice(). The prices are "$1,250.00", "$1,400.00", "$2,500.00", and "$1,395.00." Be sure to include a null price for the zero item in the list. The select list object name is DeckList.
5. Call this function with an onclick event handler when the user clicks the Price button in the DeckMenu form.
6. Write the code for the message display function. Name the function message().

*In the Lab*

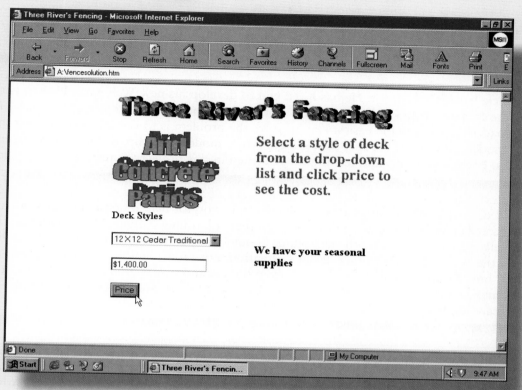

**FIGURE 3-46**

7. Set the message using a Switch statement. The case condition tests the current month.
8. If the month is April or May, the message reads, See us for fence repairs from winter damage!
9. If the month is September or October, the message reads, Call us about fall landscaping specials!
10. If none of the conditions matches, display a generic message which reads, We have your seasonal supplies.
11. Call this function by placing the JavaScript code in the table cell below the select form. A SCRIPT section has been started, and a JavaScript comment says, // Place message function call here.
12. Save the HTML file using the file name, fencesolution.htm, on the JavaScript Data Disk in drive A.
13. Activate the browser. Open the fencesolution.htm file to test the JavaScript code. If any errors occur double-check steps 1 through 11 and then save and test again. If no errors occur, print the Web page, and return to Notepad to print the HTML file. Hand in the printouts to your instructor.

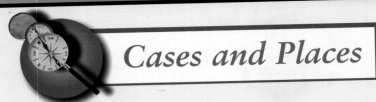

# Cases and Places

The difficulty of these case studies varies:
▶ are the least difficult; ▶▶ are more difficult; and ▶▶▶ are the most difficult.

**1** ▶  Your uncle has a used car lot. He has hired you to develop his new Web page. He wants to display pictures of the cars he has in stock, but he does not want customers to have to wait for thirty to fifty pictures to load. You tell him the easiest way to solve the problem is to use a drop-down list that shows the current models, and when the user selects a particular model, a picture displays along with the car's specifications. Use the concepts and techniques presented in this project to create the Web page.

**2** ▶  A friend of your family is an antique dealer. She calls you for help on designing a Web page. As part of the basic layout, you suggest a title and logo that is a rolling banner. After discussing this basic layout, she tells you that every month she obtains about 10 to 12 items of high value. She wants to post the items on the Web page to get other dealer's attention. For these items, you suggest a drop-down list. You describe how the user could select an item from the list and in a section next to the list, a picture, description, and asking price for the item displays. Use the concepts and techniques presented in this project to create the Web page.

**3** ▶▶  You are hired by a print shop to develop a Web page to advertise specials and promotions. Starting in late September, the owner wants to sell custom Christmas cards. She prints more than 20 varieties of Christmas cards. You realize it will take several minutes to download and display all the cards in a single Web page. You suggest using a simple description as a link, and when the user clicks the description, the card displays. To see the inside, you tell the user to drag the mouse over the picture, and the inside greeting displays. Use the concepts and techniques presented in this project to create the Web page.

**4** ▶▶  As a parent of two children at the local elementary school, you volunteer to develop a Web page for the school. The principal wants the page to be a monthly calendar of events. Design a table of seven columns and five rows and place individual days in the table cells. To make the page more interesting, add a countdown to special events. For example, during the month of November, count down until Thanksgiving, where PTA members will provide dinner to less fortunate community members. In addition, on the days when no events are planned, you want random images to display in the table cells. Use the concepts and techniques presented in this project to create the Web page.

**5** ▶▶▶  You volunteer to develop a Web site for your daughter's local Girl Scout troop. The troop raises money by organizing sporting events, and the Web page will promote the upcoming events. For example, to raise money, the troop organizes bowling, golfing, and fishing tournaments. Local businesses donate prize money or gifts for winners. While discussing the design of the Web page with troop leaders, everyone agrees that through links, each event will display on its own page, and that the page displays the number of days until that event. To show thanks for local business support, you suggest that the Web page display the logo of the businesses that support the event in a rolling banner. In addition, it is agreed that pictures of previous years' winners display in another rolling banner for each event. Use the concepts and techniques presented in this project to create the Web page.